Dedicated

To

Our beloved Parents

SPPU New Syllabus

MTC-122

GRAPH THEORY

[2 Credits]

Mathematics : Paper - II

For

First Year B.Sc. (Computer Science)

Semester - II

New Syllabus as per CBCS Pattern

from June 2019

M. D. Bhagat
Ex-Head Dept. of Mathematics
Tuljaram Chaturchand College
Baramati (Dist. Pune)

R. S. Bhamare
Ex-Head of P.G. Dept. of Mathematics
New Arts, Science & Commerce College
Ahmednagar

N. M. Phatangare
Assistant Prof. Dept. of Mathematics
Fergusson College,
Pune 411 004

Dr. S. G. Purane
Associate Prof. & HOD of Mathematics
PES's Jamkhed Mahavidyalaya
Jamkhed, Ahmednagar 413 201

Dr. A. S. Khairnar
Assistant Professor & HOD of Mathematics
MES's Abasaheb Garware College,
Pune 411 004

S. D. Manjarekar
Assistant Professor
Department of Mathematics
MGV's Loknete Vyankatrao Hiray
Arts, Science & Commerce College, Nashik 422 003

NIRALI PRAKASHAN
ADVANCEMENT OF KNOWLEDGE

N5059

F.Y.B.Sc. (Computer Science) Graph Theory **ISBN 978-93-89533-68-2**

First Edition : October 2019

Published By:

NIRALI PRAKASHAN

Abhyudaya Pragati, 1312, Shivaji Nagar
Off J.M. Road, PUNE – 411005
Tel - (020) 25512336/37/39, Fax - (020) 25511379
Email : niralipune@pragationline.com

➢ DISTRIBUTION CENTRES

PUNE

Nirali Prakashan (For orders within Pune) : 119, Budhwar Peth, Jogeshwari Mandir Lane, Pune 411002, Maharashtra, Tel : (020) 2445 2044, Mobile : 9657703145
Email : niralilocal@pragationline.com

Nirali Prakashan (For orders outside Pune) : S. No. 28/27, Dhayari, Near Asian College Pune 411041
Tel : (020) 24690204; Mobile : 9657703143
Email : bookorder@pragationline.com

MUMBAI

Nirali Prakashan : 385, S.V.P. Road, Rasdhara Co-op. Hsg. Society Ltd., Girgaum, Mumbai 400004, Maharashtra;
Mobile : 9320129587 Tel : (022) 2385 6339 / 2386 9976,
Fax : (022) 2386 9976
Email : niralimumbai@pragationline.com

➢ DISTRIBUTION BRANCHES

JALGAON

Nirali Prakashan : 34, V. V. Golani Market, Navi Peth, Jalgaon 425001, Maharashtra, Tel : (0257) 222 0395, Mob : 94234 91860;
Email : niralijalgaon@pragationline.com

KOLHAPUR

Nirali Prakashan : New Mahadvar Road, Kedar Plaza, 1st Floor Opp. IDBI Bank, Kolhapur 416 012, Maharashtra. Mob : 9850046155;
Email : niralikolhapur@pragationline.com

NAGPUR

Nirali Prakashan : Above Maratha Mandir, Shop No. 3, First Floor, Rani Jhanshi Square, Sitabuldi, Nagpur 440012, Maharashtra
Tel : (0712) 254 7129;
Email : niralinagpur@pragationline.com

DELHI

Nirali Prakashan : 4593/15, Basement, Agarwal Lane, Ansari Road, Daryaganj Near Times of India Building, New Delhi 110002
Mob : 08505972553, Email : niralidelhi@pragationline.com

BENGALURU

Nirali Prakashan : Maitri Ground Floor, Jaya Apartments, No. 99, 6th Cross, 6th Main, Malleswaram, Bengaluru 560003, Karnataka;
Mob : 9449043034
Email: niralibangalore@pragationline.com

Other Branches : Hyderabad, Chennai

niralipune@pragationline.com | www.pragationline.com

Also find us on f www.facebook.com/niralibooks

Preface ...

We have great pleasure in presenting this text book on **GRAPH THEORY** to the students of F.Y.B.Sc. Computer Science Semester - II, Mathematics Paper - II. This book is written strictly according to the new revised syllabus (CBCS Pattern) of Savitribai Phule Pune University to be implemented from June 2019.

We have taken utmost care to present the matter systematically and with proper flow of mathematical concepts. We begin the Chapter by Introduction and at the end the Summary of the Chapter is provided. We have added one significant feature: **"Think Over It"** in this new **edition**. Here, we have posed questions of simple, difficult and intuitive type in nature. It is expected that the students should think over it and try to find the answers. This will assess the understanding of the knowledge of the Chapter.

The book contains good number of solved problems and the number of graded problems in the exercises.

We are thankful to **Shri Dineshbhai Furia, Shri Jignesh Furia,** Mrs. Anagha Medhekar (Proof Reading and Co-ordination), Mr. Ilyas Shaikh, Mrs. Anjali Muley (Fig. Drawing) and the staff of Nirali Prakashan for the great efforts that they have taken to publish the book in time.

We welcome the valuable suggestions from our colleagues' and readers for the improvement of the book.

PUNE **AUTHORS**

2019

✍ ✍ ✍

Syllabus ...

1. An Introduction to Graph (10 Lectures)

1.1 Definitions, Basic terminologies and properties of graph, Graph models.

1.2 Special types of graphs, Basic terminologies, Properties and examples of directed graphs. Types of diagraphs.

1.3 Some applications of special types of graph.

1.4 Matrix representation and elementary results, Isomorphism of graphs.

2. Connected Graph (08 Lectures)

2.1 Walk, trail, path, cycle, elementary properties of connectedness. Counting paths between vertices (by Warshall's algorithm).

2.2 Cut edge (Bridge), Cut vertex, Cut set, Vertex connectivity, Edge connectivity and Properties.

2.3 Shortest path problem, Dijkstra's algorithm.

3. Euler and Hamilton Path (08 Lectures)

3.1 The Konigsberg bridge problem, Euler trail, Path, Circuit and tour, Elementary properties and Fleury's algorithm.

3.2 Hamilton path, Circuit, Elementary properties and examples.

3.3 Introduction of Travelling salesman problem, Chinese postman problem.

4. Trees (10 Lectures)

4.1 Definitions, Basic terminologies, Properties and applications of trees.

4.2 Weighted graph, Definition and properties of spanning tree, shortest spanning tree, Kruskal's algorithm, Prim's algorithm.

4.3 M-ary tree, Binary tree, Definitions and properties, Tree traversal preorder, Inorder, Postorder, Infix, Prefix, Postfix notations and examples.

✍✍✍

Contents ...

Chapter **1**...

An Introduction to Graph

Frank Harary

Frank Harary (March 11, 1921 - January 4, 2005) was a prolific American mathematician, who specialized in graph theory. He was widely recognized as one of the "fathers" of modern graph theory. Harary was a master of clear exposition and together with his many doctoral students, he standardized the terminology of graphs.

He broadened the reach of this field to include physics, psychology, sociology, and even anthropology. Gifted with a keen sense of humor. Harary challenged and entertained audiences at levels of mathematical sophistication. A particular trick he employed was to turn theorems into games - for instance, students would try to add red edges to a graph on six vertices in order to create a red triangle, while another group of students tried to add edges to create a blue triangle (and each edge of the graph had to be either blue or red). Because of the simplest case of Ramsey theory, one team or the other would have to win.

1.1 Introduction

A graph consists of two types of objects viz. vertices and edges such that each edge is associated with unordered pair of vertices. Consider the situation which describes the road map of a city joining some important places like garden (g), hospital (h), bus station (b), railway station (r), swimming tank (s), temple (t) and telephone booth (p). By taking into consideration their locations, we can represent this situation diagrammatically as shown below.

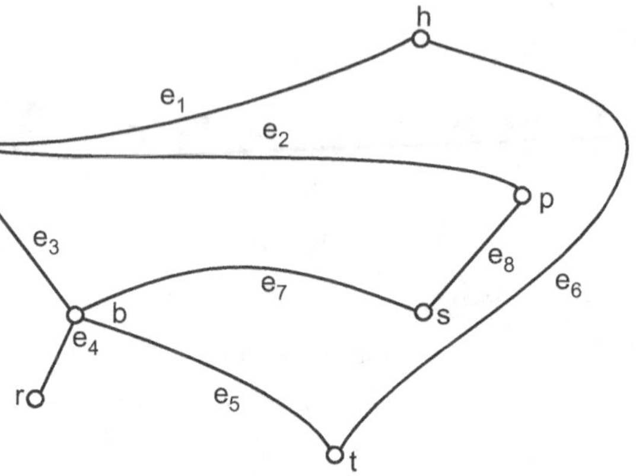

Fig. 1.1

This diagram represents a graph with 7 vertices g, b, r, t, s, p, h and 8 edges e_1, e_2, e_3, e_4, e_5, e_6, e_7, e_8.

Some other examples of graphs are :

(i) Communication lines joining military stations of a country.

(ii) A river together with its tributories and subtributories.

(iii) Ranking of workers in an office according to their ranks.

(iv) A plot of land with the walls to prevent the water from flowing.

(v) Railway route map of the country.

(vi) Nerves in the human body.

Definition: A graph G = G (V, E) consists of two sets : A non-empty set V called vertex set whose elements are called vertices (or nodes) and a set E called edge set whose elements are called edges, such that each edge $e \in E$ is associated with an unordered pair (v_1, v_2) of vertices $v_1, v_2 \in V$.

If both the sets V and E are finite then the graph is called a **finite graph**. If both the sets V and E or either of them is infinite set then the graph is called an **infinite graph**. For our purpose, the word graph would mean a finite graph.

In the above definition whether the edge e_i is associated with vertex pair (v_j, v_k) or (v_k, v_j) is immaterial. This means we are not yet assigning the directions to the edges. Such graphs in which the edges are not assigned the directions are called undirected graphs.

Fig. 1.1 shows the diagrammatic representation of a graph. In the diagrammatic representation of a graph, the vertices are denoted by small circles and the edges are denoted either by straight lines or curved lines. Another way of representing a graph is to list the edges as vertex pairs. Thus, a graph shown in Fig. 1.1 can be represented as {(g, h), (g, p), (g, b), (h, t), (p, s), (s, b), (b, t), (b, r)}.

If the edge set E of a graph G is empty then G is called a null graph. The null graphs N_1, N_2, N_3, N_4 of 1, 2, 3, 4 vertices respectively are shown below.

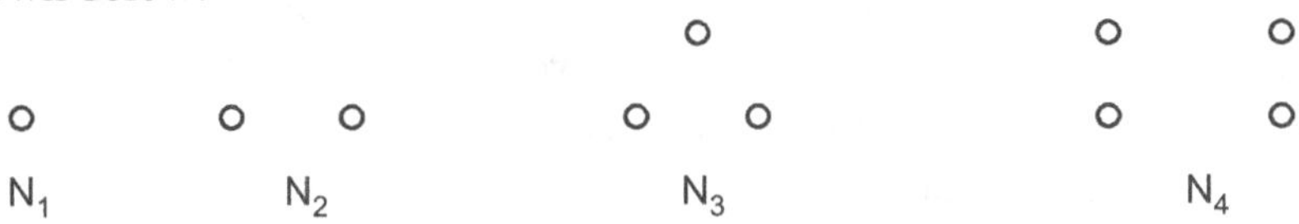

Fig. 1.2

In the graph G (V, E), if the edge e_i is associated with the vertex pair (v_j, v_k) then v_j, v_k are end vertices of e_i and equivalently we say that edge e_i is incident on v_j and v_k. Also, in this case, the vertices v_j and v_k are said to be adjacent vertices. The two edges e_i and e_j are called adjacent if they have a vertex in common. In the graph of Fig. 1.1, the vertices h and t are adjacent vertices but h and p are not adjacent because there is no edge joining h and p. Also the edges e_2 and e_8 are adjacent edges as they have a vertex p in common.

In the graph G (V, E) if two edges have the same end vertices then they are called parallel edges. If an edge e_i of a graph G has its two end vertices coincident then e_i is said to form a loop at that vertex. A graph without loops and without parallel edges is called a simple graph (or linear graph). A graph with parallel edges but having no loop is called a multigraph. A graph having parallel edges and loops is called a pseudograph.

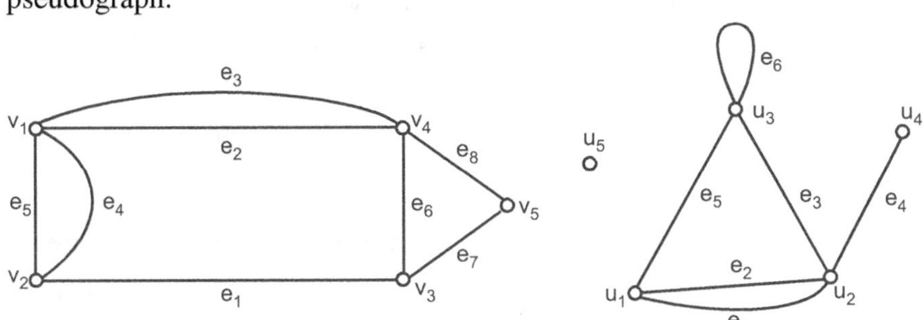

(a) **(b)**

Fig. 1.3

Fig. 1.3 (a) shows a multigraph having e_2 and e_3 as parallel edges and also e_4 and e_5 as parallel edges.

Fig. 1.3 (b) shows a pseudograph. Here e_1 and e_2 are parallel edges and the edge e_6 forms a loop at the vertex u_3.

Degree of a vertex : Let v be a vertex in a graph G(V, E). The number of edges incident on v is called the degree of v and is denoted by d (v).

We note that every edge of the graph G contributes two degrees, one at each end vertex. Also the loop at the vertex v contributes two degrees at v. The total degree of the graph G is the sum of the degrees of all the vertices. Hence, we have the following result.

Theorem 1 The total degree of a graph G is equal to twice the number of edges in G.

This result is known as Hand Shaking Lemma; the name follows from the fact that at a party if n hand shakes occur then because each hand shake involves two hands, the total number of hands involved in hand shakes is 2n.

A vertex of degree 1 in a graph is called a pendant vertex and the corresponding edge is called a pendant edge. A vertex of degree 0 is called isolated vertex.

In Fig. 1.3 (a) we have $d(v_1) = 4$, $d(v_2) = 3$, $d(v_3) = 3$, $d(v_4) = 4$, $d(v_5) = 2$. The total degree is $4 + 3 + 3 + 4 + 2 = 16$. Also there are 8 edges and $2 \times 8 = 16$. This verifies Hand Shaking Lemma.

In Fig. 1.3 (b), $d(u_1) = 3$, $d(u_2) = 4$, $d(u_3) = 4$, $d(u_4) = 1$, $d(u_5) = 0$. Here u_4 is a pendant vertex and e_4 is a pendant edge. The vertex u_5 is isolated vertex. We note that the edge e_6 which forms a loop at u_3 contributes 2 degrees at u_3.

As a corollary to Hand Shaking Lemma i.e. theorem 1, we have the following result. ■

Theorem 2 In a graph G (V, E) the number of vertices of odd degree is even. **(April 10)**

Proof : Let G (V, E) be a graph with p vertices and q edges. Then by Hand Shaking Lemma, the total degree of G is 2q.

i.e. $$\sum_{i=1}^{p} d(v_i) = 2q$$

We separate the sum on left hand side into two parts viz. in the first part we consider vertices of even degree and in the second part the vertices of odd degree.

$$\therefore \quad \sum_{\substack{\text{even degree} \\ \text{vertices}}} d(v_i) + \sum_{\substack{\text{odd degree} \\ \text{vertices}}} d(v_j) = 2q$$

The first sum on left side is even. Also the right side 2q is even. Therefore, the second sum on left side must be even.

i.e. $$\sum_{\substack{\text{odd degree} \\ \text{vertices}}} d(v_j) \text{ is even number.}$$

Hence, the number of odd degree vertices must be even. ■

Example 1 : The Holywood graph

The Hollywood graph represents actors by vertices and connects two vertices when the actors represented by these vertices have worked together on a movie. This graph is a simple graph because its edges are undirected, it contains no multiple edges, and it contains no loops.

Example 2 : Round-Robin Tournaments

A tournament where each team plays with each other team exactly once is called a round-robin tournament. Such tournaments can be modeled using Directed graphs where each team is represented by a vertex. Note that (a, b) is an edge if team a beats team b. This graph is a simple directed graph, containing no loops or multiple directed edges. In Fig. 1.4, we see that Team 1 is undefeated in this tournament, and Team 3 is winless.

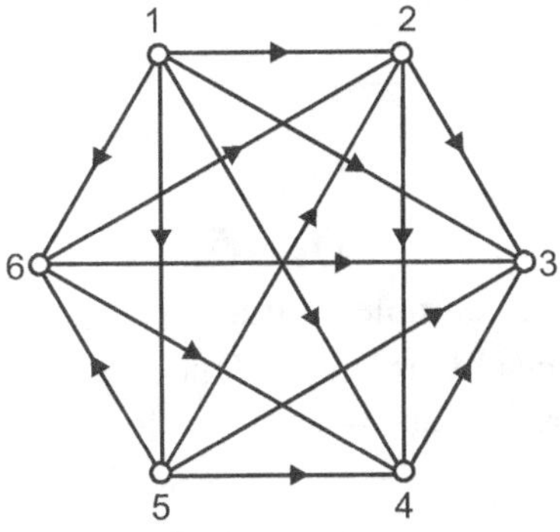

Fig. 1.4

Example 3 : The Web Graph

The world wide web can be modeled as a directed graph where each web page is represented by a vertex and where an edge starts at the web page a and ends at other removed somewhere on the web almost every second, the web graph changes on an almost continual basis. Many people are studying the properties of the web graph to better understand the nature of the web.

1.2 Types of Graphs

(i) Weighted graph : A weighted graph is a graph in which every edge is assigned to it some positive number called weight of that edge. If we interpret the vertices of the graph as cities and the edges as the roads joining the cities, then the weight w (e_i) of edge e_i joining the cities v_j and v_k may be actual length of the road or it may be the cost of constructing that road or it may be the bus fare for travelling from v_j to v_k.

The total weight of the graph G is the sum of the weights of all edges of G.

(ii) Complete graph : A simple graph with n vertices such that there exists an edge between every pair of vertices is called a complete graph and it is denoted by K_n.

The graphs K_1, K_2, K_3, K_4, K_5 are shown below.

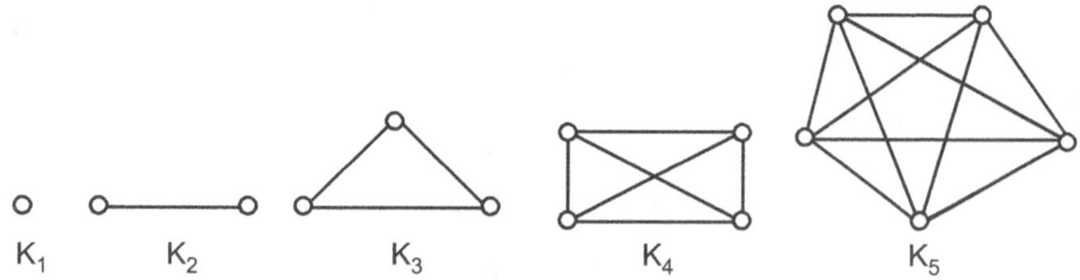

Fig. 1.5

We note that in a complete graph K_n, each vertex is joined to remaining n – 1 vertices by an edge. Hence, the degree of each vertex is n – 1. The total degree is n(n – 1). Therefore, the number of edges in K_n is $\frac{n(n-1)}{2}$.

(iii) Regular graph : Let K be a positive integer. A simple graph G in which every vertex is of degree K is called k-regular graph. A graph G is called regular if it is K-regular for some positive integer K. A graph G shown below is 2-regular.

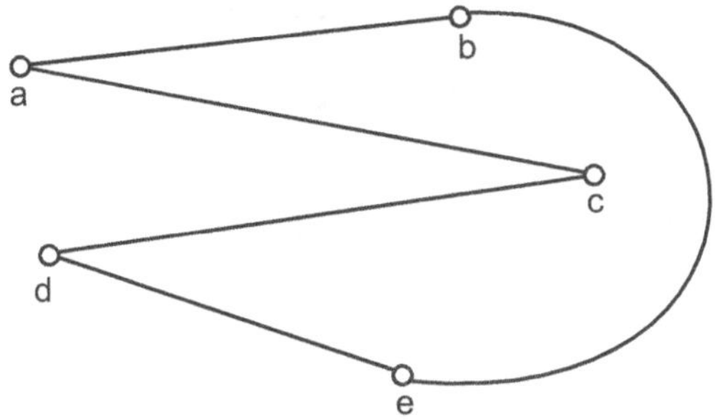

Fig. 1.6

A complete graph K_n is n – 1 regular. We see that a complete graph is regular but regular graph need not be complete.

(iv) Bipartite graph (Oct. 03, May 99) : Let G(V, E) be a simple graph. If the vertex set V of G can be partitioned into two non-empty disjoint subsets V_1 and V_2 ($V_1 \cup V_2 = V$, $V_1 \cap V_2 = \phi$) in such a way that every edge of G has its one end vertex in V_1 and the other end vertex in V_2; then G is called a bipartite graph and the collection $\{V_1, V_2\}$ is called a bipartition.

A bipartite graph in which there exists an edge between every vertex in V_1 and every vertex in V_2 is called a complete bipartite graph. A complete bipartite graph with bipartition V_1, V_2 having m vertices in V_1 and n vertices in V_2 is denoted by $K_{m, n}$. Following figures illustrate this.

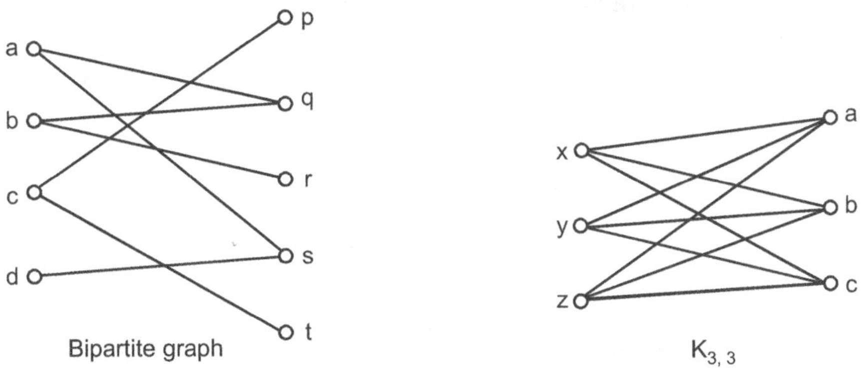

Fig. 1.7

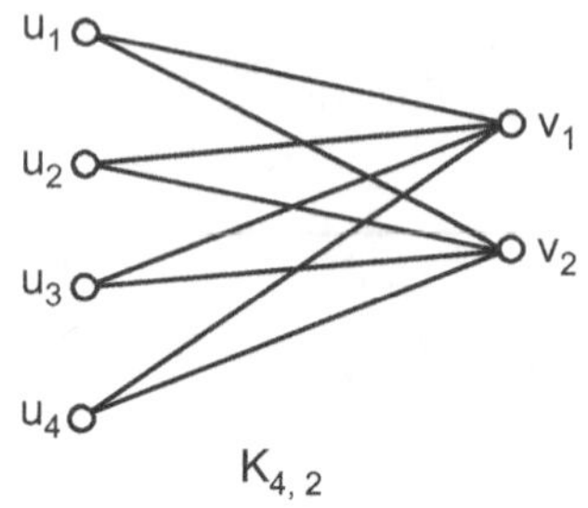

Fig. 1.8

In $K_{m, n}$ every vertex in

$V_1 = \{u_1, u_2, ..., u_m\}$ is joined to every vertex in $V_2 = \{v_1, v_2, ... v_n\}$. Therefore $K_{m, n}$ has mn edges.

The graph $K_{1, n}$ is called a star.

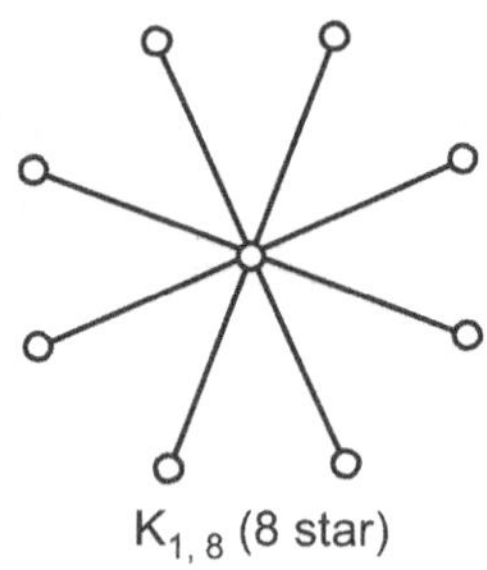

Fig. 1.9

From the star graph, we get a wheel graph.

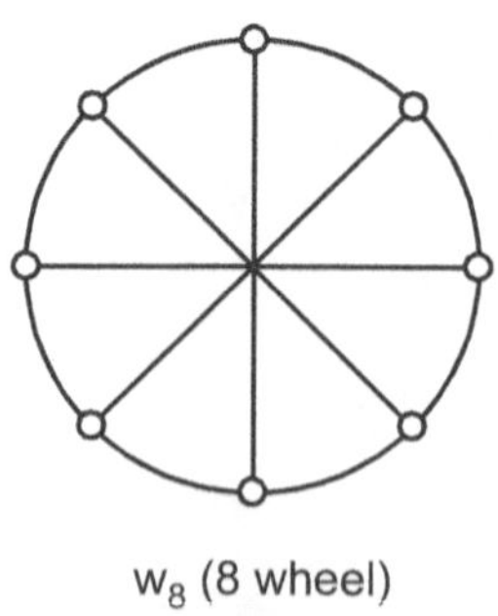

Fig. 1.10

Consider the graph shown below.

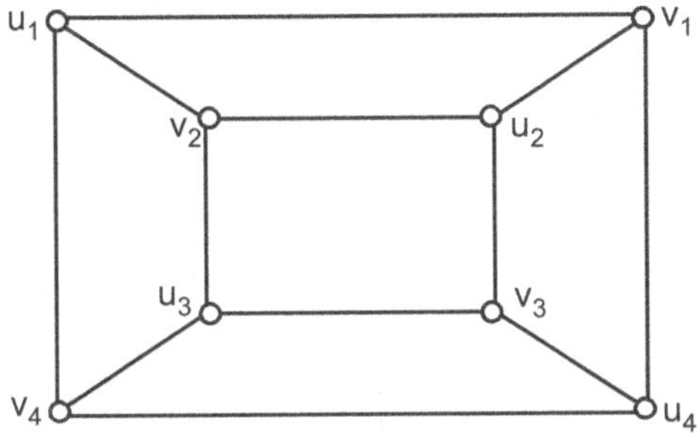

Fig. 1.11

In this graph, we observe that every edge is such that it joins u type vertex to v type vertex.

Therefore, $V_1 = \{u_1, u_2, u_3, u_4\}$ and $V_2 = \{v_1, v_2, v_3, v_4\}$ is a bipartition of the vertex set. We can redraw the above graph as below.

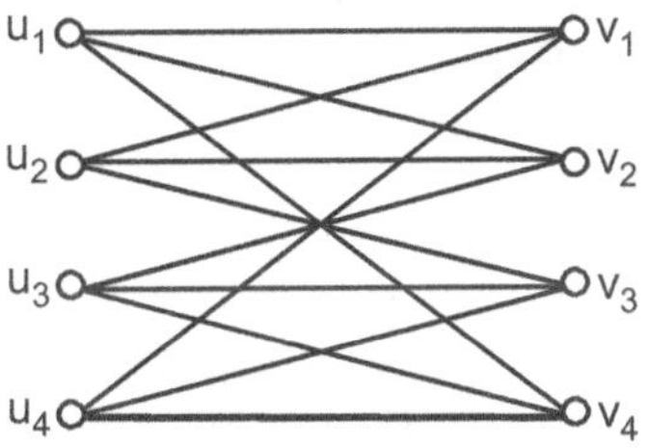

Fig. 1.12

It is a bipartite graph.

Cycles : The cycle C_n, $n \geq 3$, consists of n vertices 1, 2, …, n and edges {1, 2}, {2, 3}, …, {n – 1, n}, and {n, 1}. The cycles C_3, C_4, C_5 and C_6 are shown in the following figure.

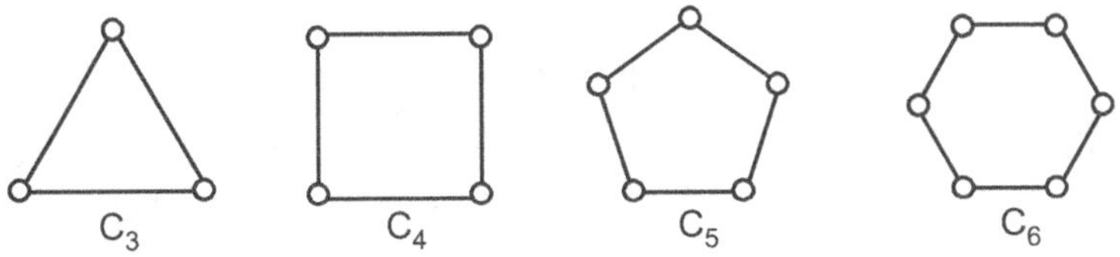

Fig. 1.13

Wheels : We obtain the wheel W_n when we add an additional vertex to the cycle C_n, for $n \geq 3$, and connect this new vertex to each of the n vertices in C_n, by new edges. The wheels W_3, W_4, W_5 and W_6 are shown in the following figure.

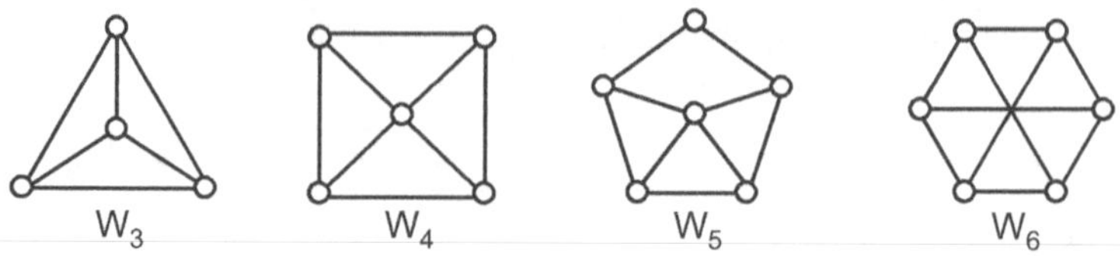

Fig. 1.14

n-Cubes : The n-dimensional hypercube, or n-cube, denoted by Q_n, is the graph that has vertices representing the 2^n bit strings of length n. Two vertices are adjacent if and only if the bit strings that they represent differ in exactly one bit position. The graphs Q_1, Q_2 and Q_3 are shown in the following figure.

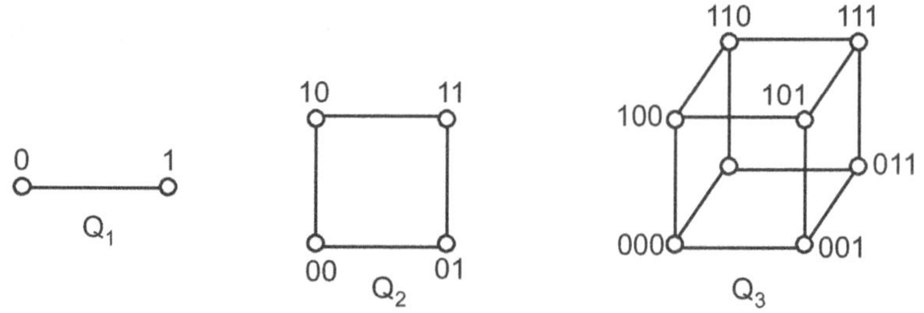

Fig. 1.15

Complete Bipartite Graphs : The complete bipartite graph $K_{m;\ n}$ is the graph that has its vertex set partitioned into two subsets of m and n vertices, respectively. There is an edge between two vertices if and only if one vertex is in the first subset and the other vertex is in the second subset. The complete bipartite graphs $K_{2,\ 3}$, $K_{3,\ 3}$, $K_{3,\ 5}$ and $K_{2,\ 6}$ are shown in the following figure.

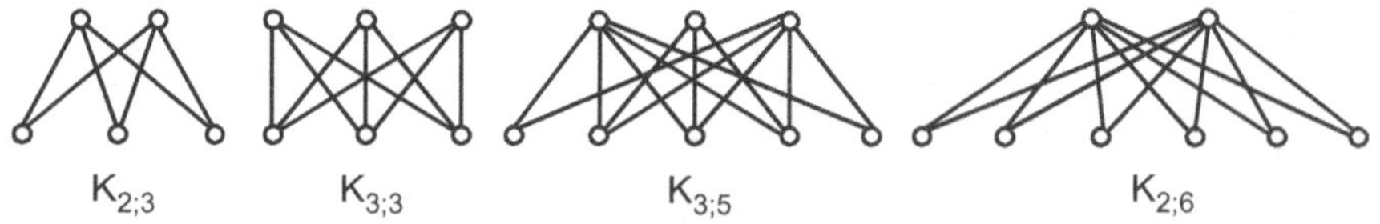

Fig. 1.16

Subgraph : A subgraph of a graph G = (V, E) is a graph H = (W, F), where $W \subseteq V$ and $F \subseteq E$. A subgraph H of G is a proper subgraph of G if $H \neq G$.

Example : Few subgraphs of K_4 are shown in the following figure.

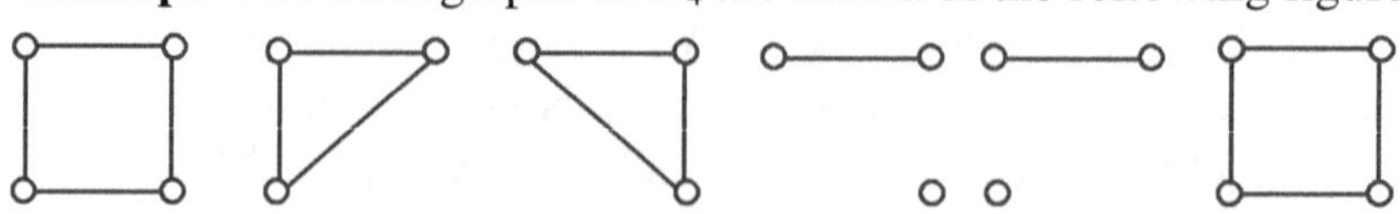

Fig. 1.17

Union of Two Graphs : The union of two simple graphs $G_1 = (V_1, E_1)$ and $G_2 = (V_2, E_2)$ is the simple graph with vertex set $V_1 \cup V_2$ and edge set $E_1 \cup E_2$. The union of G_1 and G_2 is denoted by $G_1 \cup G_2$.

Example : The two graphs G_1 and G_2 and their union is shown below.

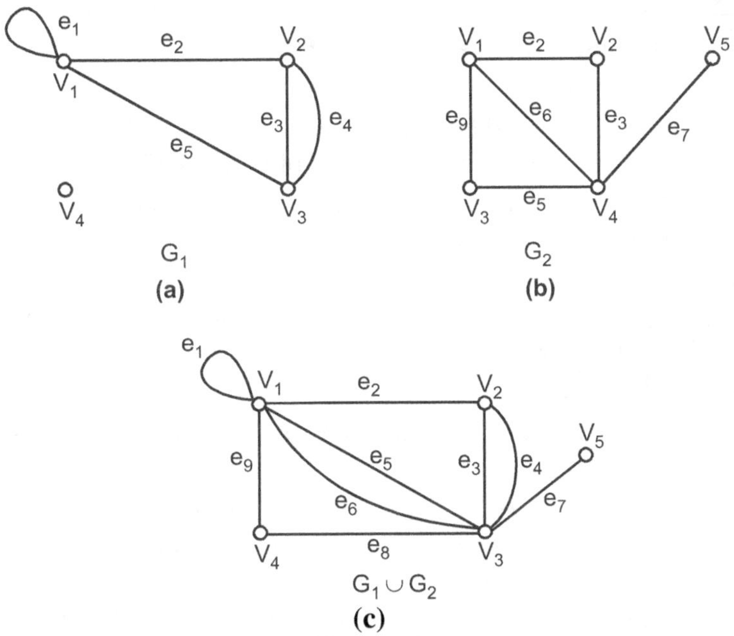

Fig. 1.18

1.3 Isomorphism

Definition : The two graphs G (V, E) and G' (V', E') are said to be isomorphic if

(i) there exists a bijective mapping $f_V : V \rightarrow V'$

(ii) there exists a bijective mapping $f_E : E \rightarrow E'$ such that

(iii) whenever e is an edge in G with its end vertices a and b then the edge f_E (e) in G' has its end vertices f_V (a) and f_V (b).

The condition (iii) in the definition is described by saying that under isomorphism, the incidence relationship is preserved.

When two graphs G and G' are isomorphic, we write $G \cong G'$ (G is isomorphic to G').

The relation of isomorphism between graphs is an equivalence relation. (Left as an exercise).

Remark : From the definition of isomorphism, it immediately follows that if $G \cong G'$ then

(i) G and G' have equal number of vertices.

(ii) G and G' have equal number of edges.

Theorem 3 Let G(V, E) and G'(V', E') be isomorphic graphs under the objective mappings $f_V : V \to V'$ and $f_E : E \to E'$.

Then

(i) $d(x) = d(f_V(x))$ for any x in V.

(ii) G and G' contain equal number of vertices of the same degree.

(iii) If $e \in E$ has end vertices a and b then the end vertices of $f_E(e)$ have the same degrees as a and b.

Proof : It is given that $G \cong G'$. By definition, there exist bijective mappings $f_V : V \to V'$ and $f_E : E \to E'$ such that the incidence relationship is preserved.

(i) Let now $x \in V$.

If an edge e is incident on x in G then by isomorphism the edge $f_E(e)$ is incident on $f_V(x)$ in G'.

As this is true for every edge that is incident on x, the number of edges incident on x is exactly equal to the number of edges incident on $f_V(x)$. Therefore $d(x) = d(f_V(x))$.

(ii) Let $x_1, x_2, \ldots, x_m$ be m vertices of degree r in G. Then $f_V(x_1), \ldots, f_V(x_m)$ are vertices of degree r in G' by (i). If possible, let $y \neq f_V(x_i)$ be another vertex in G' of degree r. Then there exist $x \in V$ such that $f_V(x) = y$ and $x \neq x_i$ since f_V is a bijective map. Now, $d(x) = d(y) = r$.

Hence, $x = x_i$ for some i and this is a contradiction.

Hence, proved.

(iii) $e \in E$ has end vertices a and b. Therefore, $f_E(e)$ has end vertices $f_V(a)$ and $f_V(b)$ by isomorphism.

$\therefore$ $d(a) = d(f_V(a))$ and $d(b) = d(f_V(b))$ by (i). Hence proved.

As mentioned in the remark and by the part (ii) of the above theorem, we have the following result. The necessary conditions for two graphs G and G' to be isomorphic are

(a) they have equal number of vertices,

(b) they have equal number of edges,

(c) they have equal number of vertices of the same degree.

However, these conditions are not sufficient. It is seen from the following two graphs G_1 and G_2.

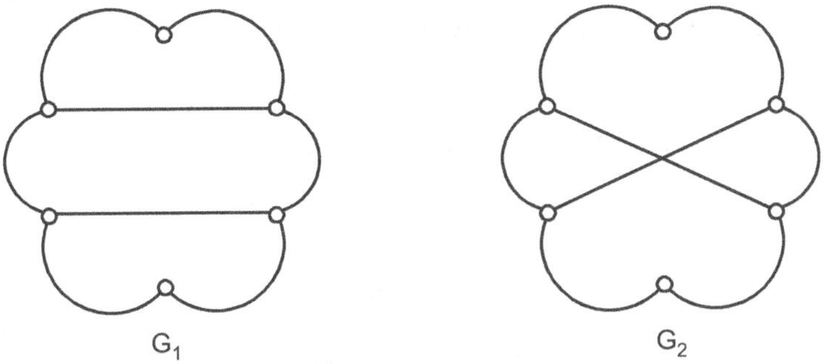

Fig. 1.19

These two graphs have six vertices and eight edges each.

Also in both the graphs there are two vertices of degree 2 and four vertices of degree 3. Thus, the three necessary conditions are satisfied.

Now in G_1 a vertex of degree 2 has two adjacent vertices of degree 3 which are themselves adjacent. But in G_2 a vertex of degree 2 has two adjacent vertices of degree 3 and they are not adjacent. Therefore, G_1 and G_2 are not isomorphic. ■

Note : In order to show that the two graphs are isomorphic, first we check that the three necessary conditions for isomorphism are satisfied and then establish bijective mappings between vertex sets and edge sets of two graphs in such a way that the incidence relationship is preserved.

In case of simple graphs, we need to establish a bijective mapping between vertex sets only and check that whenever edge exists between a and b in G then there exists an edge between f(a) and f(b) also. This is because there exists unique edge between two vertices of a simple graph (provided it exists).

1.4 Matrix Representation of a Graph

We have seen that a graph is represented in two different ways :

(i) by listing the edges as vertex pairs and (ii) by a diagram.

There is another way of representing a graph i.e. by using matrices and this representation is used by a computer. We study two types of matrix representations of a graph; one by adjacency matrix and the other by incidence matrix of a graph.

Adjacency Matrix : Let G be a graph with n vertices $v_1, v_2, \ldots, v_n$. Then the adjacency matrix A(G) of G is $n \times n$ matrix in which the $(i - j)^{th}$ element a_{ij} is the number of edges in G joining the vertex pair (v_i, v_j).

Consider the graph G with 5 vertices shown below.

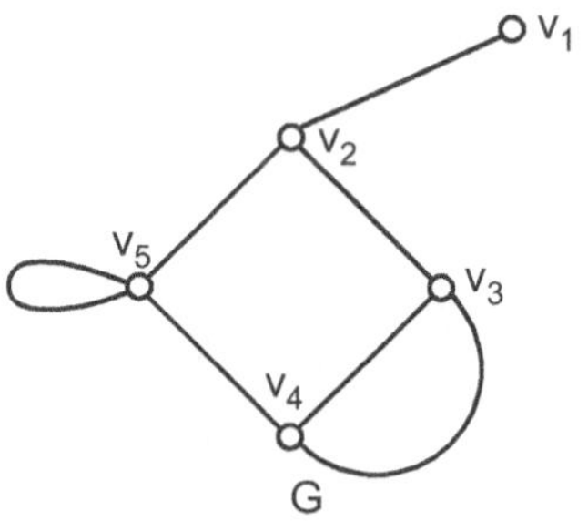

Fig. 1.20

The adjacency matrix corresponding to this graph is

$$\begin{array}{c} \\ v_1 \\ v_2 \\ v_3 \\ v_4 \\ v_5 \end{array} \begin{array}{c} \begin{array}{ccccc} v_1 & v_2 & v_3 & v_4 & v_5 \end{array} \\ \begin{bmatrix} 0 & 1 & 0 & 0 & 0 \\ 1 & 0 & 1 & 0 & 1 \\ 0 & 1 & 0 & 2 & 0 \\ 0 & 0 & 2 & 0 & 1 \\ 0 & 1 & 0 & 1 & 1 \end{bmatrix} \end{array}$$

We have the following observations about the adjacency matrix of a graph :

(i) As the number of edges joining v_i, v_j is the same as v_j, v_i, we have $a_{ij} = a_{ji}$.

Therefore, the adjacency matrix of a graph is a symmetric matrix.

(ii) The diagonal entries on the main diagonal (top left to bottom right) are 0 except when there is a loop. If there are loops at the vertex v_i then a_{ii} = number of loops at v_i.

(iii) If there is no loop at the vertex v_i then the sum of all the entries in the column of v_i gives the degree of v_i.

(iv) If there are no parallel edges and loops in G then all the entries of A(G) will be 0 or 1.

(v) If two graphs G_1 and G_2 are isomorphic then we can obtain $A(G_1)$ from $A(G_2)$ by permuting rows of $A(G_1)$ into themselves and that for columns in the same way and converse is also true.

Now we consider the converse problem i.e. given a $n \times n$ symmetric matrix whose elements are non-negative integers then to draw a graph associated with this matrix. This is done simply by joining the vertices v_i, v_j by the number of edges equal to a_{ij}.

Incidence Matrix : Let G be a graph with n vertices $v_1, v_2, \ldots, v_n$ and q edges $e_1, e_2, \ldots, e_q$. Then the incidence matrix $M = [m_{ij}]$ is $n \times q$ matrix in which the entry m_{ij} represents the number of times the vertex v_i is incident on the edge e_j.

$$\text{i.e. } m_{ij} = \begin{cases} 0 \text{ if } v_i \text{ is not end vertex of } e_j \\ 1 \text{ if } v_i \text{ is end vertex of } e_j \text{ (not loop)} \\ 2 \text{ if } v_i \text{ is end vertex of } e_j \text{ (loop)} \end{cases}$$

We also denote incidence matrix of graph G by I(G).

For example, consider the following graph.

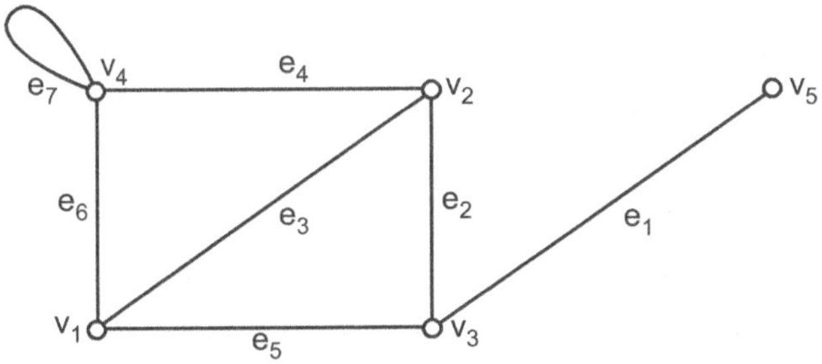

Fig. 1.21

This graph has 5 vertices and 7 edges. Therefore. incidence matrix is 5×7 matrix.

$$\begin{array}{c} \\ v_1 \\ v_2 \\ v_3 \\ v_4 \\ v_5 \end{array} \begin{array}{c} \begin{array}{ccccccc} e_1 & e_2 & e_3 & e_4 & e_5 & e_6 & e_7 \end{array} \\ \begin{bmatrix} 0 & 0 & 1 & 0 & 1 & 1 & 0 \\ 0 & 1 & 1 & 1 & 0 & 0 & 0 \\ 1 & 1 & 0 & 0 & 1 & 0 & 0 \\ 0 & 0 & 0 & 1 & 0 & 1 & 2 \\ 1 & 0 & 0 & 0 & 0 & 0 & 0 \end{bmatrix} \end{array}$$

We observe that the sum of the entries in the row of v_i gives the degree of v_i. Also the sum of the entries in each column is 2; its being the contribution of 2 degrees by any edge.

If two graphs are isomorphic then we can obtain $I(G_2)$ from $I(G_1)$ by permuting rows of $I(G_1)$ into themselves and permuting columns into themselves in the same way. Also converse is true.

Illustrative Examples

Example 1.1 : *Let G be a graph with p vertices, r of which have degree k and the others have degree k + 1. Prove that r = (k + 1) p – 2q, where q is the number of edges in G.*

Solution : A graph G has p vertices and q edges.

By hand shaking lemma, the total degree is 2q. ... (1)

Also out of p vertices, r of them have degree k and remaining p – r vertices have degree k + 1.

$\therefore$ Total degree $= rk + (p - r)(k + 1)$ ... (2)

From equations (1) and (2), we have,

$$rk + (p - r)(k + 1) = 2q$$

$$\therefore \quad -r + p(k + 1) = 2q$$

$$\therefore \quad r = p(k + 1) - 2q$$

Example 1.2 : *A graph G has n vertices and n – 1 edges. Prove that G has either a vertex of degree 1 or an isolated vertex.*

Solution : A graph G has n vertices and n – 1 edges.

By hand shaking lemma, the total degree is 2 (n – 1) = 2n – 2.

Assume that G does not have a vertex of degree 1 and no isolated vertex.

Then degree of each of n vertices is greater than or equal to 2. Therefore, total degree $\geq$ 2n. This contradicts to the fact that the total degree is 2n – 2.

Hence our assumption is wrong.

$\therefore$ G must have a vertex of degree 1 or an isolated vertex.

Example 1.3 : *How many edges are there in a graph with 10 vertices each of degree 6 ?*

Solution : Graph G has 10 vertices each of degree 6.

Therefore, total degree is $10 \times 6 = 60$. We know that each edge in a graph contributes 2 degrees. Therefore, the number of edges $= \frac{60}{2} = 30$.

Example 1.4 : *The five military stations of a country are to be connected by express highway roads. The cost in ₹ crores of constructing a road between two stations is given in the following table. The infinity cost implies that a road cannot be constructed between two stations due to the geographical conditions.*

	a	b	c	d	e
a	–	4	5	∞	∞
b	4	–	∞	7	∞
c	5	∞	–	6	∞
d	∞	7	6	–	2
e	∞	∞	∞	2	–

(a) *Represent the situation by a graph.*

(b) *Find the degree of each vertex.*

(c) *Find the total weight of the graph.*

Solution : (a)

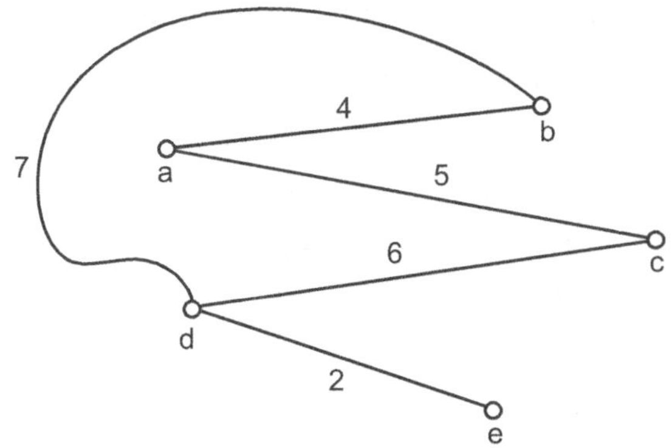

Fig. 1.22

(b) d(a) = 2, d(b) = 2, d(c) = 2, d(d) = 3, d(e) = 1.

(c) Total weight of the graph is $4 + 5 + 7 + 6 + 2 = 24$ crores ₹.

Example 1.5 : *Show that the following two graphs are isomorphic.*

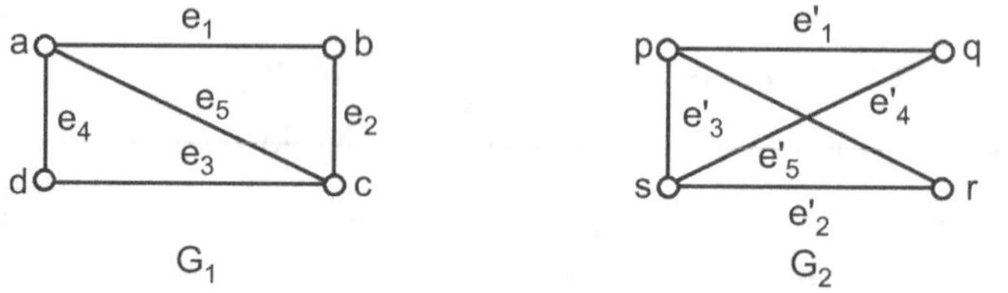

Fig. 1.23

Solution : Consider the bijective mapping between vertex sets as below.

$$a \rightarrow p$$
$$b \rightarrow q$$
$$c \rightarrow s$$
$$d \rightarrow r$$

We now establish the bijective mapping between edge sets in such a way that the incidence relationship is preserved.

In the graph G_1, there is an edge e_1 between vertices a and b.

In the graph G_2, the edge joining f (a) = p and f (b) = q is e_1'.

Therefore, we associate e_1 with e_1'. Similar argument for remaining edges gives the following mapping between edge sets :

$$e_1 \rightarrow e_1'$$
$$e_2 \rightarrow e_4'$$
$$e_3 \rightarrow e_2'$$
$$e_4 \rightarrow e_5'$$
$$e_5 \rightarrow e_3'$$

Hence, $G_1 \cong G_2$

Example 1.6 : *Determine which of the following pairs of graphs is isomorphic. Justify.*

(a)

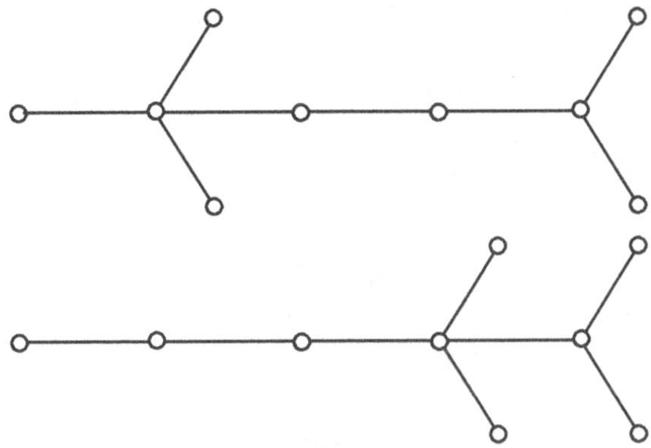

Fig. 1.24 (a)

(b)

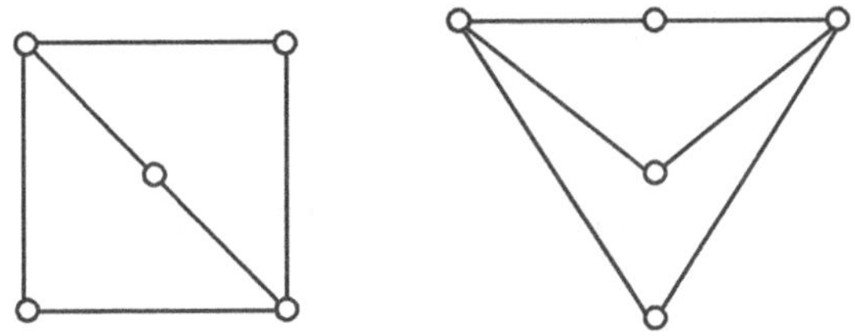

Fig. 1.24 (b)

Solution : (a) The two given graphs are

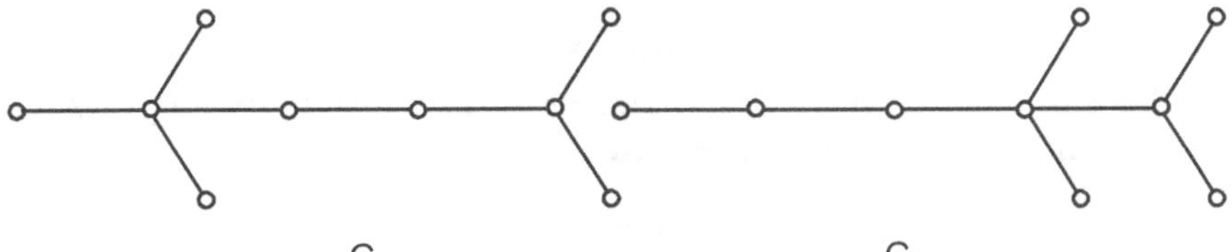

Fig. 1.25 (a)

These two graphs have 9 vertices and 8 edges each.

Also in both the graphs there are 5 vertices of degree 1, 2 vertices of degree 2, 1 vertex of degree 3, and 1 vertex of degree 4.

The necessary conditions for isomorphism are satisfied. However, they are not isomorphic because in the graph G_2, a vertex of degree 3 is adjacent to the vertex of degree 4 and in G_1 a vertex of degree 3 is not adjacent to the vertex of degree 4.

(b) The two given graphs are

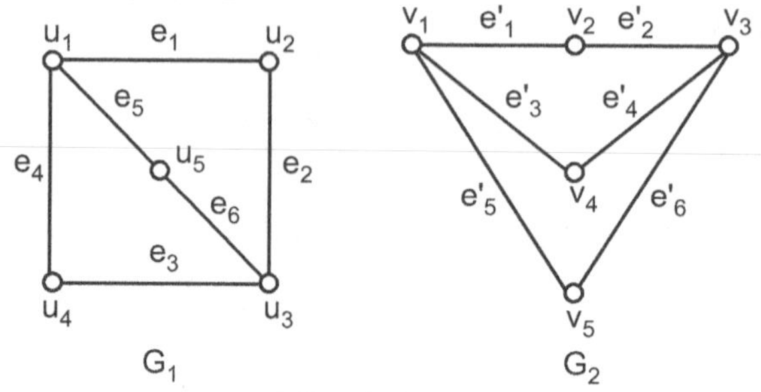

Fig. 1.25 (b)

These two graphs have 5 vertices and 6 edges each.

Also in both the graphs there are 3 vertices of degree 2 and 2 vertices of degree 3.

The necessary conditions for isomorphism are satisfied.

Now a vertex u_1 of degree 3 in G_1 corresponds to a vertex v_1 of degree 3 in G_2. Similarly, u_3 in G_1 corresponds to v_3 in G_2.

Then, $$u_5 \leftrightarrow v_2$$
$$u_2 \leftrightarrow v_4$$
and $$u_4 \leftrightarrow v_5$$

Thus, the bijective mapping between vertex sets is

$$u_1 \rightarrow v_1$$
$$u_2 \rightarrow v_4$$
$$u_3 \rightarrow v_3$$
$$u_4 \rightarrow v_5$$
$$u_5 \rightarrow v_2$$

Now in order to preserve the incidence relationship, following is the bijective mapping between edge sets.

$$e_1 \rightarrow e'_3$$
$$e_2 \rightarrow e'_4$$
$$e_3 \rightarrow e'_6$$
$$e_4 \rightarrow e'_5$$
$$e_5 \rightarrow e'_1$$
$$e_6 \rightarrow e'_2$$

Thus, $$G_1 \cong G_2$$

Example 1.7 : *Show that the following two graphs are isomorphic.*

(a) (b)

1.26 (A)

Solution : Given two graphs

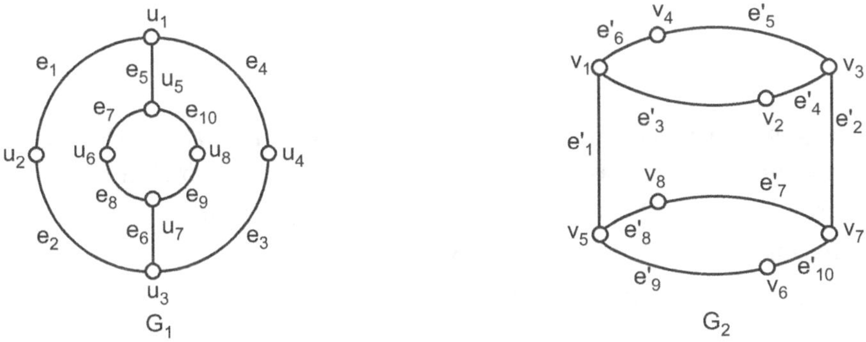

(c) (d)

Fig. 1.26 (B)

Two graphs have equal number of vertices i.e. 8 and equal number of edges e.g. 10.

Also G_1 and G_2 have equal number of vertices of the same degree.

The following one-one correspondence between vertices and edges preserves the incidence relationship.

$u_1 - v_5$	$e_1 - e'_9$
$u_2 - v_6$	$e_2 - e'_{10}$
$u_3 - v_7$	$e_3 - e'_7$
$u_4 - v_8$	$e_4 - e'_8$
$u_5 - v_1$	$e_5 - e'_1$
$u_6 - v_2$	$e_6 - e'_2$

u_7 – v_3	e_7 – e'_3
u_8 – v_4	e_8 – e'_4
	e_9 – e'_5
	e_{10} – e'_6

Hence, G_1 and G_2 are isomorphic.

Example 1.8 : *Draw a multigraph corresponding to the adjacency matrix.*

$$\begin{array}{c} \\ v_1 \\ v_2 \\ v_3 \\ v_4 \end{array} \begin{array}{c} \begin{array}{cccc} v_1 & v_2 & v_3 & v_4 \end{array} \\ \begin{bmatrix} 1 & 1 & 1 & 2 \\ 1 & 0 & 0 & 0 \\ 1 & 0 & 0 & 2 \\ 2 & 0 & 2 & 2 \end{bmatrix} \end{array}$$

Solution : The given matrix is 4 × 4 symmetric matrix. Hence, the associated graph G has 4 vertices. We see that $a_{11} = 1$ which implies that there is a loop at the vertex v_1. Also there are 2 loops at v_4. Further, $a_{14} = 2$ means there are 2 edges joining v_1 and v_4.

Similarly for other entries of the matrix.

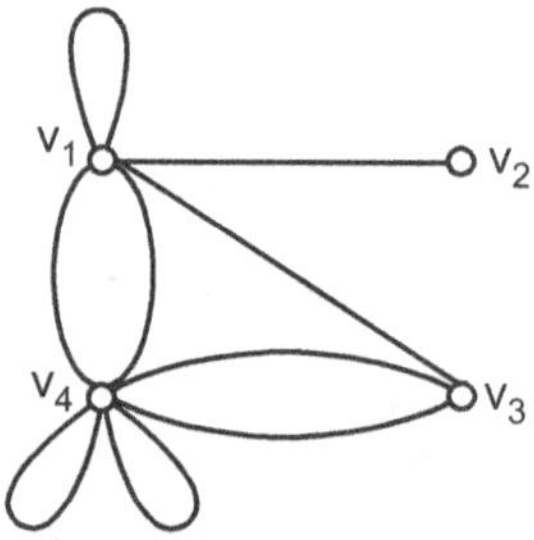

Fig. 1.27

Example 1.9 : *Draw the graph represented by the incidence matrix*

$$\begin{array}{c} \\ v_1 \\ v_2 \\ v_3 \\ v_4 \\ v_5 \end{array} \begin{array}{c} \begin{array}{cccccc} e_1 & e_2 & e_3 & e_4 & e_5 & e_6 \end{array} \\ \begin{bmatrix} 0 & 1 & 0 & 0 & 1 & 1 \\ 0 & 1 & 2 & 0 & 1 & 0 \\ 0 & 0 & 0 & 0 & 0 & 1 \\ 1 & 0 & 0 & 1 & 0 & 0 \\ 1 & 0 & 0 & 1 & 0 & 0 \end{bmatrix} \end{array}$$

Solution : The given matrix M is 5×6 matrix. Therefore, associated graph has 5 vertices and 6 edges. We see that edge e_1 has v_4 and v_5 as its end vertices. Similarly, e_2 has v_1 and v_2 as its end vertices. The edge e_3 forms a loop at v_2. The graph is as shown below.

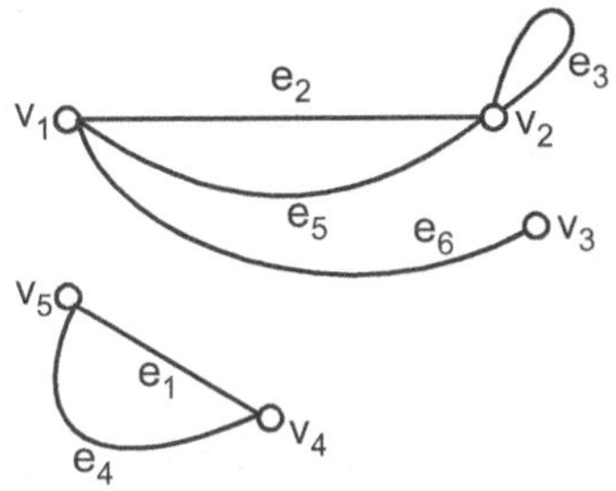

Fig. 1.28

We note that the identical columns in the incidence matrix correspond to parallel edges of the associated graph.

Example 1.10 : *Draw the following graphs :*

(i) *Non-complete bipartite graph.*

(ii) *Complete graph which is complete bipartite.*

(iii) *Regular graph but not complete.*

(iv) *$^3R_6$ i.e. 3 regular graph with 6 vertices.*

(v) *Wheel graph with outside 5 vertices.*

(vi) *Star of outside 5 vertices.*

Solution :

(i) Non-complete bipartite graph.

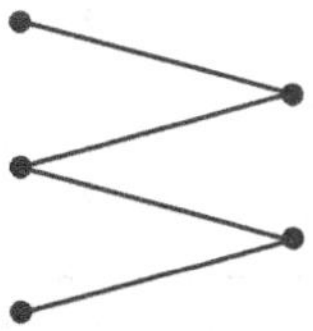

Fig. 1.29

(ii) Complete graph which is complete bipartite.

Fig. 1.30

(iii) Regular graph but not complete.

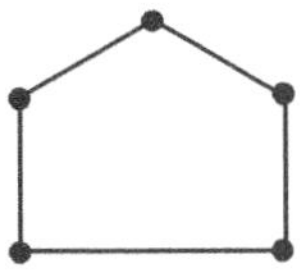

Fig. 1.31

(iv) $^3R_6$ i.e. 3 regular graph with 6 vertices.

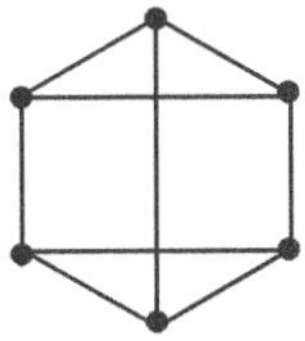

Fig. 1.32

(v) Wheel graph with outside 5 vertices.

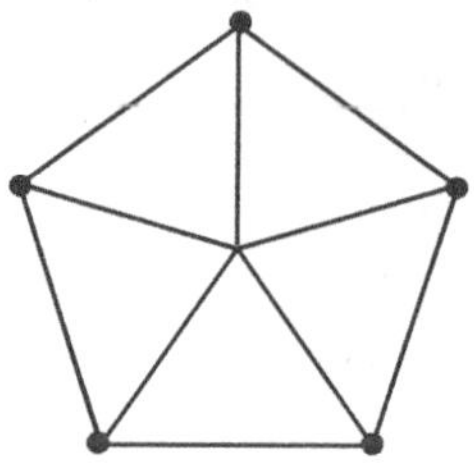

Fig. 1.33

(vi) Star of outside 5 vertices.

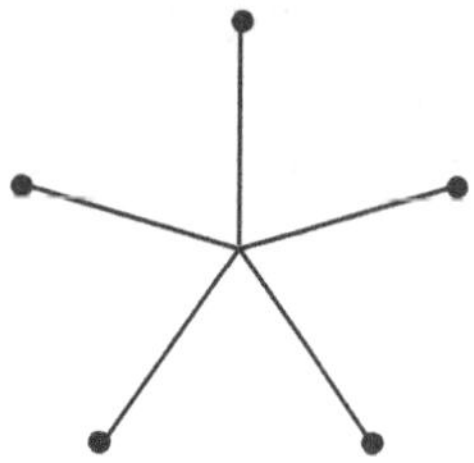

Fig. 1.34

Example 1.11 : *Find adjacency matrix of following graph.*

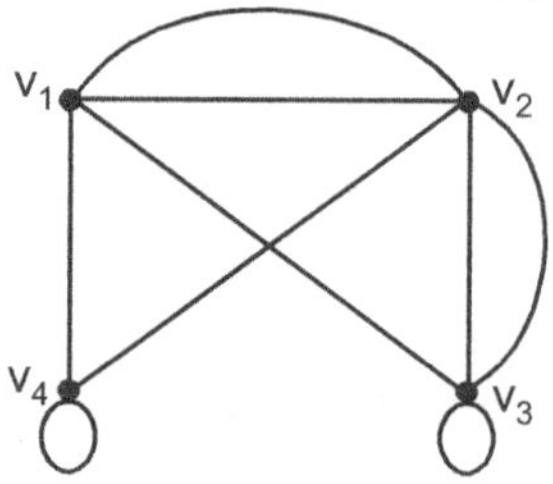

Fig. 1.35

Solution : Graph G has 4 vertices. Adjacency matrix of it is given below :

	v_1	v_2	v_3	v_4
v_1	0	2	1	1
v_2	2	0	2	1
v_3	1	2	1	0
v_4	1	1	0	1

Example 1.12 : *Write incidence and adjacency matrix of the following graph :*

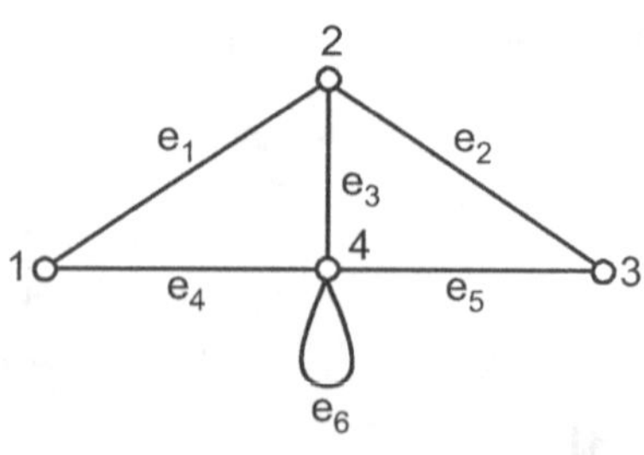

Fig. 1.36

Solution : Give graph G has 4 vertices and 6 edges. Incidence matrix $I(G) = [m_{ij}]$.

$i = 1, 2, 3, 4,\ \ j = 1, 2, 3, 4, 5, 6$ is 4×6 matrix.

$$M(G) = \begin{array}{c} \\ 1 \\ 2 \\ 3 \\ 4 \end{array}\begin{array}{c} \begin{array}{cccccc} e_1 & e_2 & e_3 & e_4 & e_5 & e_6 \end{array} \\ \begin{bmatrix} 1 & 0 & 0 & 1 & 0 & 0 \\ 1 & 1 & 1 & 0 & 0 & 0 \\ 0 & 1 & 0 & 0 & 1 & 0 \\ 0 & 0 & 1 & 1 & 1 & 2 \end{bmatrix} \end{array}$$

Graph G has 4 vertices. The adjacency matrix A(G) is 4×4 matrix.

$$A(G) = \begin{array}{c} \\ 1 \\ 2 \\ 3 \\ 4 \end{array}\begin{array}{c} \begin{array}{cccc} 1 & 2 & 3 & 4 \end{array} \\ \begin{bmatrix} 0 & 1 & 0 & 1 \\ 1 & 0 & 1 & 1 \\ 0 & 1 & 0 & 1 \\ 1 & 1 & 1 & 1 \end{bmatrix} \end{array}$$

Example 1.13 : *Draw the graph represented by the adjacency matrix.*

$$\begin{array}{c} \\ p \\ q \\ r \\ s \end{array}\begin{array}{c} \begin{array}{cccc} p & q & r & s \end{array} \\ \begin{bmatrix} 0 & 1 & 2 & 0 \\ 1 & 2 & 1 & 1 \\ 2 & 1 & 0 & 0 \\ 0 & 1 & 0 & 0 \end{bmatrix} \end{array}$$

Solution : Adjacency matrix has four rows and four columns. Therefore, the graph of given adjacency matrix is given in Fig. 1.37 below.

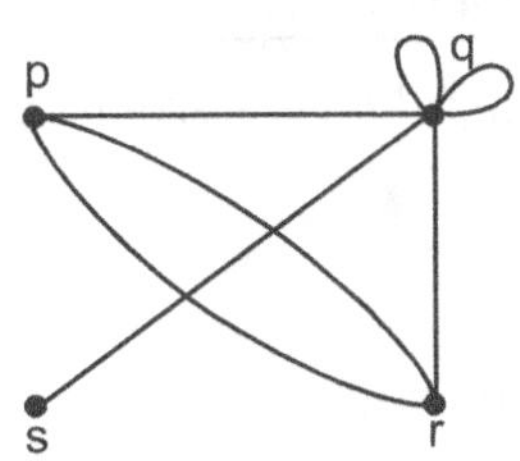

Fig. 1.37

Example 1.14 : *Consider a circle centered (1, 1) and having radius 3 units. Is it a graph? Justify.*

Solution : Circle with centre (1, 1) and radius 3 is not graph because circumference of circle does not form an edge.

Example 1.15 : *State Handshaking lemma and justify with proper example.*

Solution : Statement of Handshaking lemma : The sum of the degrees of all the vertices is equal to twice the number of edges in graph.

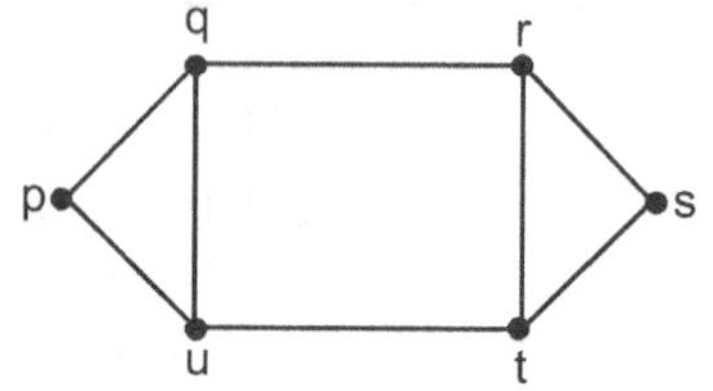

Fig. 1.38

$$d(p) = 2$$
$$d(q) = 3$$
$$d(r) = 3$$
$$d(s) = 2$$
$$d(t) = 3$$
$$d(u) = 3$$

$$\Rightarrow \sum_{V \in G} d(v) = 2 + 3 + 3 + 2 + 3 + 3 = 16$$

number of edges of graph are 8.

$$\therefore \quad \sum_{V \in G} d(v) = 2.8 = 2 \times \text{number of edges in G.}$$

$\therefore$ Handshaking lemma is verified.

Example 1.16 : *For the following graphs G_1 and G_2, find $G_1 \times G_2$.*

Fig. 1.39

Solution : The vertex set of $G_1 \times G_2$ is (a, p), (a, q), (b, p), (b, q), (c, p), (c, q), (d, p), (d, q).

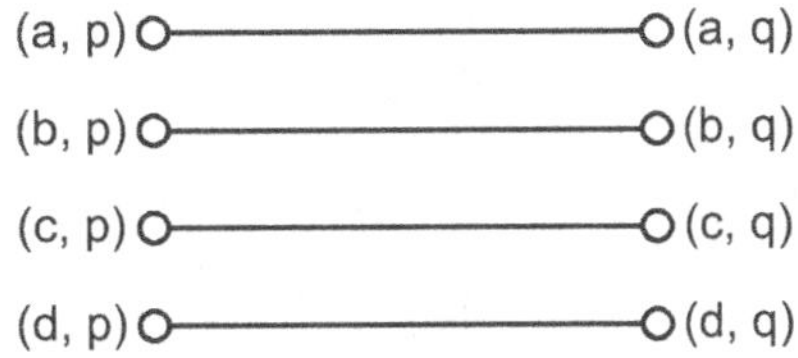

Fig. 1.39 (c)

By keeping 'a' fixed, we make a copy of G_2. Similarly, by keeping 'b', 'c', 'd' fixed, we make copy of G_2.

Also by keeping 'p' fixed and 'q' fixed, we make a copy of G_1. The resulting graph $G_1 \times G_2$ is as below.

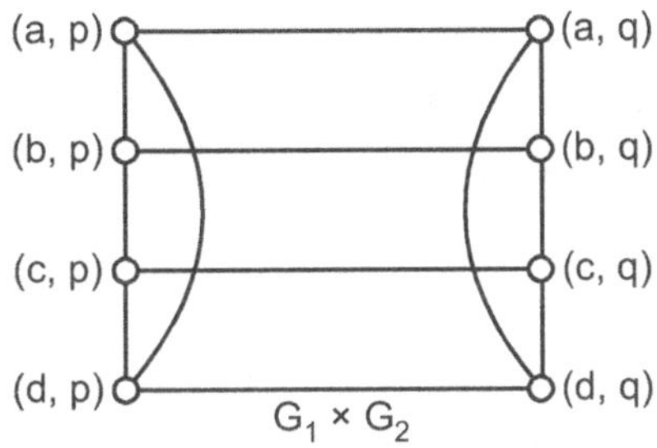

Fig. 1.39 (d)

Example 1.17 : *How many edges are there in a graph with 10 vertices with each of degree 6 ?*

Solution : Given that G(V, E) is a graph with $|V| = 10$ and $d(v) = 6 \; \forall \; v \in V$.

∴ By handshaking lemma,

$$\sum_{V \in G} d(v) = 2|E|$$

$$\therefore \quad \sum_{V \in G} 6 = 2|E| \qquad (\because \; d(v) = 6 \; \forall \; v \in V)$$

$$\therefore \quad 6 \times |V| = |E|$$

$$\therefore \quad \boxed{30 = |E|}$$

Example 1.18 : *Find the smallest integer n such that k_n has atleast 600 edges.*

Solution : Given that k_n has atleast 600 edges

$\therefore$ $$|E| \geq 600$$

But by handshaking lemma, for k_n, we have

$$|E| = \frac{n(n-1)}{2}$$

$\therefore$ We have, $$\frac{n(n-1)}{2} \geq 600$$

$$n(n-1) \geq 1200$$

i.e. we have $35 \times 34 = 1190 < 1200$ and $36 \times 35 = 1260 > 1200$

$\therefore$ $$\boxed{n = 36}$$

Example 1.19 : *Let G be k regular graph and k is odd integer. Prove that number of edges in G is multiple of k.*

Solution : Given that G(V, E) is a graph with $d(v) = k \ \forall \ v \in V$ and k is odd.

By handshaking lemma,

$$\sum_{v \in V} d(v) = 2|E|$$

$\therefore$ $$\sum_{v \in V} k = 2|E| \qquad (\because d(v) = k \ \forall \ v \in V)$$

$\therefore$ $$k \times |V| = 2|E|$$

$(\because 2|E|$ is even and K is odd $\Rightarrow |V|$ is even)

$\therefore$ $$k \times \left(\frac{|V|}{2}\right) = |E|$$

$\therefore$ Hence proved.

Example 1.20 : *Let G be a simple graph with atleast two vertices. Show that G contains atleast two vertices of same degree.*

Solution : Given that G(V, E) be a graph with $|V| \geq 2$.

Let $$|V| = n$$

we observe that,

G has vertex of degree n iff G does not have an isolated vertex. ... (1)

Let A_i = set of vertices in G having degree i, we have atmost n – 1 such non-empty sets.

Namely $A_0, A_1, A_2 \ldots A_n$ (from equation (1) A_0 or A_n is empty)

If we want to put vertices in V into sets A_i's, by pigeon-hole principle atleast two A_i's contain more than 2 vertices say u, v.

Hence we get, $d(v) = d(u)$

Example 1.21 : *Which complete bipartite graphs are complete graphs ?*

Solution : K_1 and K_2 are only complete bipartite graphs which are complete graphs.

[$\because$ If G is complete bipartite graph with partition $\forall = X \cup Y$ then $|X| \ngtr$ and $|Y| \ngtr 1$ otherwise G will not be complete graph]

Example 1.22 : *Show that the following graphs are isomorphic.*

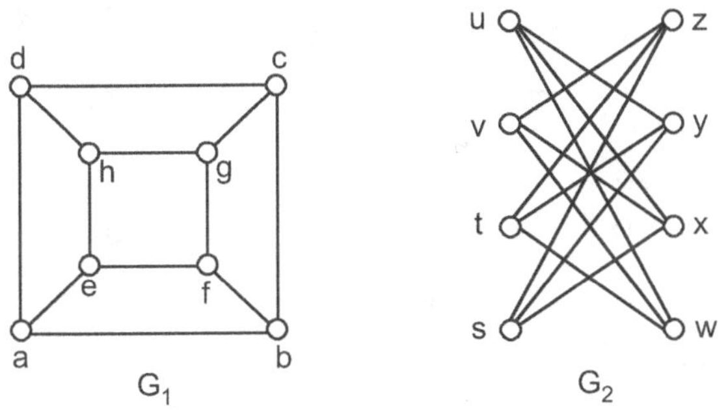

(a) **(b)**

Fig. 1.40

Solution : Define map from vertex set of G_1 to vertex set of G_2 by

$f(a) = u$, $f(b) = w$, $f(c) = v$, $f(d) = x$

$f(e) = y$, $f(f) = t$, $f(g) = z$, $f(h) = s$

[$\because$ Motivation to define f is we can redraw graph G_1 as

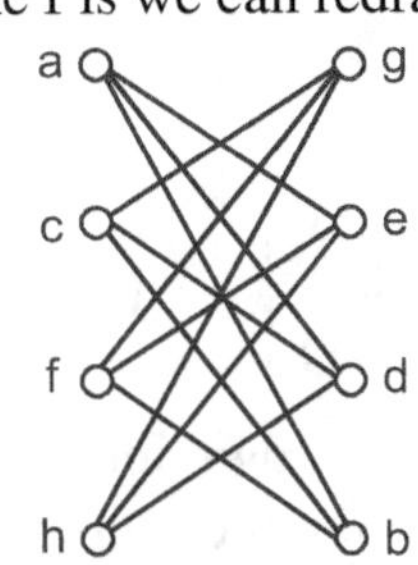

Fig. 1.41

Clearly f preserves adjacency relationship.

$\therefore$ f is isomorphism.

Hence both graphs are isomorphic

Example 1.23 : *Write all possible adjacency matrices and incidence matrices for following graphs*

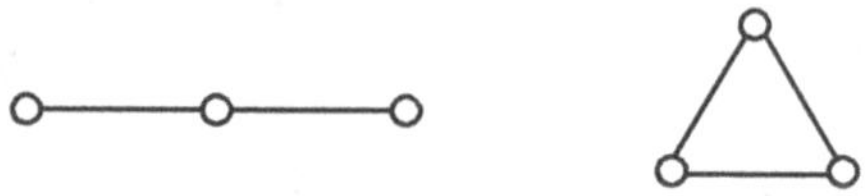

Fig. 1.42 (a)

Solution : Consider the graph

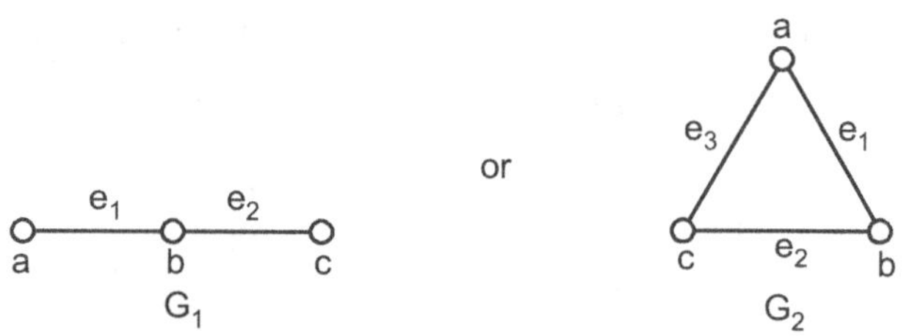

(i) (ii)

Fig. 1.42 (b)

$\therefore$ Adjacency matrices are

$$A(G_1) = \begin{array}{c} \\ a \\ b \\ c \end{array} \begin{array}{c} \begin{array}{ccc} a & b & c \end{array} \\ \begin{bmatrix} 0 & 1 & 0 \\ 1 & 0 & 1 \\ 0 & 1 & 0 \end{bmatrix} \end{array}, \quad A(G_2) = \begin{array}{c} \\ a \\ b \\ c \end{array} \begin{array}{c} \begin{array}{ccc} a & b & c \end{array} \\ \begin{bmatrix} 0 & 1 & 1 \\ 1 & 0 & 1 \\ 1 & 1 & 0 \end{bmatrix} \end{array}$$

Permuting rows into themselves and columns into themselves in similar way as that of rows, we get another adjacency matrices. Now incidence matrices are

$$I(G_1) = \begin{array}{c} \\ a \\ b \\ c \end{array} \begin{array}{c} \begin{array}{cc} e_1 & e_2 \end{array} \\ \begin{bmatrix} 1 & 0 \\ 1 & 1 \\ 0 & 1 \end{bmatrix} \end{array} \quad I(G_2) = \begin{array}{c} \\ a \\ b \\ c \end{array} \begin{array}{c} \begin{array}{ccc} e_1 & e_2 & e_3 \end{array} \\ \begin{bmatrix} 1 & 0 & 1 \\ 1 & 1 & 0 \\ 0 & 1 & 1 \end{bmatrix} \end{array}$$

Permuting the headings of rows into themselves and column into themselves and changing entries accordingly, we get another incidence matrices.

Example 1.24 : *Draw the graphs of the following adjacency matrix.*

$$\begin{bmatrix} 0 & 1 & 0 & 0 \\ 1 & 0 & 2 & 2 \\ 0 & 2 & 1 & 2 \\ 0 & 2 & 2 & 1 \end{bmatrix}$$

Solution : Let G be a graph with A(G) as shown above.

$$\therefore \quad A(G) = \begin{array}{c} \\ a \\ b \\ c \\ d \end{array} \begin{array}{c} \begin{array}{cccc} a & b & c & d \end{array} \\ \begin{bmatrix} 0 & 1 & 0 & 0 \\ 1 & 0 & 2 & 2 \\ 0 & 2 & 1 & 2 \\ 0 & 2 & 2 & 1 \end{bmatrix} \end{array}$$

where a, b, c, d are vertices of G

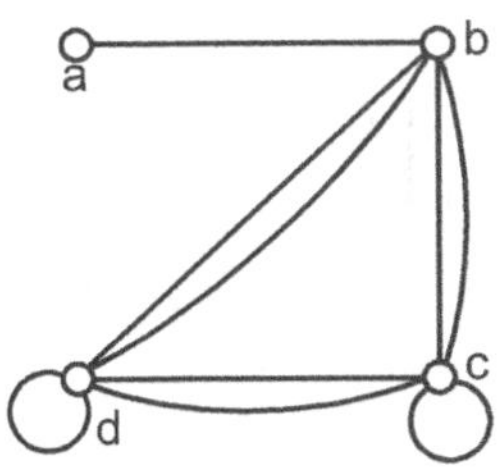

Fig. 1.43

Example 1.25 : *Let G be a bipartite graph, show that we can list the vertices of G so that corresponding adjacency matrix of G has the form*

$$A(G) = \begin{bmatrix} O & C \\ D & O \end{bmatrix}$$

Solution : Let vertex set V of G has partition

$\{X, Y\}$ i.e. $X \cup Y = V \quad X \cap Y = \phi$

and no two vertices of X are adjacent and no two vertices of Y are adjacent.

Let $X = \{x_1, x_2 \ldots x_m\}$

$Y = \{y_1, y_2 \ldots y_l\}$

Write A(G) with row headings $x_1, x_2 \ldots x_m, y_1 \ldots y_l$ and column headings $x_1, x_2, \ldots, x_m, y_1 \ldots y_l$.

We get, $$A(G) = \begin{bmatrix} O & C \\ D & O \end{bmatrix}$$

Example 1.26 : *Consider the graph G*

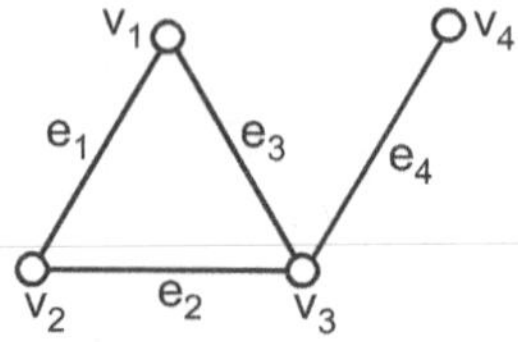

Fig. 1.44

Find A(G) and I(G).

Solution :

$$A(G) = \begin{array}{c} \\ v_1 \\ v_2 \\ v_3 \\ v_4 \end{array} \begin{array}{c} \begin{array}{cccc} v_1 & v_2 & v_3 & v_4 \end{array} \\ \begin{bmatrix} 0 & 1 & 1 & 0 \\ 1 & 0 & 1 & 0 \\ 0 & 1 & 1 & 1 \\ 0 & 0 & 1 & 0 \end{bmatrix} \end{array} \qquad I(G) = \begin{array}{c} \\ v_1 \\ v_2 \\ v_3 \\ v_4 \end{array} \begin{array}{c} \begin{array}{cccc} e_1 & e_2 & e_3 & e_4 \end{array} \\ \begin{bmatrix} 1 & 0 & 1 & 0 \\ 1 & 1 & 0 & 0 \\ 0 & 1 & 1 & 1 \\ 0 & 0 & 0 & 1 \end{bmatrix} \end{array}$$

Example 1.27 : *Find all non-isomorphic complete bipartite graphs with 7 vertices.*

Solution :

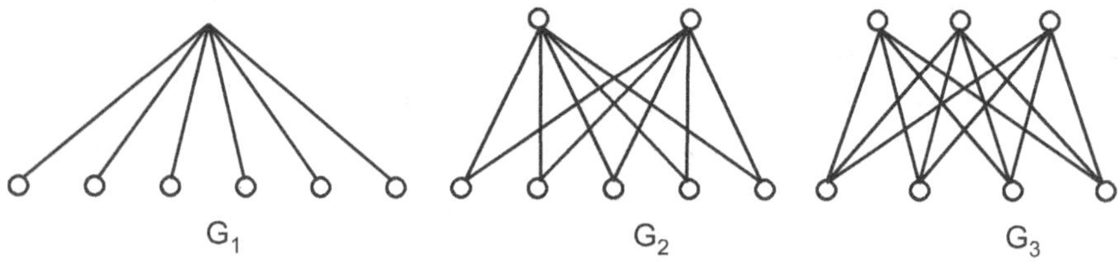

Fig. 1.45

Remark : Number of non-isomorphic complete bipartite graph of n vertices are number of 2 partitions of n i.e. equal to $\frac{n}{2}$ if n is even and $\frac{n-1}{2}$ if n is odd.

Example 1.28 : *Prove that it is impossible to have a group of 9 people at a party such that each one knows exactly five of the others in the group.*

Solution : Let us represent persons at party by set of vertices $(p_1, p_2, p_3, p_4, p_5, p_6, p_7, p_8, p_9\}$ we join p_i to p_j by an edge, if p_i knows p_j (obviously p_j knows p_i)

∴ Each p_i has degree 5.

∴ Sum of degrees $= 5 \times 9 = 45$

But by handshaking lemma sum of degrees

$= 2 \times |E|$ where $|E|$ = number of edges

∴ $45 = 2 \times |E|$

∴ 45 is even, which is absurd.

∴ Hence it is impossible to have a group of 9 people at a party such that each one knows exactly five of others in the group.

Think Over It

The degree sequence of a graph is the sequence of the degrees of the vertices of the graph in non-increasing order. For example, degree sequence of the graph G (as shown below) is 4, 4, 4, 3, 2,1, 0.

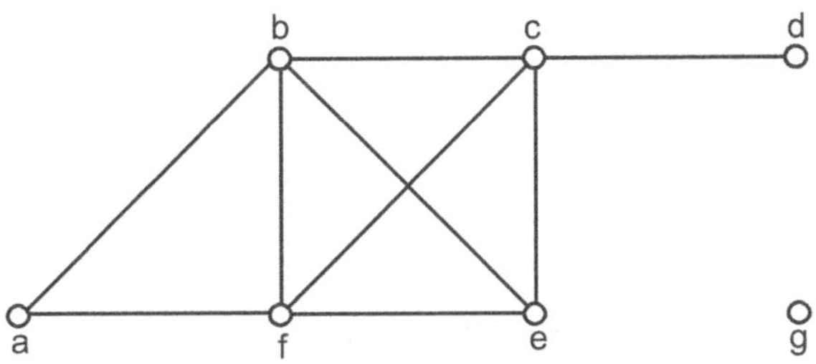

Fig. 1.46

Q.1 Find degree sequence of each of the following graphs

(a) K_4 (b) C_4

(c) W_4 (d) $K_{2, 3}$ (e) Q_3

Q.2 How many edges does a graph have if its degree sequence is 4, 3, 3, 2,? Draw such a graph.

Q.3 Determine whether each of these sequences is graphic. For those that are draw a graph having the given degree sequence

(a) 5, 4, 3, 2, 1, 0 (b) 6, 5, 4, 3, 2, 1

(c) 2, 2, 2, 2, 2, 2 (d) 3, 3, 3, 2, 2, 2

(e) 3, 3, 2, 2, 2, 2 (f) 1, 1, 1, 1, 1, 1

Summary

1. A graph in which each edge connects two different vertices and where no two edges connect the same pair of vertices is called a **simple graph**.
2. Graphs that may have multiple edges connecting the same vertices are called **multigraphs.**
3. A **directed graph** (or digraph) (V, E) consists of a non-empty set of vertices V and a set of directed edges (or arcs) E. Each directed edge is associated with an ordered pair of vertices. The directed edge associated with the ordered pair (u, v) is said to start at u and end at v.
4. If directed graph has no loops and has no multiple directed edges, then it is called a **simple directed graph**.
5. The degree of a vertex in an undirected graph is the number of edges incident with it, except that a loop at a vertex contributes twice to the degree of that vertex. The degree of the vertex is denoted by deg( ).
6. **The Handshaking Theorem :** Let G = (V, E) be an undirected graph with e edges.

   Then, $$2e = \sum_{u \in V} \deg(u)$$
7. An undirected graph has an even number of vertices of odd degree.
8. In a graph with directed edges the in-degree of a vertex v, denoted by $\deg^{-}(v)_i$ is the number of edges with v as their terminal vertex. The out degree of v_1 denoted by $\deg^{+}(v)_1$ is the number of edges with v_1 as their initial vertex.
9. Let G = (V, E) be a simple graph, with V = {1, 2, …, n}.

   The **adjacency matrix** of G is A = $[a_{ij}]$ where,

   $$a_{ij} = \begin{cases} 1, & \text{if } \{i, j\} \text{ is an edge of G} \\ 0, & \text{otherwise} \end{cases}$$
10. Let G = (V, E) be an undirected graph and V = {1, 2, …, n}.

    E = $\{e_1, e_2, \ldots, e_n\}$. Then the **incidence matrix** of G is

    $$M = [m_{ij}] \text{ where, } m_{ij} = \begin{cases} 1, & \text{when edge } e_j \text{ is incident with i} \\ 0, & \text{otherwise} \end{cases}$$

11. The simple graphs $G_1 = (V_1, E_1)$ and $G_2 = (V_2, E_2)$ are isomorphic if there is a one-to-one and onto function $f : V_1 \rightarrow V_2$ with the property that a and b are adjacent in G_1 if and only if f(a) and f(b) are adjacent in G_2, for all a and b in V_1. Such a function f is called an isomorphism.

Exercise

[A] Say True or False : Justify !

1. A circle with centre at (2, 3) and radius unity is a graph.
2. There is no simple graph with 10 vertices and 46 edges.
3. There exists a 5-regular graph on 7 vertices.
4. $K_{m, n}$ is regular if m = n.
5. Handshaking lemma is true for multigraph also.
6. There is a group of nine people at a party such that one knows exactly five of the others in the group.
7. There is simple graph with 10 vertices and 46 edges.
8. There is 5 regular graph with 7 vertices.
9. $K_{m, n}$ is regular iff m = n.
10. 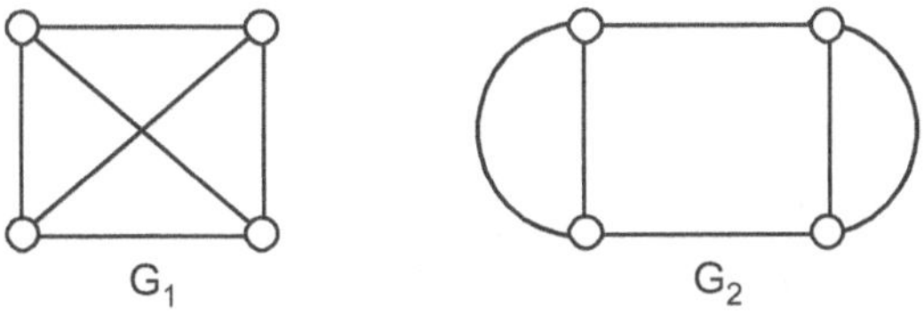 are isomorphic.
11. Adjacency matrix of graph is symmetric matrix.
12. 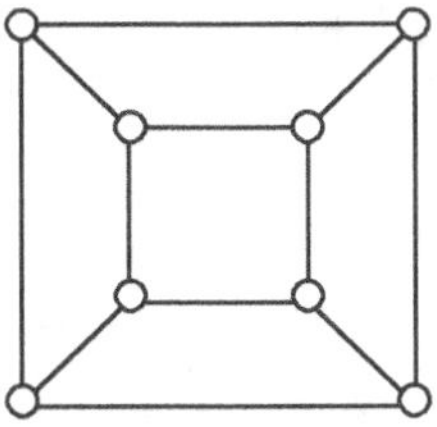 is a bipartite graph
13. Incidence matrix of null graph is zero matrix. But adjacency matrix of null graph is non-zero matrix.
14. Isomorphism of graphs is an equivalence relation on set of all graphs.

[B] Multiple Choice Questions : Choose the Correct Alternative

1. Let G be regular graph on odd number of vertices then degree of each vertex in G is possibly
   (a) 21 (b) 20
   (c) 19 (d) 17
2. The number of graphs on 3 vertices upto isomorphism are
   (a) 4 (b) 5
   (c) 6 (d) 7
3. The smallest number of vertices in K_n with 600 edges are
   (a) 35 (b) 36
   (c) 37 (d) 38
4. Which of the following are complete graphs.
   (a) $K_{1, 1}$ (b) $K_{2, 1}$
   (c) $K_{1, 2}$ (d) $K_{2, 2}$
5. Which of the following is an adjacency matrix of a simple graph ?
   (a) $\begin{bmatrix} 1 & 2 & 3 \\ 4 & 5 & 0 \\ 0 & 0 & 0 \end{bmatrix}$ (b) $\begin{bmatrix} 1 & 2 & 3 \\ 4 & 5 & 0 \end{bmatrix}$
   (c) $\begin{bmatrix} 0 & 1 & 1 \\ 1 & 0 & 1 \\ 1 & 1 & 0 \end{bmatrix}$ (d) $\begin{bmatrix} 0 & 1 & 1 \\ 0 & 0 & 1 \\ 1 & 0 & 1 \end{bmatrix}$
6. Let $A(G) = \begin{bmatrix} 1 & 0 & 1 \\ 0 & 1 & 2 \\ 2 & 1 & 0 \end{bmatrix}$ $A(G') = \begin{bmatrix} 0 & 1 & 2 \\ 1 & 0 & 1 \\ 2 & 1 & 0 \end{bmatrix}$

   are adjacency matrices of graphs G and G' then
   (a) $G \cong G'$
   (b) $G \cong G'$
   (c) Sometimes $G \cong G'$ but not always
   (d) $G = G'$
7. The number of 2 regular graphs on 4 vertices, upto isomorphism are
   (a) 2 (b) 3
   (c) 4 (d) 5

8. Which of the following is an incidence matrix of a simple graph?

(a) $\begin{bmatrix} 1 & 2 & 3 \\ 4 & 5 & 6 \\ 0 & 1 & 2 \end{bmatrix}$ (b) $\begin{bmatrix} 0 & 1 & 1 \\ 1 & 0 & 1 \\ 1 & 1 & 0 \end{bmatrix}$

(c) $\begin{bmatrix} 0 & 0 & 1 & 0 & 1 \\ 1 & 0 & 1 & 1 & 1 \\ 1 & 1 & 1 & 1 & 1 \end{bmatrix}$ (d) $\begin{bmatrix} 0 & 0 & 1 & 0 \\ 0 & 1 & 0 & 1 \\ 0 & 0 & 1 & 1 \end{bmatrix}$

9. Let G be a simple graph with atleast two vertices then
   (a) $G \cong K_3$
   (b) $G \cong K_{2,4}$
   (c) G has atleast two vertices of same degree
   (d) G is null graph

10. Let G be a graph with vertices v_1, v_2, v_3, v_4 then we have possibly.
   (a) $d(v_1) = 1$ $d(v_2) = 2$ $d(v_3) = 3$ $d(v_4) = 5$
   (b) $d(v_1) = 1$ $d(v_2) = 1$ $d(v_3) = 2$ $d(v_4) = 1$
   (c) $d(v_1) = 3$ $d(v_2) = 2$ $d(v_3) = 5$ $d(v_4) = 0$
   (d) $d(v_1) = 0$ $d(v_2) = 2$ $d(v_3) = 2$ $d(v_3) = 3$

[C] Theory Questions :

1. Give one application of graph in brief.
2. State and prove handshaking lemma.
3. Prove that any simple graph on n vertices has atmost $\frac{n(n-1)}{2}$ edges.
4. Let G_1, G_2 and G_3 be three graphs. If $G_1 \cong G_2$ and $G_2 \cong G_3$ then show that $G_1 \cong G_3$.
5. Let G_1 and G_2 be two graphs such that $G_1 \cong G_2$. If G_1 has 20 vertices of degree 4 then show that G_2 also has 20 vertices at degree 4.
6. Prove that isomorphism of graphs is an equivalence relation.
7. A man has a boat with carrying capacity of two objects only, himself and other. He wants to pass a goat, a bundle of grass and tiger from a bank of river to opposite bank of the river through the boat. Show that it is possible for him to do this. Explain this in terms of a graph.
8. Define a complete graph and a regular graph.
9. Define adjacency matrix and incidence matrix of a graph. What is the difference between them ?

[D] Numerical Problems :

1. Draw all simple non-isomorphic graphs on 3 vertices.
2. Draw all simple non-isomorphic graphs on 4 vertices.
3. Show that the following pairs of graphs are isomorphic :

(a)

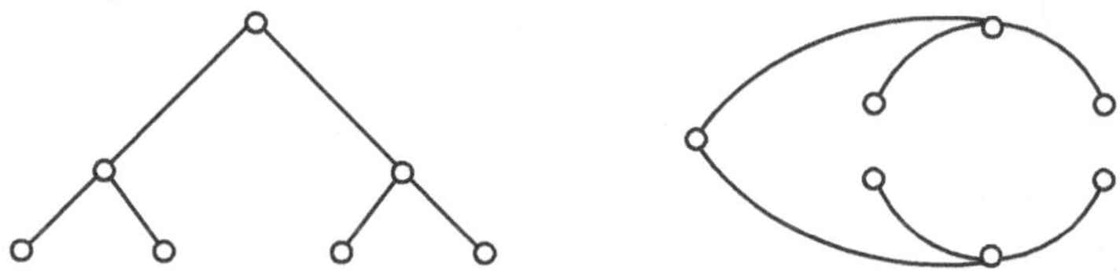

Fig. 1.47 (a)

(b)

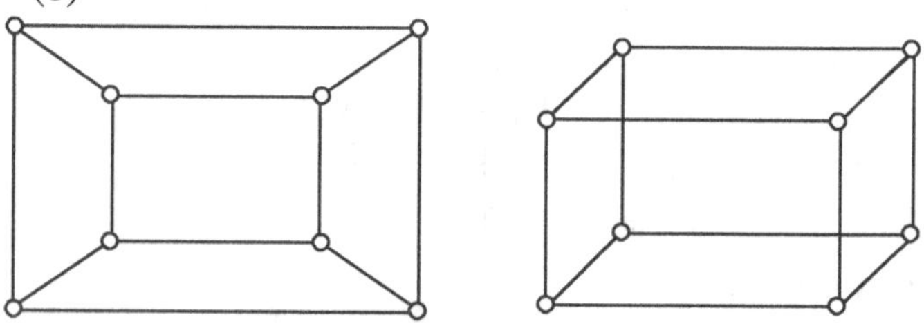

Fig. 1.47 (b)

4. Explain why the two given graphs are not isomorphic although the necessary conditions for isomorphism are satisfied.

(a)

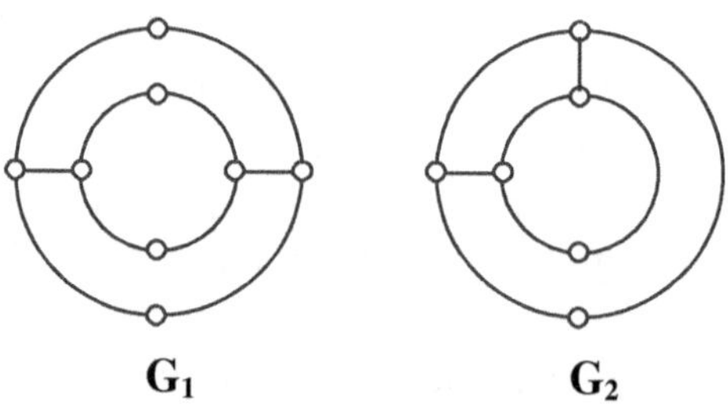

Fig. 1.48 (a)

(b)

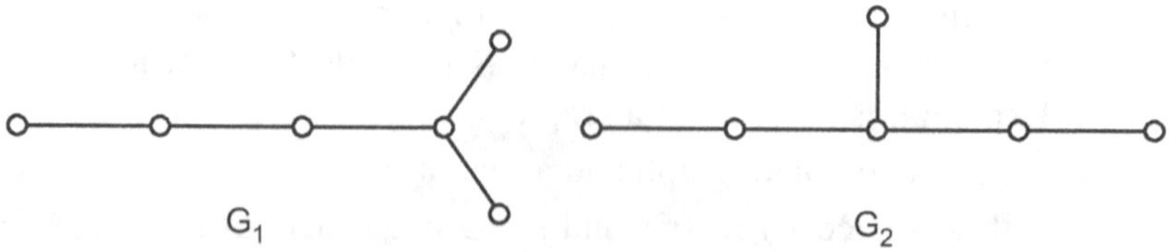

Fig. 1.48 (b)

5. Examine whether the following pairs of graphs are isomorphic or not.

(a)

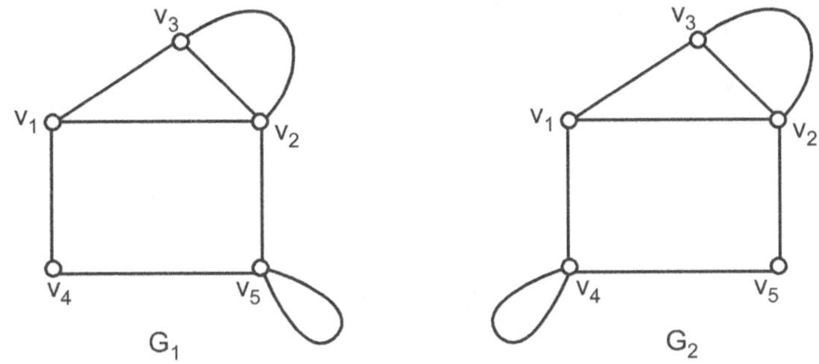

Fig. 1.49 (a)

(b)

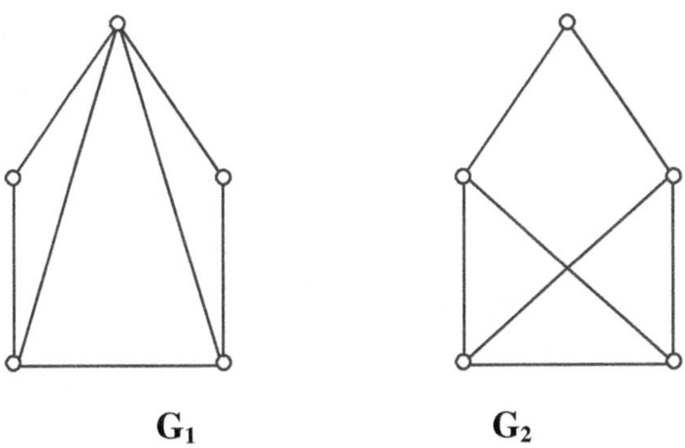

Fig. 1.49 (b)

(c)

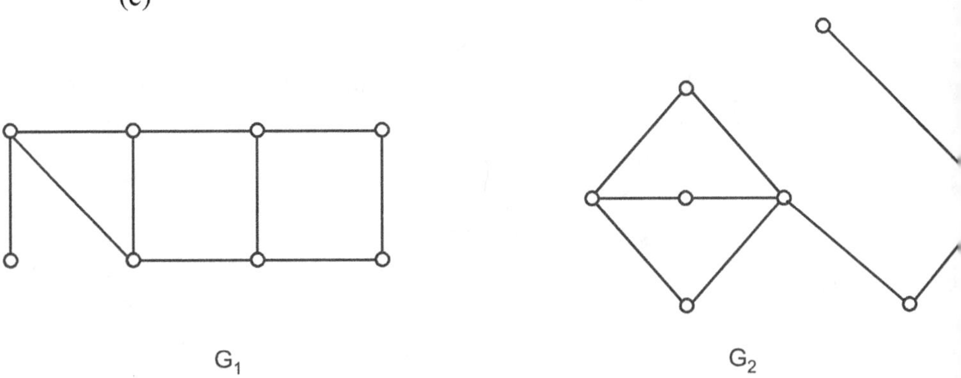

Fig. 1.49 (c)

(d)

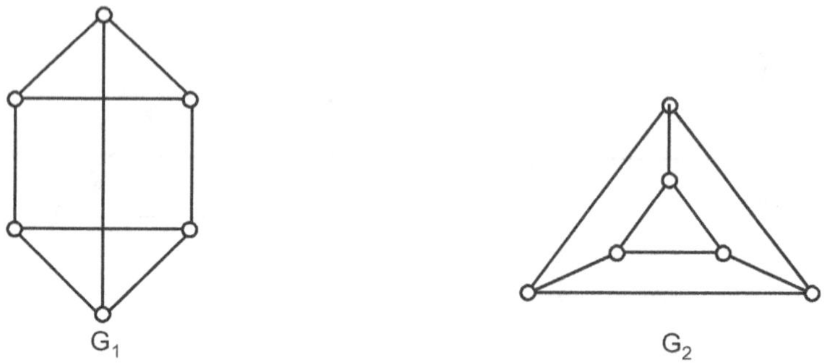

Fig. 1.49 (d)

(e)

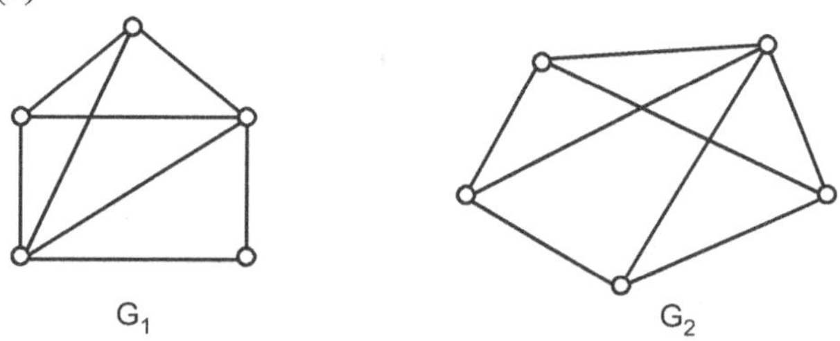

Fig. 1.49 (e)

(f)

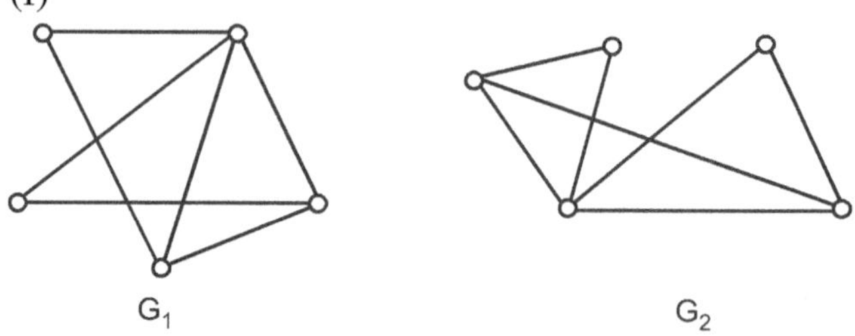

Fig. 1.49 (f)

6. Find the isomorphic pair out of three graphs shown below. Justify.

(a)

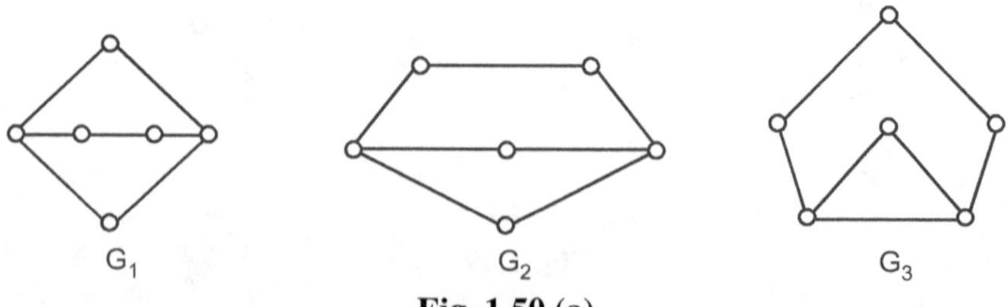

Fig. 1.50 (a)

(b)

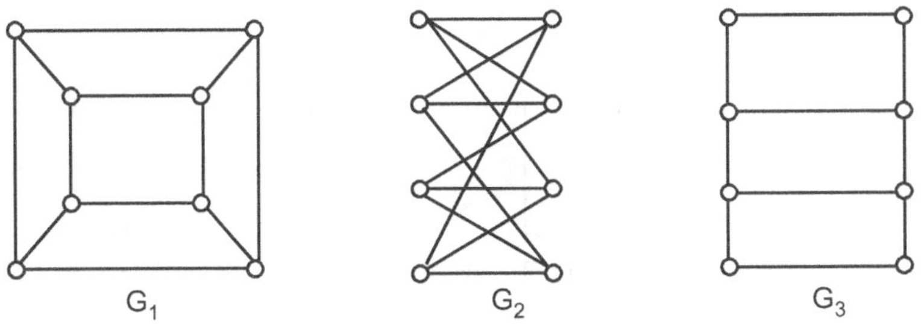

Fig. 1.50 (b)

7. Show that the following two graphs are isomorphic.

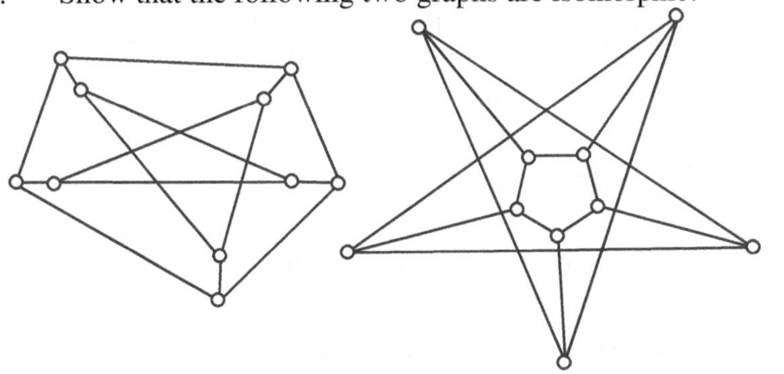

Fig. 1.51

8. Find the adjacency matrix and incidence matrix of the graph.

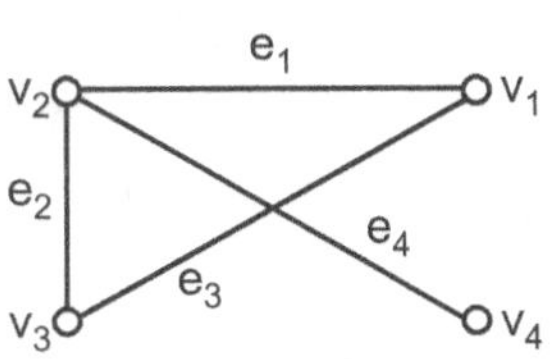

Fig. 1.52 (a)

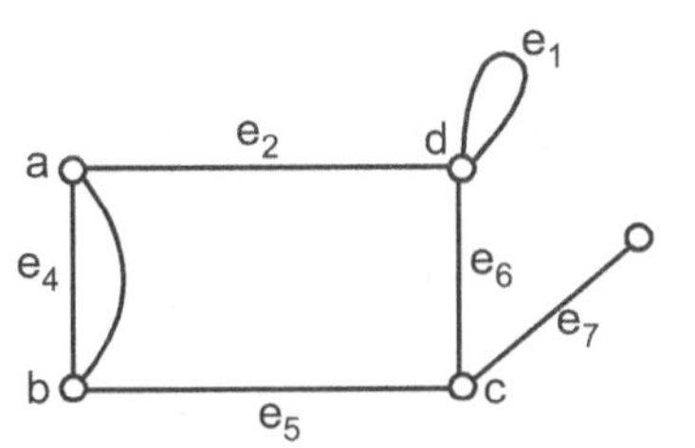

Fig. 1.52 (b)

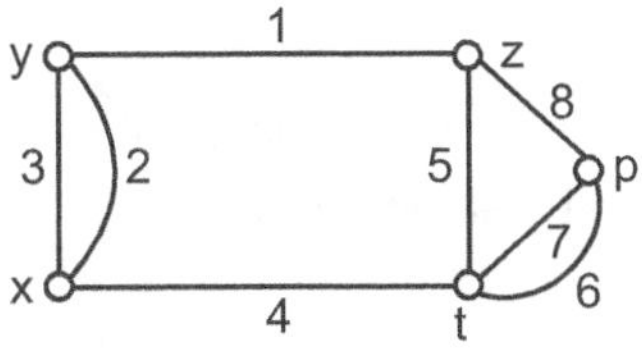

Fig. 1.52 (c)

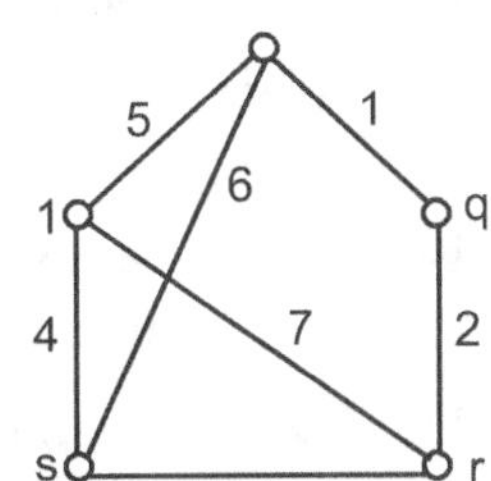

Fig. 1.52 (d)

9. The adjacency matrix of the graph is given below. Draw the graph.

(a) $\begin{bmatrix} 1 & 1 & 2 & 0 \\ 1 & 2 & 1 & 3 \\ 2 & 1 & 0 & 1 \\ 0 & 3 & 1 & 0 \end{bmatrix}$ (b) $\begin{bmatrix} 1 & 3 & 0 & 0 \\ 3 & 0 & 2 & 1 \\ 0 & 2 & 1 & 2 \\ 0 & 1 & 2 & 0 \end{bmatrix}$

(c) $\begin{bmatrix} 0 & 2 & 0 & 1 \\ 2 & 1 & 1 & 1 \\ 0 & 1 & 0 & 1 \\ 1 & 1 & 1 & 0 \end{bmatrix}$ (d) $\begin{bmatrix} 1 & 1 & 1 & 2 \\ 1 & 0 & 0 & 0 \\ 1 & 0 & 0 & 2 \\ 2 & 0 & 2 & 2 \end{bmatrix}$

10. Draw a graph G with vertex set {1, 2, 3, 4, 5, 6, 7} and exactly one edge between the members of each of the following pairs of vertices : (1, 2), (1, 3) (2, 4), (2, 5), (3, 6), (3, 7). Is G simple ?

11. Determine the number of edges in a graph with 6 vertices, 2 of degree 4 and 4 of degree 2.

Draw two such graphs one simple and the other not simple.

12. Verify hand shaking lemma for the graph shown in Fig. 1.53.

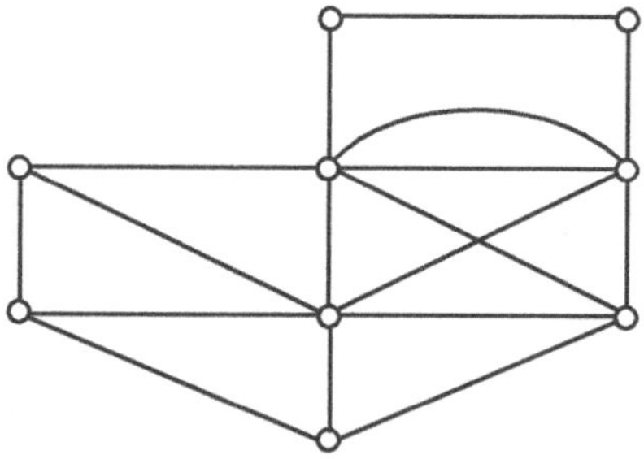

Fig. 1.53

13. Prove that it is impossible to have a group of nine people at a party such that each one knows exactly five of the others in the group.

14. Let G be a simple graph with at least two vertices. Show that G contains at least two vertices of the same degree.

15. Draw the graphs $K_{2,4}$ and $K_{3,2}$.

16. Find the smallest integer n such that K_n has at least 600 edges.

17. G is a K-regular graph where K is odd number. Prove that the number of edges in G is a multiple of K.

18. Describe a graph model that represents a subway system in a large city. Should edges be directed or undirected? Should multiple edges be allowed? Should loops be allowed?

19. Describe a graph model that represents traditional marriage between men and women. Does this graph have any properties?

20. Show that in a simple graph with at least two vertices there must be two vertices that have the same degree.

21. Draw the following graphs :

(a) K_7 (b) $K_{1,8}$ (c) C_7 (d) W_9 (e) Q_4

22. For which values of n are these graphs bipartite?

(a) K_n (b) C_n (c) W_n (d) Q_n

23. How many subgraphs with at least one vertex does K_3 have?

24. How many subgraphs with at least one vertex does W_3 have?

25. Draw a subgraphs of the following graph

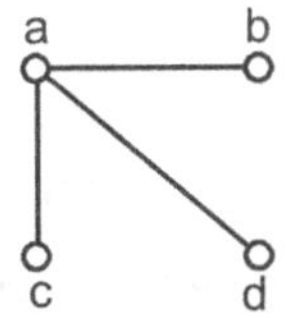

Fig. 1.54

26. How many non-isomorphic simple graphs are there with five vertices and three edges ?

27. Are the simple graphs with the following adjacency matrices isomorphic?

$$\begin{bmatrix} 0 & 0 & 1 \\ 0 & 0 & 1 \\ 1 & 1 & 0 \end{bmatrix}, \begin{bmatrix} 0 & 1 & 1 \\ 1 & 0 & 0 \\ 1 & 0 & 0 \end{bmatrix}$$

28. Determine whether the graphs without loops with these incidence matrices are isomorphic

$$\begin{bmatrix} 1 & 0 & 1 \\ 0 & 1 & 1 \\ 1 & 1 & 0 \end{bmatrix}, \begin{bmatrix} 1 & 1 & 0 \\ 1 & 0 & 1 \\ 0 & 1 & 1 \end{bmatrix}$$

29. A tree T having n vertices is such that each vertex has degree 1 or 3 only. Show that the number of vertices of degree is $\frac{n-2}{2}$.

30. Find the total number of spanning trees of the following graph.

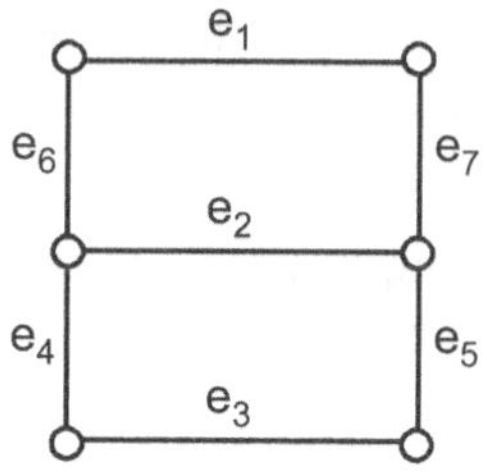

Fig. 1.55

31. Consider the graph G below :

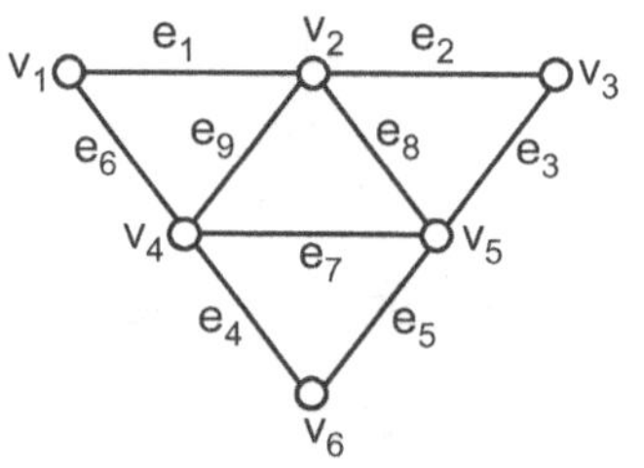

Fig. 1.56

Show that G has 54 spanning trees.

Answers

[A] (1) False (2) True (3) False (4) True (5) True (6) False (7) False (8) False (9) True (10) True (11) True (12) True (13) False (14) True

[B] (1) - (b) (2) - (a) (3) - (a) (4) - (a) (5) - (c) (6) - (a) (7) - (a) (8) - (b) (9) - (c) (10) - (c)

[D] 1.

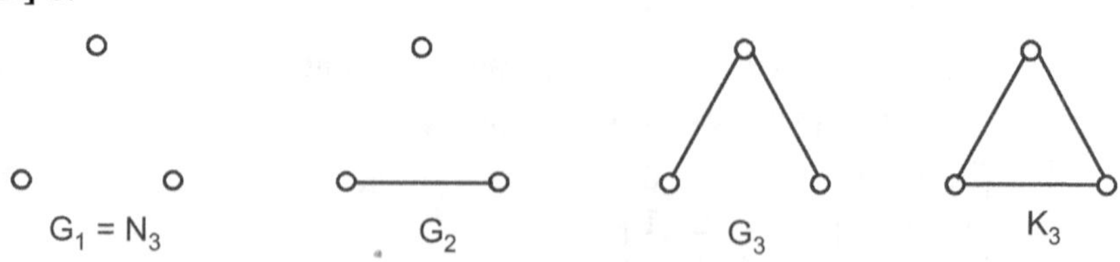

Fig. 1.57

2.

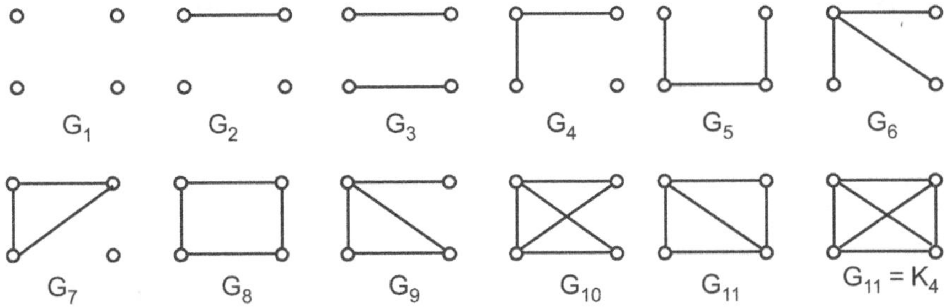

Fig. 1.58

4. (a) In G_2, any two vertices of degree 3 are adjacent. This does not hold in G_1.

(b) In G_1, a vertex of degree 3 has two adjacent vertices of degree 1 and one adjacent vertex of degree 2. In G_2, a vertex of degree 3 has one adjacent vertex of degree 1 and two adjacent vertices of degree 2.

5. (a) Not isomorphic. In G_1, the degree 4 vertices are adjacent but in G_2, degree 4 vertices are not adjacent.

(b) Not isomorphic. G_1 has a vertex of degree 4 but G_2 does not have a vertex of degree 4.

(c) Not isomorphic. Number of edges in two graphs is not equal.

(d) Isomorphic

(e) Not isomorphic. G_1 has two vertices of degree 4 but G_2 has only one vertex of degree 4.

(f) Isomorphic

6. (a) $G_1 \cong G_2$, (b) $G_2 \cong G_3$.

8. (a)

$$A(G) = \begin{array}{c} \\ v_1 \\ v_2 \\ v_3 \\ v_4 \end{array} \begin{array}{c} \begin{array}{cccc} v_1 & v_2 & v_3 & v_4 \end{array} \\ \begin{bmatrix} 0 & 1 & 1 & 0 \\ 1 & 0 & 1 & 1 \\ 1 & 1 & 0 & 0 \\ 0 & 1 & 0 & 0 \end{bmatrix} \end{array}$$

$M(G) =$

	e_1	e_2	e_3	e_4
v_1	1	0	1	0
v_2	1	1	0	1
v_3	0	1	1	0
v_4	0	0	0	1

(b) $A(G) =$

	a	b	c	d	e
a	0	2	0	1	0
b	2	0	1	0	0
c	0	1	0	1	1
d	1	0	1	1	0
e	0	0	1	0	0

$M(G) =$

	e_1	e_2	e_3	e_4	e_5	e_6	e_7
a	0	1	1	1	0	0	0
b	0	0	1	1	1	0	0
c	0	0	0	0	1	1	1
d	2	1	0	0	0	1	0
e	0	0	0	0	0	0	1

(c) $A(G) =$

	x	y	z	t	p
x	0	2	0	1	0
y	2	0	1	0	0
z	0	1	0	1	1
t	1	0	1	0	2
p	0	0	1	2	0

$M(G) =$

	1	2	3	4	5	6	7	8
x	0	1	1	1	0	0	0	0
y	1	1	1	0	0	0	0	0
z	1	0	0	0	1	0	0	1
t	0	0	0	1	1	1	1	0
p	0	0	0	0	0	1		

(d)

$$A(G) = \begin{array}{c} \\ p \\ q \\ r \\ s \\ t \end{array} \begin{array}{c} \begin{array}{ccccc} p & q & r & s & t \end{array} \\ \begin{bmatrix} 0 & 1 & 0 & 1 & 1 \\ 1 & 0 & 1 & 0 & 0 \\ 0 & 1 & 0 & 1 & 1 \\ 1 & 0 & 1 & 0 & 1 \\ 1 & 0 & 1 & 1 & 0 \end{bmatrix} \end{array}$$

$$M(G) = \begin{array}{c} \\ p \\ q \\ r \\ s \\ t \end{array} \begin{array}{c} \begin{array}{ccccccc} 1 & 2 & 3 & 4 & 5 & 6 & 7 \end{array} \\ \begin{bmatrix} 1 & 0 & 0 & 0 & 1 & 1 & 0 \\ 1 & 1 & 0 & 0 & 0 & 0 & 0 \\ 0 & 1 & 1 & 0 & 0 & 0 & 1 \\ 0 & 0 & 1 & 1 & 0 & 1 & 0 \\ 0 & 0 & 0 & 1 & 1 & 0 & 1 \end{bmatrix} \end{array}$$

9. (a)

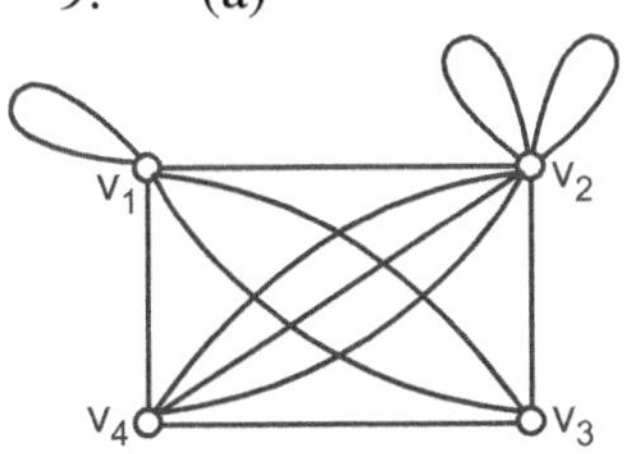

Fig. 1.59 (a)

(b)

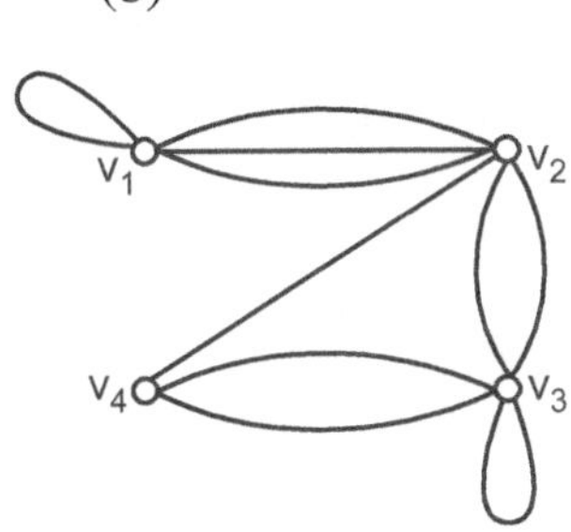

Fig. 1.59 (b)

(c)

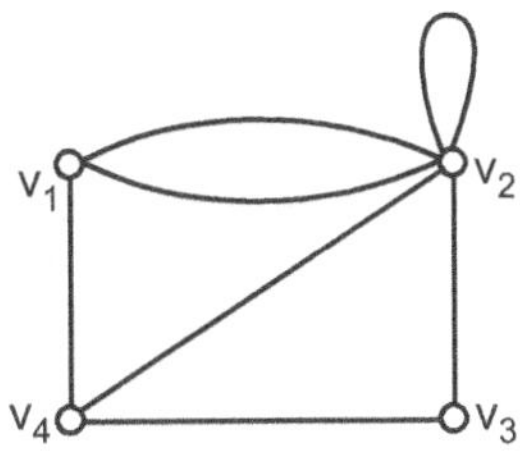

Fig. 1.59 (c)

(d)

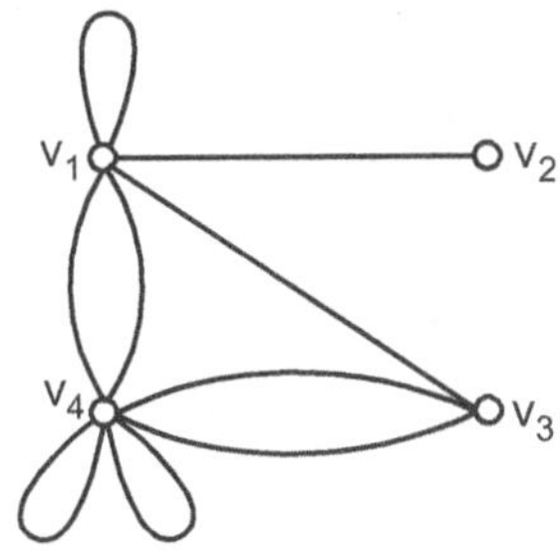

Fig. 1.59 (d)

10.

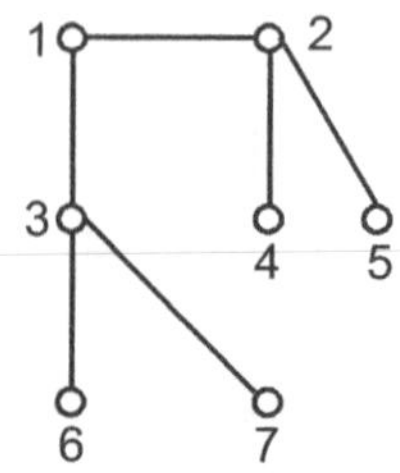

Fig. 1.60

Yes this graph is simple.

11. 8

15.

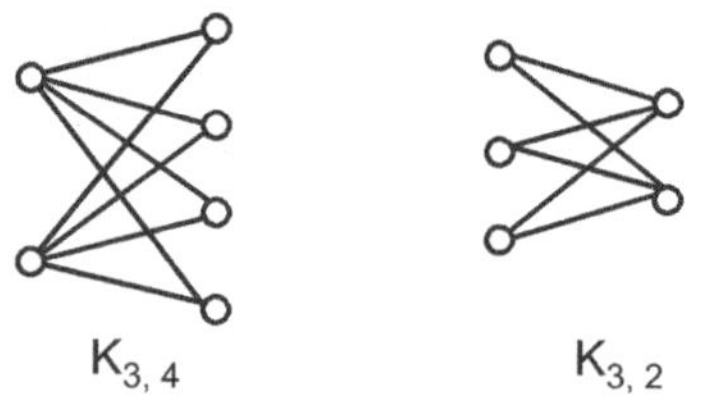

Fig. 1.61

30. 15

✍ ✍ ✍

Chapter **2**...

Connected Graphs

Edsger Wybe Dijkstra

Dijkstra completed his studies in theoretical physics at the university, graduating in 1956. Also in 1956 the Mathematical Centre competed building a new computer and wanted to give a public demonstration.

He published this shortest algorithm, together with his very efficient algorithm for the shortest spanning tree, were published in the two page paper *A Note on Two Problems in Connexion with Graphs* (1959). Also in 1959 he was awarded his Ph.D. from the University of Amsterdam for his thesis *Communication with an Automatic Computer.*

In 1962 Dijkstra was appointed Professor of Mathematics at the Eindhoven University of Technology. At this time Eindhoven had no Computer Science Department, nor of course did other universities.

In 1972 Dijkstra won the ACM Turing Award which is considered the most prestigious award in Computer Science.

2.1 Introduction

We are now acquainted with the adjacency and incidence relationships in a graph. These relationships lead us to various concepts like path, cycle etc. which in turn enable us to give the definition of a connected graph. First we define those concepts.

Walk : Let G be a graph. A finite alternating sequence $\{v_1\ e_1,\ v_2\ e_2 \dots v_i\ e_i\ v_{i+1} \dots v_n\}$ of vertices and edges of G, beginning and ending with a vertex such that every edge involved in it is incident on a vertex which precedes and succeeds it, is called a walk in G.

This definition clearly allows the repetition of a vertex/edge in a walk.

Consider the graph given below.

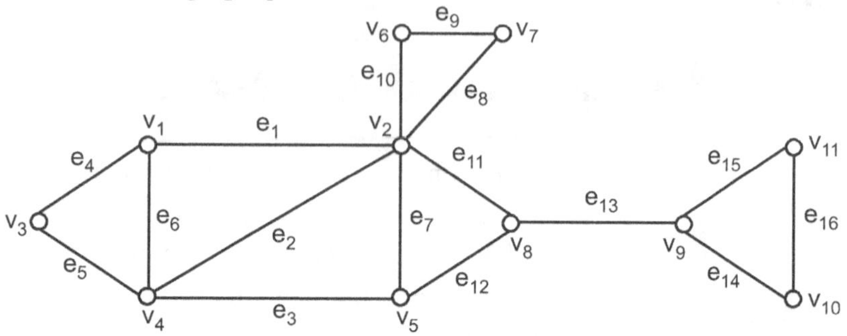

Fig. 2.1

The following are some walks in G :

W_1 : $v_4\, e_2\, v_2\, e_{10}\, v_6\, e_9\, v_7\, e_8\, v_2\, e_{11}\, v_8\, e_{13}\, v_9\, e_{13}\, v_8\, e_{12}\, v_5$

W_2 : $v_4\, e_2\, v_2\, e_{10}\, v_6\, e_9\, v_7\, e_8\, v_2\, e_7\, v_5$

W_3 : $v_1\, e_1\, v_2\, e_{10}\, v_6\, e_9\, v_7\, e_8\, v_2\, e_2\, v_4\, e_6\, v_1$

W_4 : $v_3\, e_5\, v_4\, e_3\, v_5\, e_{12}\, v_8$

W_5 : $v_4\, e_2\, v_2\, e_{11}\, v_8\, e_{12}\, v_5\, e_3\, v_4$

These walks differ from one another in a slight manner. For example, in the walk W_1, there is a repetition of v_2 and v_5, also the edge e_{13} is repeated. But in W_2, a vertex v_2 is repeated without repetition of any edge.

Trail : A walk in which there is no repetition of any edge is called a trail.

Thus, the walk W_2 is a trail. In any walk the vertices with which it begins and ends are called end vertices of that walk; in particular the beginning vertex is called initial vertex and the ending vertex is called terminal vertex. Any other vertex in the walk is called an intermediate vertex.

A walk is called open or closed according as its end vertices are distinct or coincident.

We see that W_3 and W_5 are closed walks and the remaining 3 are open walks.

Tour : A closed trail is called a tour. Accordingly, the walk W_3 above is a tour.

Path : A walk in which any vertex is non-repeated (hence there cannot be repetition of any edge) is called a path.

Cycle : A closed path is called a cycle (or circuit). Thus, W_4 is a path and W_5 is a cycle.

The number of edges in a path (cycle) is called length of that path (cycle).

The path W_4 above is of length 3 because there are 3 edges in it and the cycle W_5 is of length 4. A single vertex is a path of length 0. A single vertex together with a loop is a cycle of length 1 and a single edge together with its two distinct vertices is a path of length 1.

If now a and b are two vertices of a graph G then there exist in general various paths of different lengths from the vertex a to the vertex b. (Note that we are assuming the existence of at least one such path.) In the graph G above, for example,

$$p_1 \ : \ v_1 e_1 v_2 e_{11} v_8$$

$$p_2 \ : \ v_1 e_1 v_2 e_7 v_5 e_{12} v_8$$

$$p_3 \ : \ v_1 e_6 v_4 e_2 v_2 e_7 v_5 e_{12} v_8$$

are paths joining v_1 to v_8 of lengths 2, 3, 4 respectively. If P is the path of minimum length joining the vertices a and b then it is called the shortest path from a to b. The length of the shortest path joining the vertices a and b of a graph G is called the distance between a and b and it is denoted by d(a, b). In the graph G mentioned above, we see that $v_4 e_2 v_2 e_{11} v_8$ and $v_4 e_3 v_5 e_{12} v_8$ are two different shortest paths; having path length 2. Therefore, $d(v_4, v_8) = 2$.

This shows that the shortest path joining the two given vertices is not unique but its length is unique.

Theorem 1 In a graph G there exists a path from the vertex u to the vertex v if and only if there exists a walk from u to v.

Proof : First Part : We know that every path is a walk. Therefore, if there is a path from u to v then it can be considered as a walk from u to v.

Second Part : Suppose now that there is a walk W from u to v and $W : u\, e_1 v_1 e_2 v_2 \ldots v$.

If in W each vertex has frequency 1 i.e. appears only once then W is itself a path from u to v.

If not then some vertices in W are repeated. Let v_i be the first vertex which is repeated in W. Therefore, walk W is of the form

$$W \ : \ u\, e_1 v_1 \ldots e_{i-1} v_{i-1} e_i v_i e_{i+1} v_{i+1} \ldots e_j v_i \ldots v$$

From W now we delete the portion $e_{i+1} v_{i+1} \ldots e_j$.

Then W reduces to W' : u e_1 v_1 … e_i v_i … v. If there is no repetition of any vertex in W' then W' is a path from u to v. Otherwise suppose the vertex v_j is the first vertex in W' which is repeated. As before we delete the portion e_{j+1} v_{j+1} … e_k from W' and get W''. We continue this process of deletion until we get W* where there is no repetition of any vertex. Then W^* is the required path from u to v. ■

Edge Sequence :

Definition : Let G(V, E) be a graph connected or disconnected and u, v be two vertices of G. An edge sequence of length n from the vertex u to the vertex v is the set S of n edges which are arranged so that

$$S = \{(u, x_1), (x_1, x_2), (x_2, x_3), \ldots, (x_{n-1}, v)\}.$$

In the edge sequence, the repetition of vertices and edges is permitted. The edges in the edge sequence are so arranged that every edge in it from the second edge starts with a vertex in which the preceding edge ends.

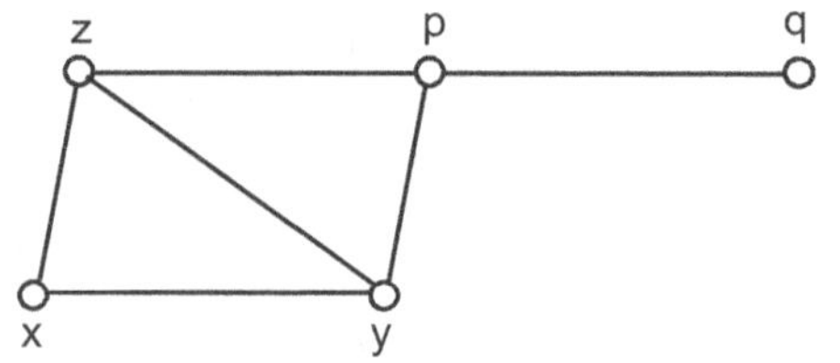

Fig. 2.2

In the above graph, consider the vertices z and q.

$$S_1 = \{(z, p), (p, q)\}$$

$$S_2 = \{(z, y), (y, p), (p, q)\}$$

$$S_3 = \{(z, x), (x, y), (y, p), (p, q)\}$$

$$S_4 = \{(z, x), (x, y), (y, z), (z, p), (p, q)\}$$

are the edge sequences of lengths 2, 3, 4, 5 respectively from the vertex z to the vertex q.

A single edge can be considered as an edge sequence of length 2 from one of its end vertex to itself. In the above graph, the set S = {(x, y), (y, x)} is an edge sequence of length 2 from x to x itself.

Suppose that G is a simple graph whose adjacency matrix is A = A(G). Then the i-jth element in the matrix A^n gives the number of edge sequences of length n from the vertex v_i to the vertex v_j. This result can be proved by induction on n.

In the above example, the adjacency matrix of G is

$$A = \begin{array}{c} \\ x \\ y \\ z \\ p \\ q \end{array} \begin{array}{c} \begin{array}{ccccc} x & y & z & p & q \end{array} \\ \begin{bmatrix} 0 & 1 & 1 & 0 & 0 \\ 1 & 0 & 1 & 1 & 0 \\ 1 & 1 & 0 & 1 & 0 \\ 0 & 1 & 1 & 0 & 1 \\ 0 & 0 & 0 & 1 & 0 \end{bmatrix} \end{array}$$

$$A^2 = \begin{bmatrix} 0 & 1 & 1 & 0 & 0 \\ 1 & 0 & 1 & 1 & 0 \\ 1 & 1 & 0 & 1 & 0 \\ 0 & 1 & 1 & 0 & 1 \\ 0 & 0 & 0 & 1 & 0 \end{bmatrix} \begin{bmatrix} 0 & 1 & 1 & 0 & 0 \\ 1 & 0 & 1 & 1 & 0 \\ 1 & 1 & 0 & 1 & 0 \\ 0 & 1 & 1 & 0 & 1 \\ 0 & 0 & 0 & 1 & 0 \end{bmatrix}$$

$$A^2 = \begin{array}{c} \\ x \\ y \\ z \\ p \\ q \end{array} \begin{array}{c} \begin{array}{ccccc} x & y & z & p & q \end{array} \\ \begin{bmatrix} 2 & 1 & 1 & 2 & 0 \\ 1 & 3 & 2 & 1 & 1 \\ 1 & 2 & 3 & 1 & 1 \\ 2 & 1 & 1 & 3 & 0 \\ 0 & 1 & 1 & 0 & 1 \end{bmatrix} \end{array}$$

Consider the row of p and column of x in the matrix A^2. The corresponding entry is 2; and in the graph G, there are exactly two edge sequences of length 2 from p to x. They are

$$S_1 = \{(p, z), (z, x)\}$$

$$\text{and } S_2 = \{(p, y), (y, x)\}$$

Again there are exactly 3 edge sequences of length 2 from z to z viz. $\{(z, p), (p, z)\}$, $\{(z, y), (y, z)\}$ and $\{(z, x), (x, z)\}$.

Further computations give us

$$A^3 = \begin{array}{c} \\ x \\ y \\ z \\ p \\ q \end{array} \begin{array}{c} \begin{array}{ccccc} x & y & z & p & q \end{array} \\ \begin{bmatrix} 2 & 5 & 5 & 2 & 2 \\ 5 & 4 & 5 & 6 & 1 \\ 5 & 5 & 4 & 6 & 1 \\ 2 & 6 & 6 & 2 & 3 \\ 2 & 1 & 1 & 3 & 0 \end{bmatrix} \end{array}$$

We see that from the vertex x to the vertex p, there are two edge sequences of length 3

viz. {(x, y), (y, z), (z, p)} and {(x, z), (z, y), (y, p)}.

Also the entry in the row of x and column of p in A^3 is 2.

Illustrative Example

Example 2.1 : *How many paths of length 4 are there from a to d in the simple graph G given below?*

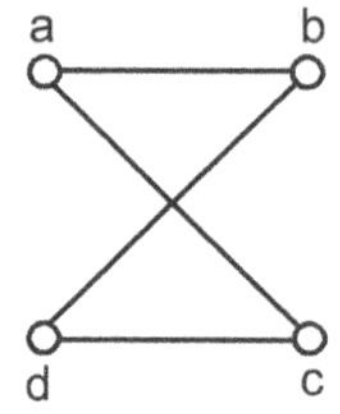

Fig. 2.3

Solution : The adjacency matrix of G is $A = \begin{bmatrix} 0 & 1 & 1 & 0 \\ 1 & 0 & 0 & 1 \\ 1 & 0 & 0 & 1 \\ 0 & 1 & 1 & 0 \end{bmatrix}$.

Hence, the number of paths of length four from a to d is the $(1, 4)^{th}$ entry of A^4.

$A^4 = \begin{bmatrix} 8 & 0 & 0 & 8 \\ 0 & 8 & 8 & 0 \\ 0 & 8 & 8 & 0 \\ 8 & 0 & 0 & 8 \end{bmatrix}$, there are exactly eight paths of length four from a to d. List all these paths.

2.2 Connected Graph

In a graph G, we say that vertex a is connected to the vertex b if there exists a path (at least one) from a to b. If a is connected to b then just by reversing the path from a to b, we get a path from b to a. Thus, if a is connected to b then b is also connected to a and we say that the pair of vertices a and b is connected.

Definition : A graph G in which every pair of vertices is connected, is called a connected graph.

If G is not connected then it is said to be disconnected. In a disconnected graph, there is at least one pair of vertices which is not connected.

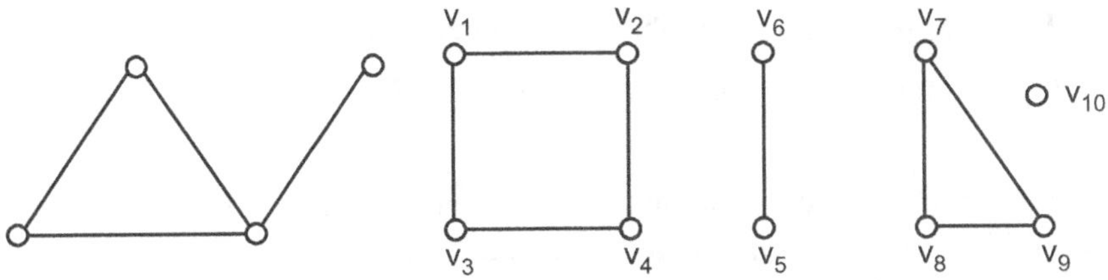

Connected graph G_1 **Disconnected graph G_2**

Fig. 2.4

A graph G_1 is connected graph with 4 vertices and 4 edges. In the graph G_2, there is no path from v_4 to v_6 or from v_6 to v_{10}. Therefore, G_2 is disconnected graph with 10 vertices and 8 edges. In addition to the two numbers (i) the number of vertices and (ii) the number of edges, there is one more number associated with any graph G.

In the Fig. 2.5, we see that the graph A is a connected subgraph of G_2 such that it is not properly contained in any other proper subgraph of G_2.

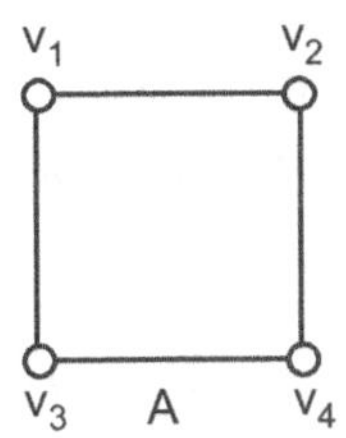

Fig. 2.5

A connected subgraph of a disconnected graph G, which is not properly contained in any proper subgraph of G is called a 'component' of G.

There are four components of the disconnected graph G_2 above. They are A, B, C, D.

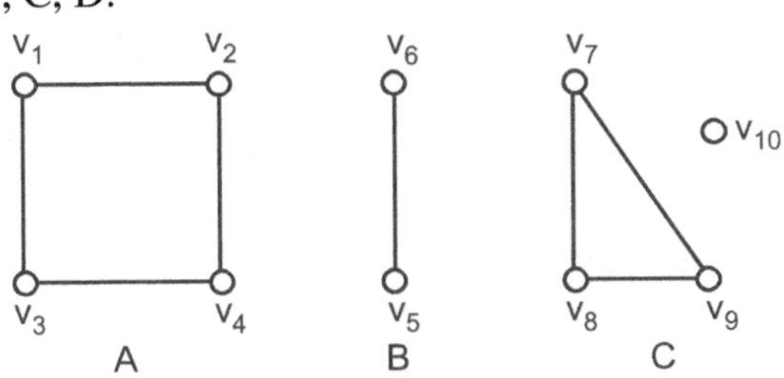

Fig. 2.6

Thus, there are three numbers associated with any graph G :

(i) number of vertices, (ii) number of edges, (iii) number of components.

The number of components in a disconnected graph G is denoted by w (G). If w (G) = 1 then G is a connected graph.

There is another way to interpret the component, which is as follows:

If v is any vertex of the graph G then consider the set H of vertices in G which are connected to v.

$$H = \{w; \text{w is connected to v}\}$$

Then the subgraph of G induced by H i.e. $\langle H \rangle$ is a component of G containing the vertex v.

Theorem 2 A graph G is disconnected if and only if its vertex set V can be partitioned into two non-empty disjoint subsets V_1 and V_2 such that there is no edge in G having one end vertex in V_1 and the other in V_2.

Proof : First Part : Let G be a disconnected graph and u be any vertex in G. Consider the component G_1 containing the vertex u. All vertices in G_1 are connected to u. As G is disconnected, there is a vertex v in G and v is not in G_1.

If V_1 is the set of vertices in G_1 and V_2 is the set of vertices v which are outside G_1, then there is no edge of G joining a vertex of V_1 to the vertex of V_2.

Second Part : Assume that the vertex set V of G can be partitioned into two non-empty disjoint subsets V_1 and V_2 such that there is no edge in G whose one end vertex is in V_1 and the other end vertex is in V_2.

If we choose a vertex u in V_1 and a vertex v in V_2 then by hypothesis, u is not connected to v. Thus, there is at least one pair of vertices of G that is not connected. Hence, G is a disconnected graph. ■

Theorem 3 The maximum number of edges in a simple graph with n vertices and k components is $\dfrac{(n-k)(n-k+1)}{2}$.

Proof : Let G be a simple graph with n vertices and k components. If $G_1, G_2, \ldots, G_k$ are k components of G having number of vertices $n_1, n_2, \ldots, n_k$ respectively, then we have

$$n_1 + n_2 + \ldots + n_k = n$$

i.e. $$\sum_{i=1}^{k} n_i = n$$

As the graph G is simple, each component G_i is also simple. Therefore, maximum number of edges in G_i is $\frac{1}{2}$ $n_i (n_i - 1)$. Hence, the total number of edges in G is

and we have

$$|E| \leq \sum_{i=1}^{k} \frac{n_i (n_i - 1)}{2} = \frac{1}{2} \sum_{i=1}^{k} n_i^2 - \frac{1}{2} \sum_{i=1}^{k} n_i = \frac{1}{2} \sum_{i=1}^{k} n_i^2 - \frac{1}{2} n \quad \dots (1)$$

But $$\left(\sum_{i=1}^{k} (n_i^2 - 1)\right)^2 = (n - k)^2 = n^2 - 2nk + k^2$$

$$\sum_{i=1}^{k} (n_i - 1)^2 + 2 \text{ (some non-negative terms)} = n^2 - 2nk + 1$$

$$\therefore \quad \sum_{i=1}^{k} n_i^2 - 2 \sum_{i=1}^{k} n_i + \sum_{i=1}^{k} 1 \leq n^2 - 2nk + k^2$$

$$\therefore \quad \sum_{i=1}^{k} n_i^2 \leq n^2 - 2nk + k + 2nk \quad \dots (2)$$

$\therefore$ From equations (1) and (2)

$$\therefore \quad |E| \leq \frac{1}{2} [n^2 - (k - 1)(2n - k)] - \frac{1}{2} n$$

$$= \frac{(n - k)(n - k + 1)}{2}$$. Hence proved. ■

Corollary : A simple graph with n vertices and more than $\frac{(n - 1)(n - 2)}{2}$ edges is connected.

Let G be a simple graph with n vertices and more than $\frac{(n - 1)(n - 2)}{2}$ edges.

$\therefore$ If G is disconnected then G has more than 2 or 2 components.

$\therefore$ Number of edges $\leq \frac{(n - 2)(n - 2 + 1)}{2}$ (by above theorem)

which contradicts to hypothesis that G has more than $\frac{(n - 1)(n - 2)}{2}$ edges.

$\therefore$ G must be connected.

Theorem 4 Let G(V, E) be a simple graph with n vertices and m edges then $n - k \leq m$ where k = number of components of graph G.

Proof : Let G be the graph with m edges, n vertices, k components.

We will prove this theorem by induction on m.

Basic step : Let m = 0.

Since, m = 0. Every vertex of a graph G is isolated.

Hence, number of components in G is k = n

Hence, $n - k = 0 = m$.

Hence, result holds true.

Induction step : Let result be true for any graph with q edges where $0 < q < m$.

Let, us remove the edges successively from the graph G until, we get the graph H with k + 1 components.

Let, the number of edges in $H = m_1 \leq m - 1$.

Now by induction hypothesis, $n - (k + 1) \leq m_1$

Hence $n - k - \leq m - 1$

That is $n - k \leq m$. Hence proof. ■

Distance between two vertices : Let G(V, E) be a connected graph. Let u, v by any two vertices in V. Distance between u and v is denoted by d(u, v) and it is defined by

$$d(u, v) = \text{the minimum of length of } u - v \text{ path in G}$$

Eccentricity of an vertex : Let G(V, E) be a connected graph. Let u be any two vertices in V. Eccentricity of u is denoted by e(u) and it is defined as

$e(u) = \max \{d(u, v) \mid v \in V\ v \neq u\}$ = It is distance of a vertex farthest from u.

Center of graph : Let G(V, E) be a connected graph. A vertex with minimum eccentricity is known as center of G and that minimum eccentricity is called as radius of the graph G. The $\max \{d(u, v) \mid u, v \in V\}$ is called as diameter of the graph G. That is diameter of a graph means the distance between two farthest points in the graph.

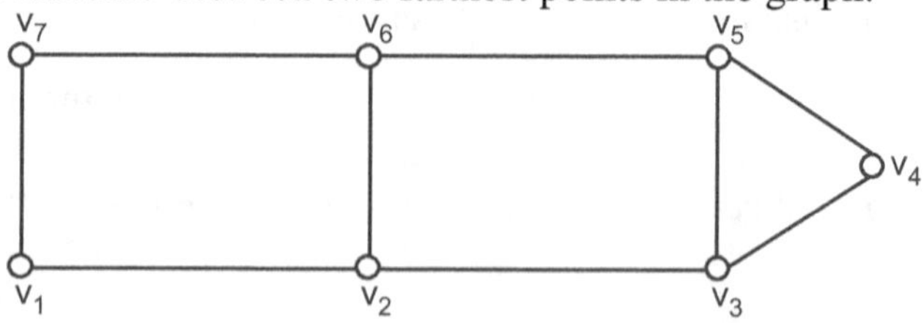

Fig. 2.7

$e(v_1) = 3$, $e(v_2) = 2$, $e(v_3) = 3$, $e(v_4) = 3$, $e(v_5) = 3$, $e(v_6) = 2$, $e(v_7) = 3$

vertices with minimum eccentricity are v_2 and v_6.

$\therefore$ $\{v_2\ v_6\}$ is center of G and G has radius 2.

Also v_1 and v_4 are farthest from each other with distance 4.

$\therefore$ Diameter of G = 4.

Theorem 5 Let G(V, E) be a connected graph.

The function d(u, v) = minimum of length of u – v path, $\forall$ u, v $\in$ V satisfies the properties.

(i) $d(u, v) \geq 0$ and $d(u, v) = 0 \Leftrightarrow = u = v$.

(ii) $d(u, v) = d(u, v)$

(iii) Triangle inequality : $d(u, v) \leq d(u, w) + d(w, v)$ for all u, v, w $\in$ V.

Proof : Let G(V, E) be a connected graph. Let any three u, v, w $\in$ V.

(i) Clearly, d(u, v) = minimum of length of u – v path ≥ 0.

Now $d(u, v) = 0$

$\Rightarrow$ Minimum of length of u – v path = 0

$\Rightarrow$ u = v. Otherwise $d(u, v) > 0$

Also $u = v \Rightarrow$ d(u, v) = minimum of length of u – v path = 0.

(ii) Clearly u – v path is also an v – u path.

Hence, minimum of length of u – v path = minimum of length of v – u path

$d(u, v) = d(v, u)$

(iii) By concanating any u – w path P_1 with any w – v path P_2, we get u – v walk P_1P_2.

Now a walk P_1P_2 contains a path u – v path P.

By definition of distance,

d(u, v) $\leq$ length of P $\leq$ length of P_1 + length of P_2.

But P_1 is arbitrary u – w path, P_2 is arbitrary w – v path, hence

d(u, v) $\leq$ inf {length of $P_1 \mid P_1$ is u – w path} + inf {length of $P_2 \mid P_2$ is w – u path}

That is $d(u, v) \leq d(u, w) + d(w, u)$ ■

Theorem 6 Let G(V, E) be a connected graph. If r = radius and d = diameter of a graph then $r \leq d \leq 2r$.

Proof : Let us take a center v_0 of G.

Now $\max \{d(v, v_0) \mid v \in V\} \leq \max \{d(v, u) \mid u, v \in V\}$

Hence $r \leq d$.

Also, $d = \max \{d(v, u) \mid u, v \in V\}$

$\leq \max \{d(v, v_0) + d(v_0, u) \mid u, v \in V\}$ (by triangle inequality of d)

$\leq \max \{d(v, v_0) \mid v \in V\} + \max \{d(v_0, u) \mid u \in V\} = r + r = 2r$ ■

2.3 Isthmus and Cut Vertex

Consider a graph G in which n is the number of vertices, e the number of edges and w (G) the number of components. In addition to these three numbers, we shall associate two more numbers with G viz. edge connectivity and vertex connectivity of G. The connectivity of a graph tells us about how much the given graph is strong or weak. Let us interpret the vertices of a graph as military stations and edges as the communication lines. In such a graph showing the communication links between various military stations, the main aim of an enemy will be to attack and destroy the weak spots so that after destroying them the communication between the remaining stations fails. As such every country tries to build its communication links in such a way that there will not be any weak spots in the corresponding graph.

The following example will be useful to clear this. Consider two graphs G_1 and G_2 with 6 vertices and 7 edges.

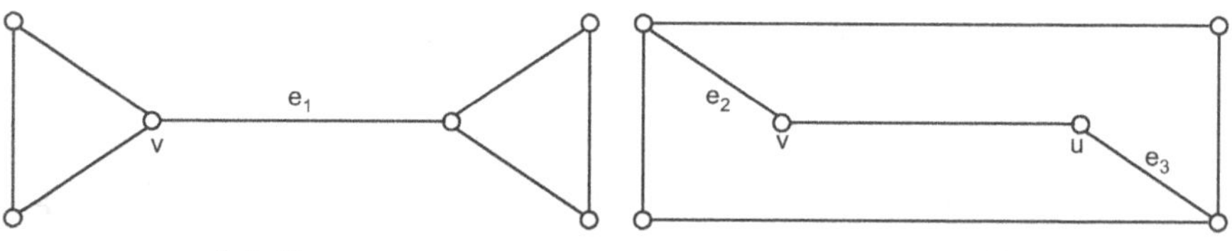

(a) G_1 (b) G_2

Fig. 2.8

The removal of single edge e_1 from G_1 results in a disconnected graph having two components as

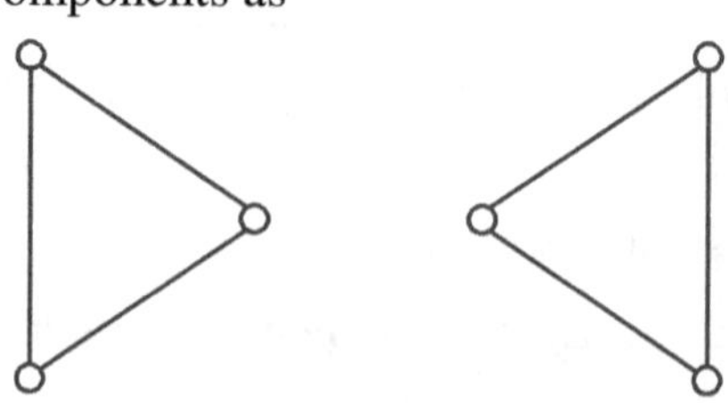

Fig. 2.9

However, after removing any single edge from G_2, the remaining graph is still connected. The enemy will be required to destroy at least two edges say e_2 and e_3 so that after their removal, the remaining graph is disconnected as

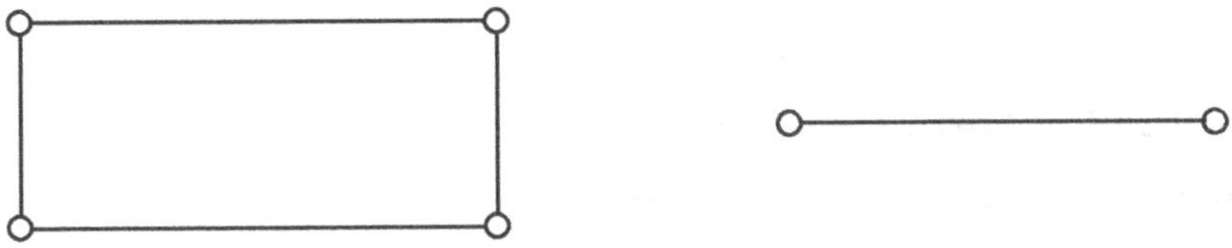

Fig. 2.10

This shows that with same number 6 of vertices and the same number 7 of edges, the graph G_2 is better connected as compared to G_1.

Again in G_1 the removal of a single vertex v results in a disconnected graph as

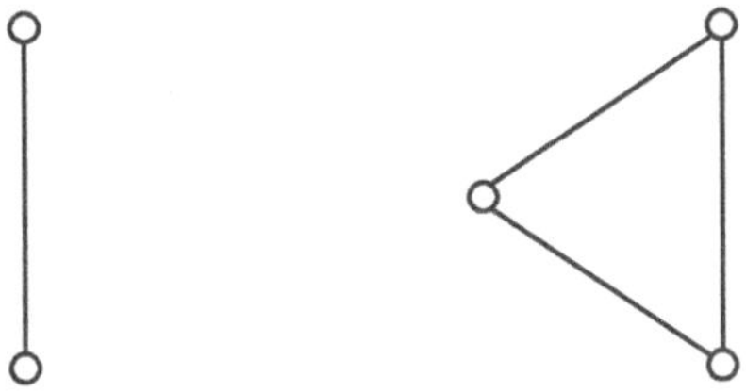

Fig. 2.11

But in the graph G_2 after removing any single vertex, the remaining 5 vertices remain connected and after removing two vertices v and w, the remaining graph is disconnected, the vertex v being isolated.

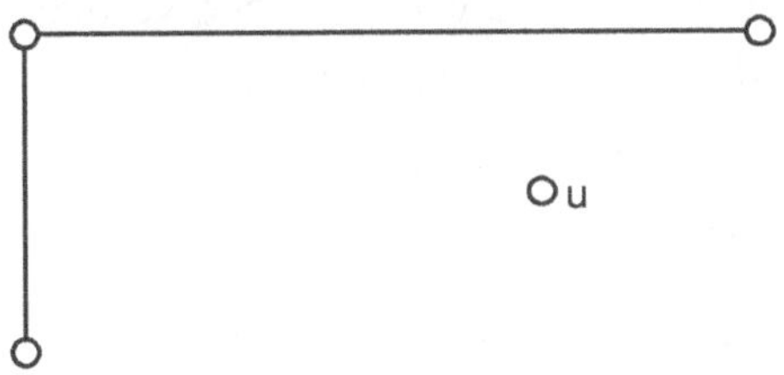

Fig. 2.12

Hence, we see again that the graph G_2 is better connected as compared to graph G_1.

Isthmus (April 2010) : An edge e of a graph G is called an isthmus (or bridge or cutedge) if $w(G - e) > w(G)$ i.e. the number of components in $G - e$ is more than that in G.

In the graph G_1 shown above, the edge e_1 is an isthmus.

We note that the removal of an isthmus from a graph G increases the number of components exactly by one and that the end vertices u and v of isthmus lie in these two different components.

Theorem 7 The edge e_i of a graph G is an isthmus if and only if e_i does not belong to any circuit in G.

Proof : First Part : In the graph G, let the edge e_i be an isthmus with u and v as its end vertices. Then by definition, G – e consists of two components and the vertices u and v lie in these two components.

We prove that e_i is not in any circuit of G.

If possible, suppose e_i is in the circuit Γ of G.

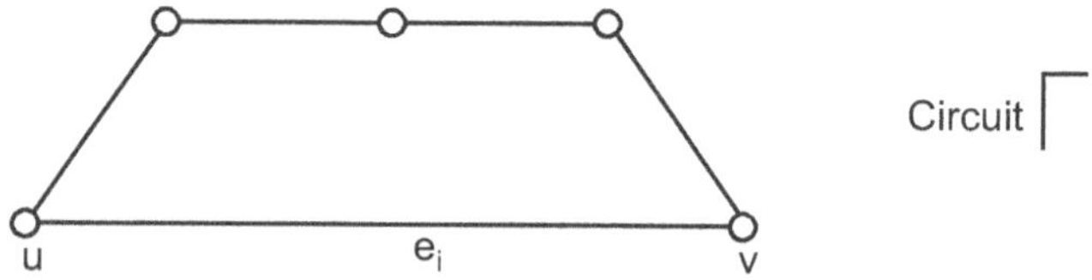

Fig. 2.13

Now by removing e_i from G, the vertices u and v still remain connected through the path p which is a part of circuit Γ. This contradicts to the definition of isthmus.

Hence, e_i cannot lie in any circuit of G.

Second Part : Assume that the edge e_i does not lie in any circuit of the graph G. Therefore, if u and v are two end vertices of e_i then u e_i v is the only path joining them. This implies that after removing the edge e_i from G, the vertices u and v are disconnected.

Hence, e_i is an isthmus.

Cut vertex : Let G (V, E) be a graph. A vertex $v \in V$ is called a cut vertex of G if $w(G - v) > w(G)$ i.e. the number of components in the graph G – v is more than that in G. A cut vertex is also called an articulation point.

We know that after removing a bridge (isthmus) from the graph G, the number of components is increased exactly by one. But after removing a cut vertex, the number of components may be increased by more.

Consider the graphs given below.

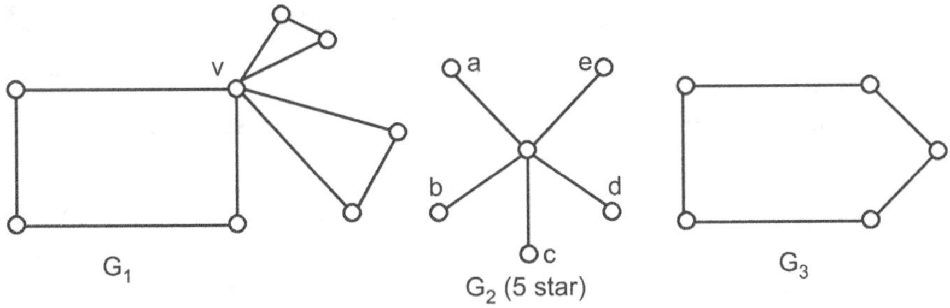

Fig. 2.14

In the graph G_1, the vertex v is a cut vertex. After removing v (and all edges incident on it), the remaining graph is as shown below.

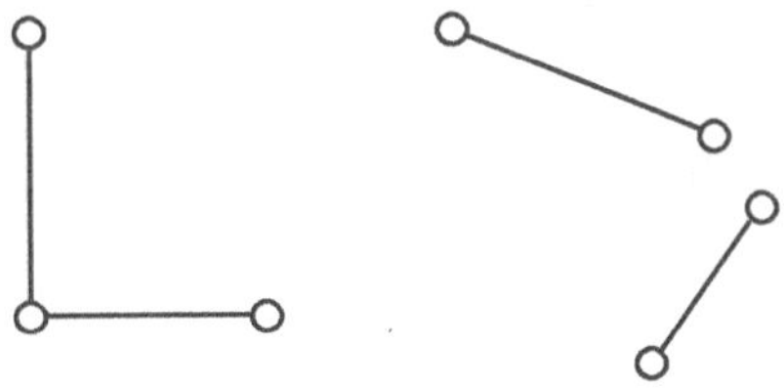

Fig. 2.15

The above graph has three components.

The graph G_2 is a 5-star and u is a cut vertex. The removal of u from G_2 makes all the 5 vertices a, b, c, d, e isolated. The graph G_3 has no cut vertex. ■

Theorem 8 In a connected graph G, the vertex v is a cut vertex iff there exist two vertices x and y in G different from v such that every path joining x and y passes through v.

Proof : First Part : Suppose v is a cut vertex in a connected graph G. Then by definition of a cut vertex, the graph G – v is disconnected and has at least two different components. Let G_1 and G_2 be two such components. We choose two vertices x and y such that x is in G_1 and y is in G_2. Initially, there was a path between x and y in the graph G but there is no path between them in the graph G – v. This implies that in the graph G every path between x and y passes through v.

Second Part : Suppose x and y are two vertices in a connected graph G ($x \neq v$, $y \neq v$) such that every path joining x and y passes through v. If now v is deleted from G then all the paths joining x and y are broken. Thus, in the graph G – v there is no path between x and y.

Therefore, G – v is a disconnected graph and the vertices x and y lie in different components. Hence, v is a cut vertex in G. ■

Theorem 9 In a connected graph G, the vertex v is a cut vertex iff there exist two or more edges e_i, e_j in G incident on v such that no circuit in G includes both e_i and e_j.

Proof : First Part : Let v be the cut vertex in the connected graph G. Then by definition, G – v is disconnected and has two or more different components. Let G_1 and G_2 be two such components. We choose a vertex x in the component G_1 such that x is adjacent to v in the graph G and e_i be the edge between x and v.

Also we choose a vertex y in the component G_2 such that y is adjacent to v in the graph G and e_j be the edge between y and v. Now e_i and e_j are incident on v in G_2.

Now, we assume that a circuit Γ in G includes both the edges e_i and e_j.

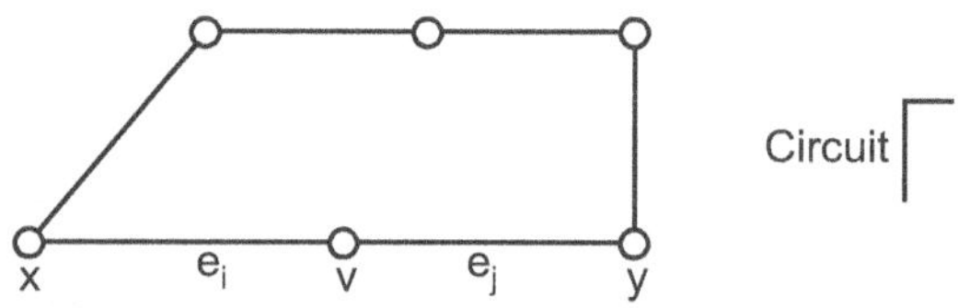

Fig. 2.16

But now we see that after removing the vertex v and edges e_i and e_j, the vertices x and y are still connected through a path which is portion of circuit Γ other than e_i and e_j. This is a contradiction because x and y are not connected in G – v. Hence, any circuit in G will not include both the edges e_i and e_j.

Second Part : Let v be a vertex in a connected graph G and e_i, e_j be two edges incident on v such that any circuit in G does not include both the edges. Let x be the other end vertex of e_i and y be the other end vertex of e_j.

We have to prove that v is a cut vertex. If possible suppose v is not a cut vertex of G. Then the graph G – v is still a connected graph. Therefore, the two vertices x and y are connected in G – v by a path say P_1.

$$P_1 \ : \ x\, e_1\, u_1\, e_2\, u_2 \ldots e_k\, y.$$

This path P_1 together with two edges e_i and e_j determine a circuit in G. But this is a contradiction to the hypothesis. Therefore, our assumption is wrong. Hence, v is a cut vertex in G. ■

Theorem 10 Let G be a connected graph with at least two vertices. Then there are at least two vertices in G which are not cut vertices.

Proof : Let G be a connected graph with n vertices where $n \geq 2$. We have to prove that in G there are at least two vertices which are not cut vertices. Assume that in G there is at the most one vertex which is not a cut vertex.

Now by connectedness all the vertices of G are connected by paths. Let u and v be two vertices in G which are farthest apart i.e. d (u, v) = diameter of G.

By our assumption one of the two vertices u and v must be a cut vertex. Suppose that v is a cut vertex.

Then G – v is disconnected graph and there exists a vertex w such that u and w are in different components of G – v.

Any path between u and w passes through the vertex v. In particular the shortest path from u to w also passes through v.

This implies that d (u, w) > d (u, v) which contradicts to the hypothesis that u and v are farthest apart. So the assumption made is wrong. Hence, in G there are at least two vertices which are not cut vertices.

Corollary : Let G be a connected graph with n vertices. We have proved in the above theorem that there are at least two vertices in G which are not cut vertices. Therefore, in G the maximum number of cut vertices is n – 2.

Edge connectivity (Definition) : The edge connectivity of a connected graph G is the number of edges in the smallest set of edges whose removal from G leaves a disconnected graph.

We shall denote the edge connectivity of G by λ (G).

The edge connectivity of a disconnected graph is defined to be 0. If a connected graph G has an isthmus then obviously λ (G) = 1.

Consider three graphs G_1, G_2, G_3 given below.

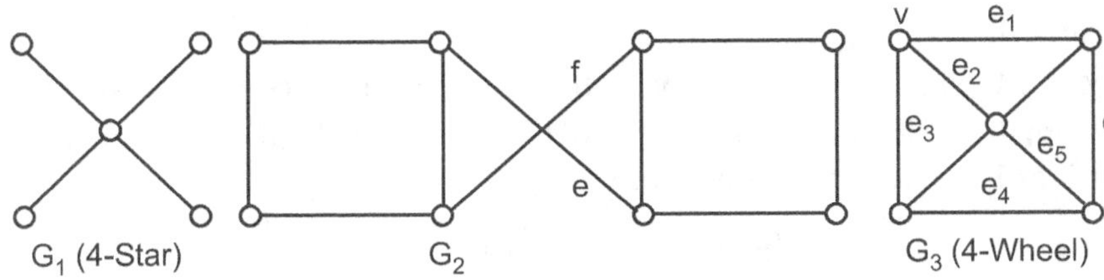

Fig. 2.17

In the graph G_1, which is a 4-star, the removal of any single edge leaves one vertex isolated while the remaining vertices remain connected. Hence $\lambda(G_1) = 1$.

In the graph G_2, the removal of any single edge does not disconnect G_2 but the deletion of two edges e and f disconnects G_2. Therefore $\lambda(G_2) = 2$.

In the graph G_3, the removal of any single edge or the removal of any two edges does not disconnect G_3. However, the removal of three edges e_1, e_2, e_3 results in a disconnected graph leaving the vertex v isolated.

Thus $\lambda(G_3) = 3$. ■

Theorem 11 The edge connectivity of a graph G cannot exceed the smallest degree of a vertex in G i.e. if d_{min} denotes the smallest degree of a vertex in G then $\lambda(G) \leq d_{min}$.

Proof : Let G be a connected graph with n vertices $v_1, v_2, v_3, \ldots, v_n$ whose degrees are $d_1, d_2, \ldots, d_n$ respectively. Suppose v_1 is the vertex of smallest degree in G.

Therefore $d_{min} = d_1$. Then there are d_1 edges incident on the vertex v_1.

The effect of removal of these d_1 edges (which are incident on v_1) from G results in a disconnected graph leaving the vertex v_1 (of minimum degree) as isolated vertex.

Therefore, $\lambda(G) \leq d_1$

$\therefore$ $\lambda(G) \leq d_{min}$ ■

Theorem 12 Let G be a connected graph with n vertices and e edges.

Then $\lambda(G) \leq \left\lfloor \frac{2e}{n} \right\rfloor$, where $\lfloor x \rfloor$ denotes the greatest integer not greater than x.

Proof : G is a connected graph with n vertices and e edges. Let d_{min} be the smallest degree of a vertex in G. Then the degree of each of n vertices is greater than or equal to d_{min}.

$\therefore$ Total degree $\geq n\, d_{min}$

$\therefore$ $2e \geq n\, d_{min}$

$$\therefore \quad n\, d_{min} \leq 2e$$

$$\therefore \quad d_{min} \leq \frac{2e}{n} \quad \ldots (1)$$

Also we know that, $\lambda(G) \leq d_{min}$ ... (2)

From (1) and (2) we have,

$$\lambda(G) \leq \frac{2e}{n}$$

Now since λ (G) must be an integer, we have $\lambda(G) \leq \left\lfloor \frac{2e}{n} \right\rfloor$; where $\left\lfloor \frac{2e}{n} \right\rfloor$ is the greatest integer not greater than $\frac{2e}{n}$. ■

Vertex Connectivity (Definition) : Let G be a simple graph. Then the vertex connectivity of G is the minimum number of vertices whose removal (deletion) from G leaves either a disconnected graph or K_1 (i.e. a single vertex). The vertex connectivity of a graph G is denoted by K (G).

The vertex connectivity of a disconnected graph is 0.

Consider the two graphs given below.

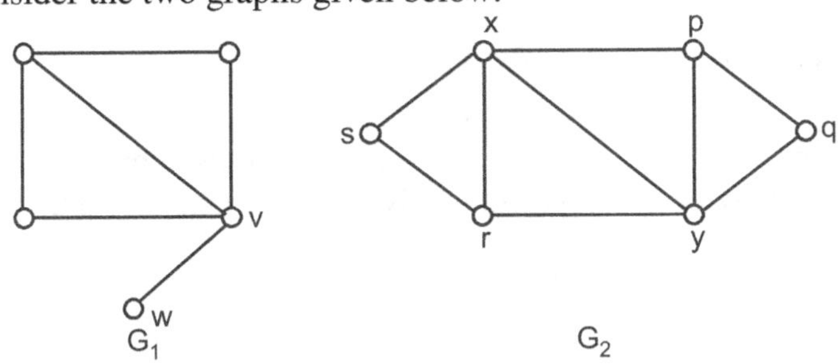

Fig. 2.18

In the graph G_1, the vertex v is a cut vertex and $K(G_1) = 1$.

In the graph G_2, the deletion of any single vertex does not result in a disconnected graph. However, after deleting the two vertices x and y, the remaining graph is disconnected as

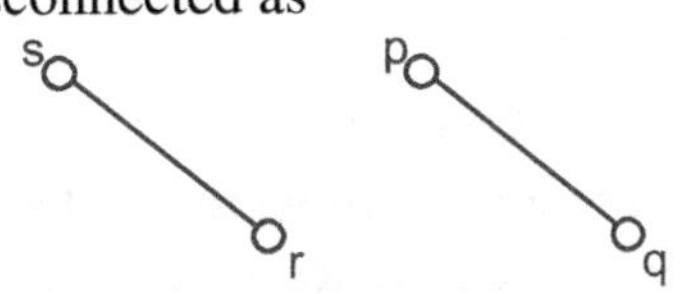

Fig. 2.19

Therefore, $K(G_2) = 2$.

Consider the complete graph K_n ($n \geq 2$) on n vertices. After deleting any one vertex say v_1 from K_1, the $n - 1$ edges joining v_1 to $v_2, v_3, ..., v_n$ are also deleted and this leaves a graph K_{n-1}. If we go on deleting in this way the vertices one by one, then after deletion of r vertices there will remain a complete graph K_{n-r}. The deletion of $n - 1$ vertices will leave K_1.

Hence, the vertex connectivity of a complete graph K_n is $n - 1$.

i.e. $$K(K_n) = n - 1$$

Theorem 13 The vertex connectivity of a graph G cannot exceed the edge connectivity of G

$$\text{i.e. } K(G) \leq \lambda(G).$$

Proof : Let G be a given graph whose edge connectivity is $\lambda(G) = \alpha$. Therefore, there exists a set of α edges in G whose removal from G leaves the disconnected graph. Suppose that after removing these edges the vertices of G are partitioned into two non-empty disjoint subsets v_1 and v_2. The end vertices of the above α edges in v_1 (or in v_2) are at the most α in number. The effect of removal of α edges from G is achieved by deleting the above end vertices which are less than or equal to α in number.

Hence, the vertex connectivity of $G \leq \alpha$.

$\therefore$ $K(G) \leq \lambda(G)$. Hence, proved.

By combining the results of the three theorems above regarding the vertex connectivity and edge connectivity of a graph G, we have, vertex connectivity $\leq$ edge connectivity $\leq \left\lfloor \frac{2e}{n} \right\rfloor$.

i.e. $$K(G) \leq \lambda(G) \leq \left\lfloor \frac{2e}{n} \right\rfloor$$

In words, the maximum vertex connectivity and edge connectivity that can be achieved with n vertices and e edges is the integral part of $\frac{2e}{n}$. ■

Connectedness in Directed Graphs :

A directed graph is **strongly connected** if there is a path from a to b and from b to a whenever a and b are vertices in the graph. A directed graph is **weakly connected** if there is a path between every two vertices in the underlying undirected graph.

Illustrative Examples

Example 2.2 : *Are the directed graphs G and H shown in the following figure strongly connected ? Are they weakly connected ?*

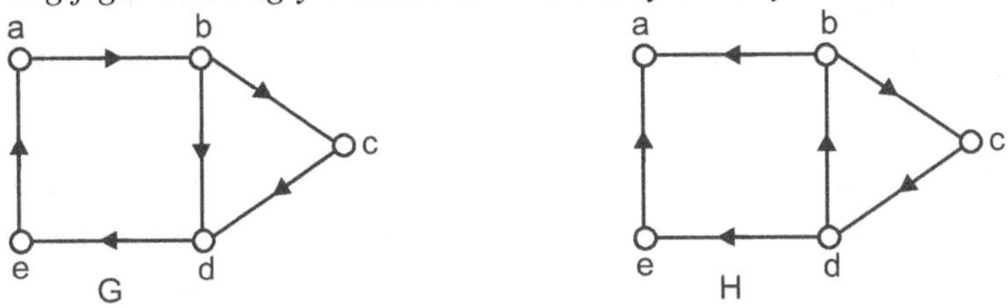

Fig. 2.20

Solution : G is strongly connected because there is a path between any two vertices in this directed graph. Hence, G is also weakly connected. The graph H is not strongly connected. There is no directed path from a to b in H. However, H is weakly connected, because there is a path between any two vertices in the underlying undirected graph of H.

Note: There are several ways that paths and circuits can help to determine whether two graphs are isomorphic. The existence of a simple circuit of a particular length is a useful invariant that can be used to show two graphs are not isomorphic.

Example 2.3 : *Determine whether the graphs G and H shown below are isomorphic.*

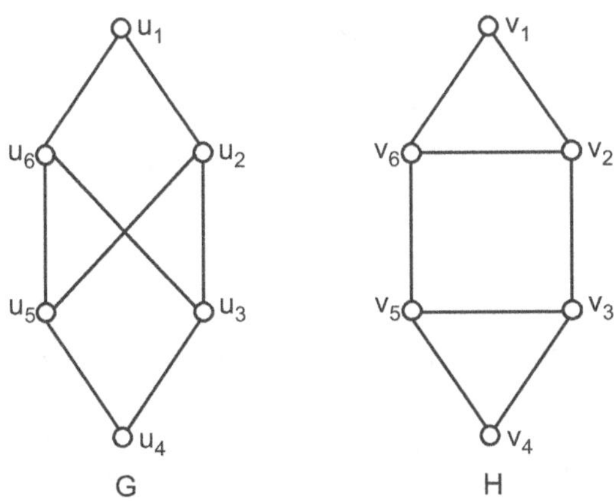

Fig. 2.21

Solution : Both G and H have six vertices and eight edges. Each has 4 vertices of degree three and two vertices of degree two. However, H has a simple circuit of length three namely v_1, v_2, v_6, v_1, whereas G has no simple circuit of length 3. Hence, G and H are not isomorphic.

2.4 Shortest Path Algorithm

We have already seen that a graph in which every edge is assigned the weight, which is a non-negative number, is called a weighted graph and the sum of the weights of all the edges is the total weight of that graph.

Let G be a connected weighted graph. If a and b are two vertices of G then by connectedness there is (at least one) a path from a to b. If P_1 : a e_1 v_1 e_2 v_2 ... b is one such path then the sum of the weights of the edges appearing in P_1 is called weight of the path P_1. Among all the paths from a to b, we are interested in that particular path whose weight is the smallest. It is called the shortest path from a to b (or geodetic path).

We can interpret this as follows. Consider the connected weighted graph G below (See Fig. 2.19).

Let us assume that x, u, v, w, p, q, r, s, y, z are 10 cities connected by roads. The positive numbers associated with the edges can be considered as actual lengths of the roads joining two cities or it may be the time or bus fare required for the journey from one city to its neighbouring city.

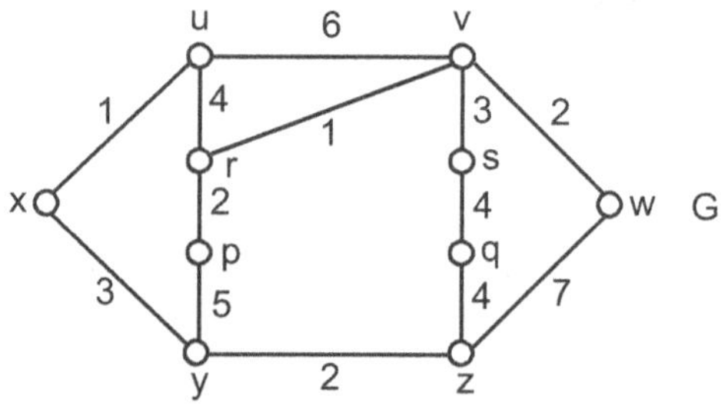

Fig. 2.22

There are 12 paths from x to w. The four of them are,

p_1 : x – u – v – w

p_2 : x – u – r – v – w

p_3 : x – u – v – s – q – z – w

p_4 : x – y – p – r – v – w

The weights of these paths are as follows :

For p_1 : $1 + 6 + 2 = 9$

For p_2 : $1 + 4 + 1 + 2 = 8$

For p_3 : $1 + 6 + 3 + 4 + 4 + 7 = 25$

For p_4 : $3 + 5 + 2 + 1 + 2 = 13$

By considering all the paths from x to w, we see that the path p_2 has the smallest weight. Therefore, p_2 is the shortest path from x to w.

In a graph with more vertices and edges, it is not very much easy just by looking to the graph, to list the various paths connecting two given particular vertices of that graph. A systematic way of finding the shortest path between the two given vertices of a connected weighted graph is provided by an algorithm - 'Dijkstra's Algorithm'. The basic principle used in Dijkstra's algorithm is the principle of optimality.

Let a and b be two vertices of a connected weighted graph and assume that the continuous curve as shown below is the shortest path from a to b (See Fig. 2.23).

Let c be any vertex of the graph which lies on this shortest path. Then the continuous curve from a to c is the shortest path from a to c. If possible suppose that the dotted path from a to c is the shortest path from a to c.

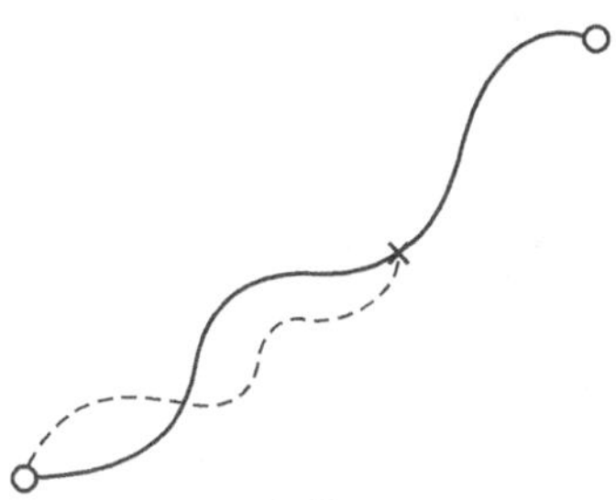

Fig. 2.23

But then the union of dotted path from a to c and continuous path from c to b will be the shortest path from a to b. This is a contradiction because shorter than shortest is impossible. The above principle is known as the principle of optimality.

Dijkstra's Algorithm : In the process of finding the shortest path from the vertex a to the vertex b of a graph G, the labelling technique is used in Dijkstra's Algorithm. We assign the labels λ (v) called temporary labels to the various vertices of G and go on updating them at every step. We shall denote by T the set of those vertices whose labels are temporary. At any stage suppose a vertex v has minimum λ value. Then this λ (v) is called permanent label of v and it is encircled in the next process. The labels of the vertices in T are updated as follows.

If w ∈ T is not adjacent to v then λ (w) will not be changed. If w ∈ T is adjacent to v then λ (w) will be changed to min {λ (w), λ (v) + weight of the edge (v w)}. This updating of λ values is the stage at which the principle of optimality has been used. We continue the process till the λ value of b is encircled i.e. b is assigned the permanent label. In the problem if we have to find the weights of the shortest paths from the vertex a to all the vertices of G then the algorithm will come to an end after every vertex has been assigned the permanent label. The permanent label assigned to any vertex is the weight of the shortest path from the starting vertex to that vertex. When the algorithm is in process, we also extend the graph from the starting vertex showing the shortest path.

We summarize the above procedure to find the weight of the shortest path from the vertex a to the vertex b.

Step 1 : Start.

Step 2 : Initialization λ (a) = 0 and λ (v) = ∞ for v ≠ a; T = v.

Step 3 : Select the vertex v of minimum λ value and assign permanent label to v.

Step 4 : If v = b then stop.

Step 5 : If v ≠ b then update the labels of vertices in T – {v}

Step 6 : Change T to T – {v}.

Step 7 : Go to step 3.

Illustrative Examples

Example 2.4 : *Consider the graph G given below.*

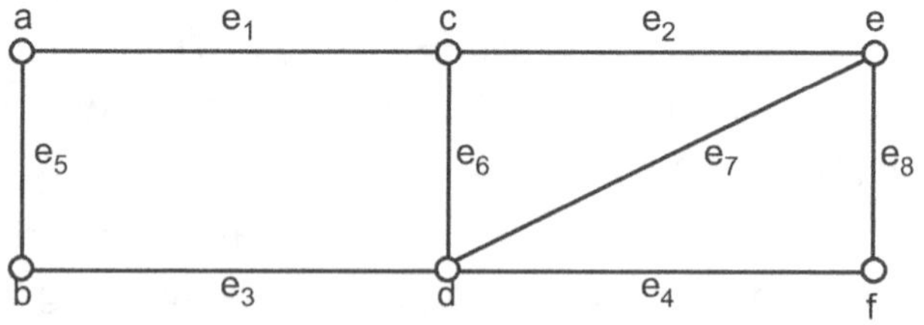

Fig. 2.24

(a) Find all paths joining a to f.

(b) What are the lengths of the paths in (a) ?

(c) Which path is the shortest path ?

(d) What is d(a, f) ?

Solution : (a) The paths joining the two vertices a and f are as follows :

p_1 : $ae_1\,ce_2\,ee_8\,f$

p_2 : $ae_1\,ce_2\,ee_7\,de_4\,f$

p_3 : $ae_1\,ce_6\,de_4\,f$

p_4 : $ae_1\,ce_6\,de_7\,ee_8\,f$

p_5 : $ae_5\,be_3\,de_4\,f$

p_6 : $ae_5\,be_3\,de_7\,ee_8\,f$

p_7 : $ae_5\,be_3\,de_6\,ce_2\,ee_8\,f$

(b) The path lengths of the 7 paths are 3, 4, 3, 4, 3, 4, 5 respectively.

(c) Among all the paths joining a and f, the paths p_1, p_3, p_5 have minimum length 3. Therefore p_1, p_3, p_5 are shortest paths.

(d) d(a, f) = length of the shortest path. Therefore, d(a, f) = 3.

Example 2.5 : *For a given graph G, the graph G^2 is a graph whose vertex set is that of G and u, v are adjacent in G^2 if $1 \leq d(u, v) \leq 2$ in G. For the following graph G, find G^2 and prepare a table of distances in G and G^2 (See Fig. 2.25).*

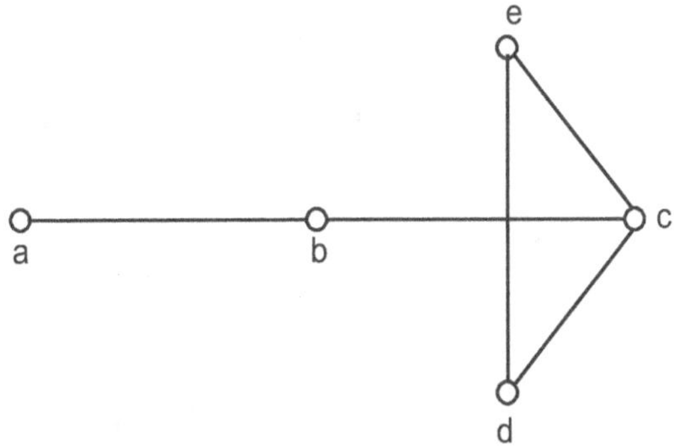

Fig. 2.25

Solution : The table showing the distances in G is as follows :

	a	b	c	d	e
a	0	1	2	3	3
b	1	0	1	2	2
c	2	1	0	1	1
d	3	2	1	0	1
e	3	2	1	1	0

The graph G^2 is as shown below.

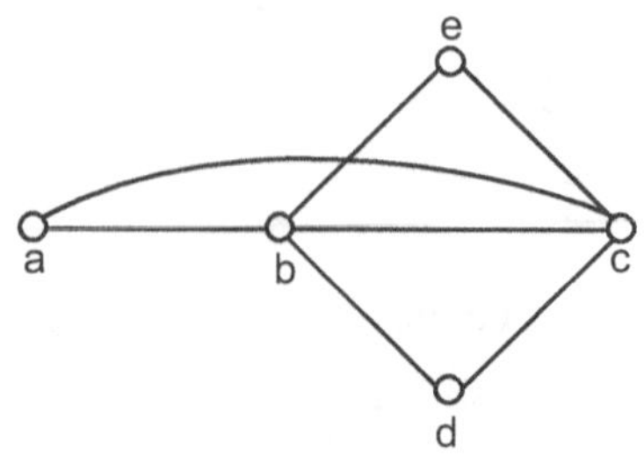

Fig. 2.26

The table showing the distances in G^2 is as follows :

	a	b	c	d	e
a	0	1	1	2	2
b	1	0	1	1	1
c	1	1	0	1	1
d	2	1	1	0	1
e	2	1	1	1	0

Example 2.6 : *Determine whether the following statement is true or false : "Every disconnected graph has an isolated vertex".*

Solution : The given statement is false.

Consider a graph G with 6 vertices a, b, c, d, e, f and 6 edges e_1, e_2, e_3, e_4, e_5, e_6.

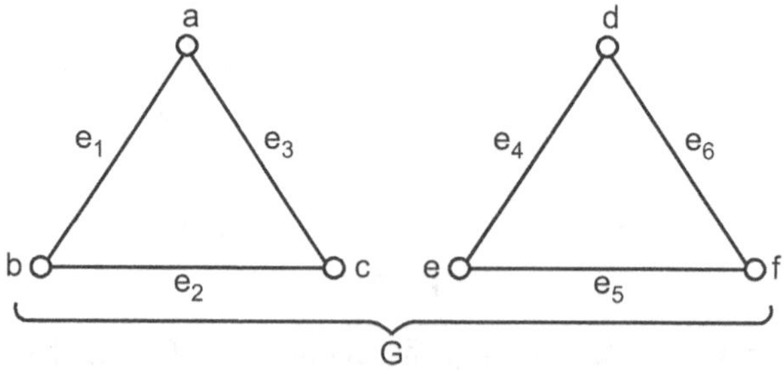

Fig. 2.27

G is a disconnected graph in which there is no isolated vertex.

Example 2.7 : *A simple graph G has vertex set {2, 3, 4, 6, 7, 8, 9, 10, 11, 12}. An edge exists between vertices x and y if $x \neq y$ and if x divides y or y divides x. Draw the graph G. Is G connected ? What is w (G) ?*

Solution : Under the given condition of divisibility, we see that the vertex pairs like (2, 4), (3, 6) etc. are adjacent. The graph is shown as below.

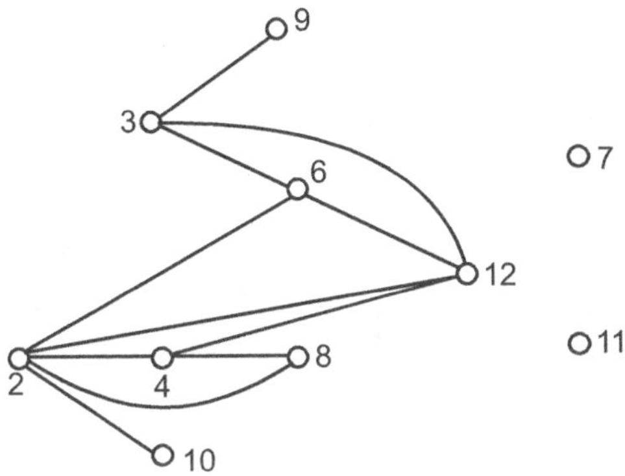

Fig. 2.28

This graph is not connected. It has three components

$$G_1 = \{2, 3, 4, 6, 8, 9, 10\}$$
$$G_2 = \{7\}$$
$$G_3 = \{11\}$$

Example 2.8 : *Find all the bridges in the following graph.*

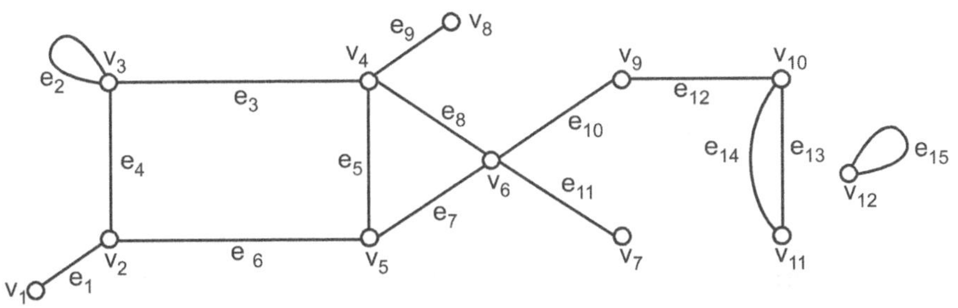

Fig. 2.29

Solution : The bridges (isthmus) in a graph are precisely those edges which does not belong to any circuit of the given graph. In the given graph, the edges e_1, e_9, e_{10}, e_{11}, e_{12} do not belong to any circuit. They are bridges.

Example 2.9 : *Show that if a simple graph G is not connected then its complement $\overline{G}$ is connected. Deduce that if G is a simple connected graph and v is a cut vertex in G then v is not a cut vertex in $\overline{G}$.*

Solution : First Part : Let G be a simple graph which is not connected. Suppose G has two different connected components G_1 and G_2. Consider any two vertices x and y in the complement $\bar{G}$. We shall prove that there exists a path from x to y in $\bar{G}$.

First suppose that the vertices x and y belong to the same component say G_1 of G.

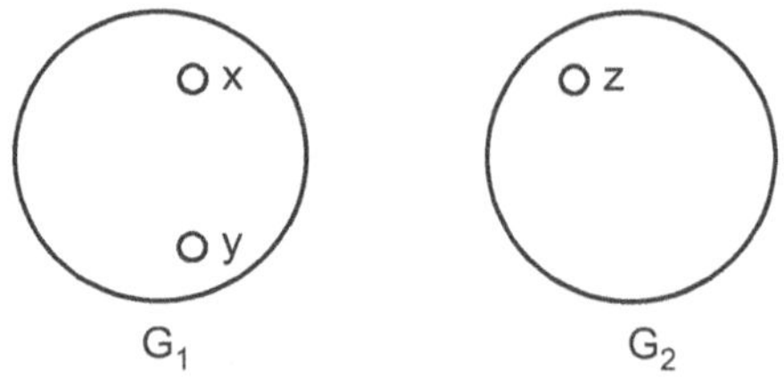

Fig. 2.30

Let z be any vertex in G_2. Then in $\bar{G}$ there exists an edge between x and z, also there exists an edge between y and z. Therefore in $\bar{G}$, x-z-y is a path from x to y. Secondly suppose x and y belong to different components say x in G_1 and y in G_2.

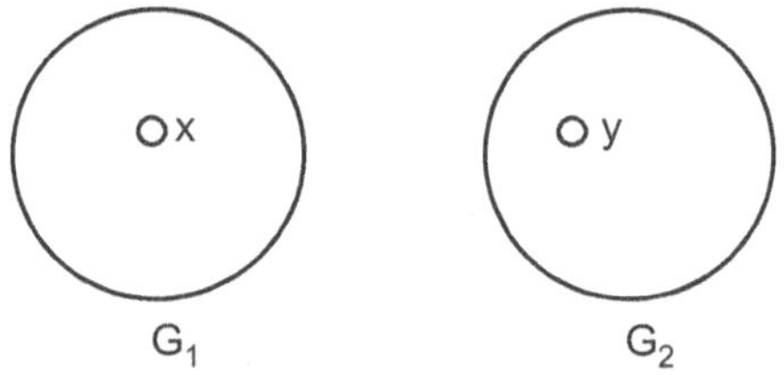

Fig. 2.31

In the graph G, the vertices x and y are not connected. However, in $\bar{G}$ there exists an edge joining x and y. Hence, there is a path from x to y in $\bar{G}$.

Thus, there exists a path between every two vertices in $\bar{G}$. So $\bar{G}$ is connected.

Second Part (Deduction) : Let G be a simple connected graph and v be a cut vertex in G. Then G – v is a simple graph which is disconnected. Therefore, by the first part, $\overline{G - v}$ is connected. But $\overline{G - v}$ = $\bar{G} - v$. Thus, $\bar{G} - v$ is connected. Hence, v is not a cut vertex in $\bar{G}$.

Example 2.10 : *What is the maximum edge connectivity of a connected graph having 5 vertices and 8 edges ? Draw two graphs G_1 and G_2 such that in G_1 the maximum edge connectivity is achieved but in G_2 it is not.*

Solution : A connected graph G has 5 vertices and 8 edges.

$$\therefore \qquad n = 5, \quad e = 8.$$

Maximum value of edge connectivity is $\left\lfloor \frac{2e}{n} \right\rfloor = \left\lfloor \frac{(2)(8)}{5} \right\rfloor = \left\lfloor \frac{16}{5} \right\rfloor = 3$

(See Fig. 2.32).

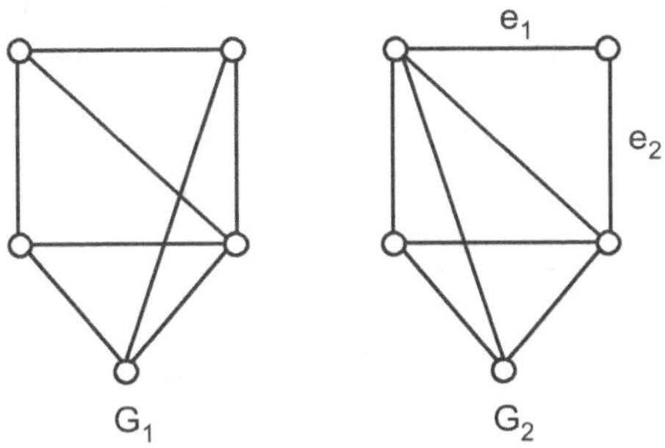

Fig. 2.32

In G_1 the removal of any single edge or any two edges does not disconnect G_1 and $d_{min} = 3$

$\therefore \quad \lambda(G_1) = 3$; maximum edge connectivity is achieved.

In G_2 there is no isthmus and the removal of e_1 and e_2 disconnects the graph G_2.

$\therefore \quad \lambda(G_2) = 2$; maximum edge connectivity is not achieved.

Example 2.11 : *Prove that a graph with n vertices and vertex connectivity K has at least $\frac{K \cdot n}{2}$ edges.*

Solution : We have for any graph G with n vertices and e edges, that

$$\text{vertex connectivity} \leq \text{edge connectivity} \leq \frac{2e}{n}.$$

Therefore, by hypothesis, $K \leq \frac{2e}{n}$

$$\therefore \qquad \frac{2e}{n} \geq K$$

$$\therefore \qquad e \geq \frac{K \cdot n}{2}.$$ Hence, proved.

Example 2.12 : *G is a connected graph with at least three vertices. Prove that if G has a bridge then G has a cut vertex.*

Solution : Let G be a connected graph with n vertices where $n \geq 3$. Assume that edge e is a bridge in G with its end vertices x and y. We shall prove that x or y (or both) is a cut vertex.

Suppose x is not a cut vertex. Therefore, G – x is a connected graph. This implies that y is the only vertex in G which is adjacent to x and remaining (at least one) vertices are connected to y. But then we see that G – y is a disconnected graph keeping the vertex x isolated and remaining vertices connected. Hence y is a cut vertex. Similarly, if y is not a cut vertex, then x is a cut vertex.

Further, if $n > 3$, then out of $n - 2$ vertices (other than x and y), it is possible that r vertices to x and $n - 2 - r$ vertices are connected to y. In this case, x and y both are cut vertices.

Example 2.13 : *By using Dijkstra's algorithm, find the shortest path from the vertex a to all vertices of the graph given below.*

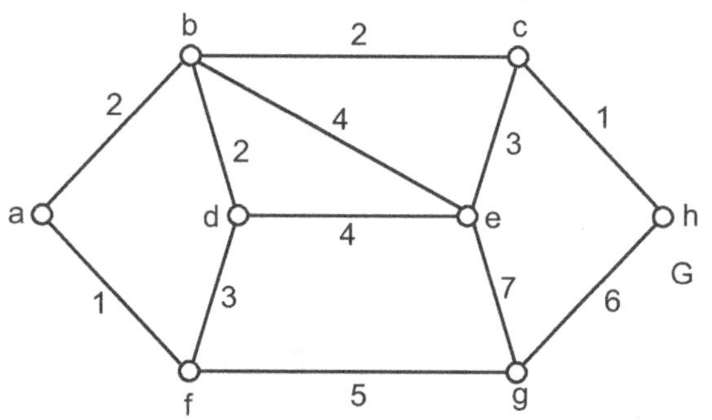

Fig. 2.33

Solution : First table :

Vertex	a	b	c	d	e	f	g	h
λ (v)	0	∞	∞	∞	∞	∞	∞	∞
T	a	b	c	d	e	f	g	h

$\lambda(a) = 0$ is minimum

The vertices in T adjacent to a are b and f.

$\lambda(b) = \min\{\infty, 2\} = 2, \ \lambda(f) = \min\{\infty, 1\} = 1.$

Second table :

Vertex	a	b	c	d	e	f	g	h
λ (v)	0	2	∞	∞	∞	1	∞	∞
T	–	b	c	d	e	f	g	h

λ (f) = 1 is minimum.

The vertices in T adjacent to f are d and g.

λ (d) = min {∞, 4} = 4, λ (g) = min {∞, 6} = 6.

Third table :

Vertex	a	b	c	d	e	f	g	h
λ (v)	0	2	∞	4	∞	1	6	∞
T	–	b	c	d	e	–	g	h

Graph showing the shortest path is

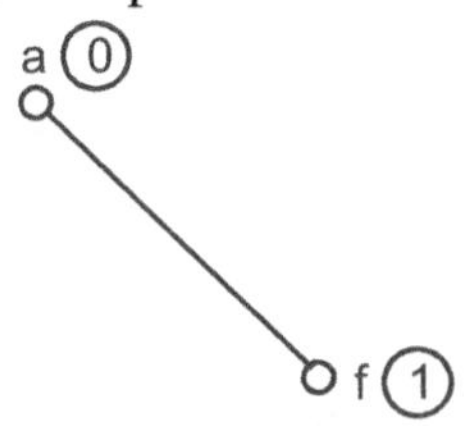

Fig. 2.34

λ (b) = 2 is minimum.

The vertices in T adjacent to b are c, d, e.

λ (c) = min {∞, 4} = 4

λ (d) = min {4, 4} = 4

λ (e) = min {∞, 6} = 6

Fourth table :

Vertex	a	b	c	d	e	f	g	h
λ (v)	0	2	4	4	6	1	6	∞
T	–	–	c	d	e	–	g	h

Graph showing the shortest path is

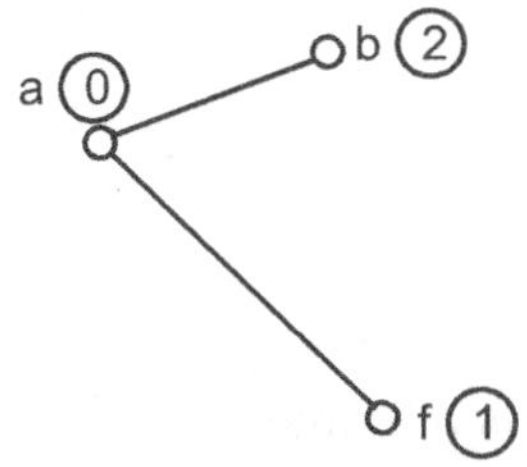

Fig. 2.35

λ (c) = 4 is minimum.

The vertices in T adjacent to c are e, h.

$$\lambda (e) = \min \{6, 7\} = 6$$
$$\lambda (h) = \min \{\infty, 5\} = 5$$

Fifth table :

Vertex	a	b	c	d	e	f	g	h
λ (v)	0	2	4	4	6	1	6	5
T	–	–	–	d	e	–	g	h

Graph showing the shortest path is

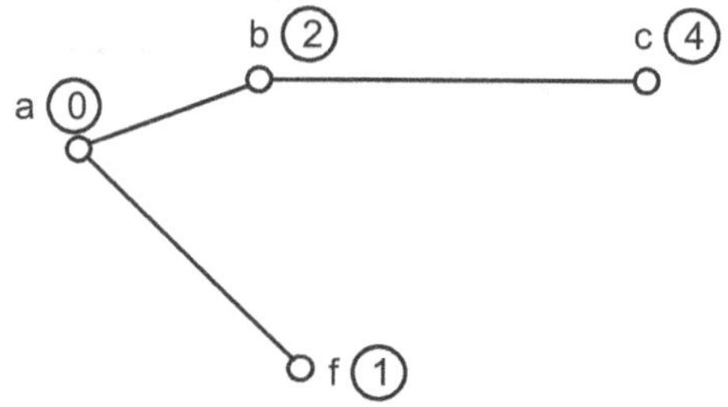

Fig. 2.36

λ (d) = 4 is minimum.

The vertices in T adjacent to d are e only. λ (e) = min {6, 8} = 6.

Sixth table :

Vertex	a	b	c	d	e	f	g	h
λ (v)	0	2	4	4	6	1	6	5
T	–	–	–	–	e	–	g	h

Graph showing the shortest path is

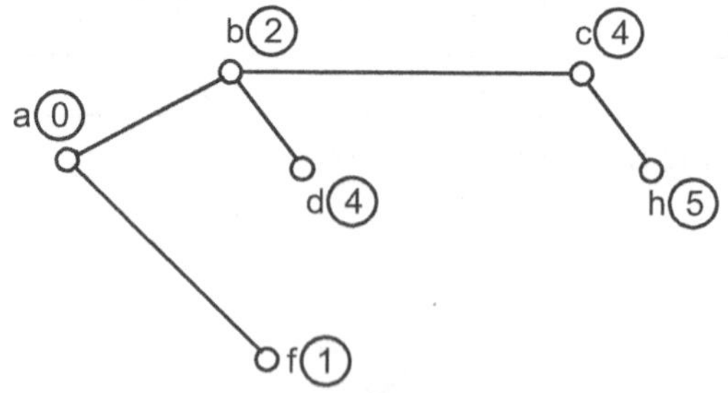

Fig. 2.37

λ (h) = 5 is minimum.

The vertices in T adjacent to h are g only. λ (g) = min {6, 11} = 6.

Seventh table :

Vertex	a	b	c	d	e	f	g	h
λ (v)	0	2	4	4	6	1	6	5
T	–	–	–	d	e	–	g	–

Graph showing the shortest path is

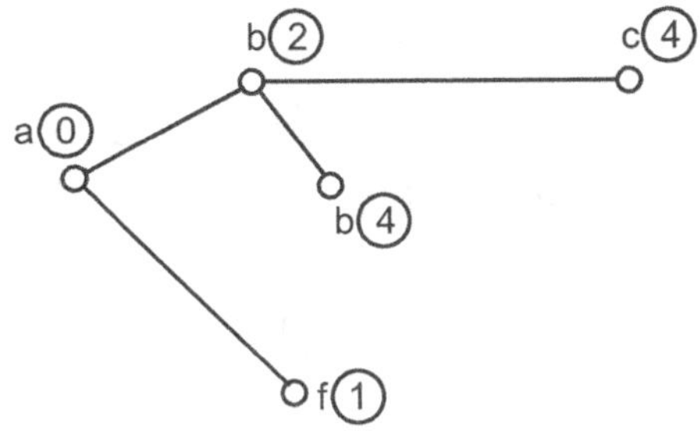

Fig. 2.38

Now, $\lambda(e) = \lambda(g) = 6$

Suppose, $\lambda(e) = 6$ is minimum and $g \in T$ is adjacent to e.

$\lambda(g) = \min\{6, 13\} = 6$

Eighth table :

Vertex	a	b	c	d	e	f	g	h
λ (v)	0	2	4	4	6	1	6	5
T	–	–	–	–		–	g	–

Graph showing the shortest path is

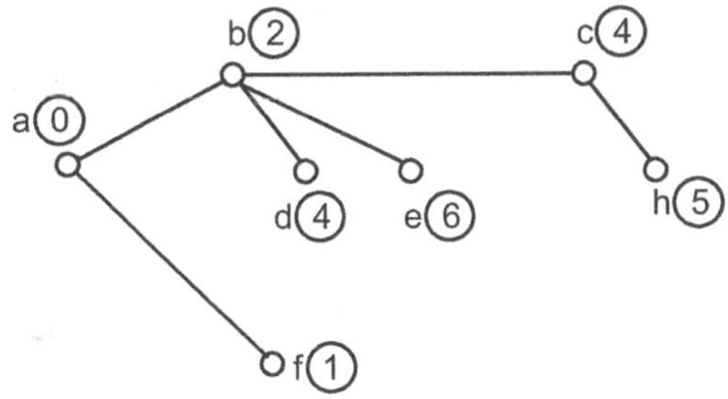

Fig. 2.39

Now, only one vertex g is remaining and λ (g) = 6. It is joined to f. Finally, the graph showing the shortest path from a to all the vertices of G is

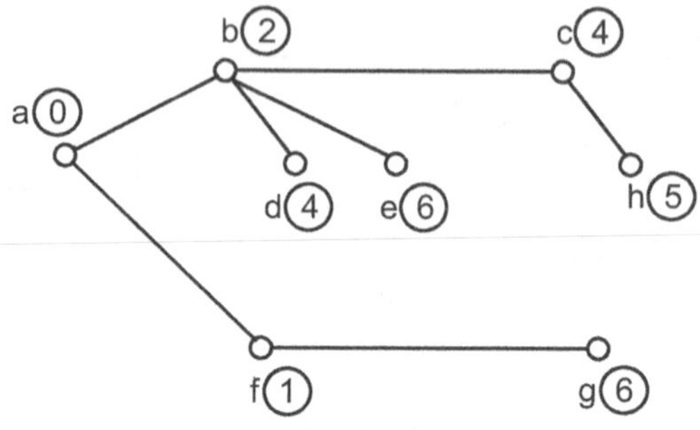

Fig. 2.40

Example 2.14 : *Find the maximum number of edges in a simple bipartite graph with n vertices.*

Solution : Let G is bipartite graph with partition. X and Y with $|X| = r$, $|Y| = s$, with $r + z = n$. It has maximum number of edges if $G = K_{r, s}$ and in this case G has number of edges equals to $r \times s$.

Now varying cardinality of X and Y, we get different possibilities of $K_{r, s}$.

Now $K_{r, s}$ has maximum number of edges if $r \times s$ is maximum.

Now we have problem

$$\max z = rs$$

$$\text{subject } r + s = n$$

$$r \geq 0, \ s \geq 0, \ r, \ s \text{ are integers}$$

From calculus, it has solution

$$r = \frac{n}{2}, \ s = \frac{n}{2} \text{ if n is even}$$

$$r = \frac{n-1}{2}, \ s = \frac{n+1}{2} \text{ if n is odd}$$

∴ In these case, we have number of edges equals to $rs = \frac{n^2}{4}$ or $rs = \frac{n^2 - 1}{4}$ respectively.

Example 2.15 : *Let V = {0, 1, 2, … 20} be a vertex set of a graph G. An edge x and y exists where x − y is divisible by 5. Draw graph G. Explain why G is not connected. What the components of G represent ?*

Solution : Here x − y ≡ 0 (mod 5) on set {0, 1, 2, … 20} is equivalence relation.

The components of G represents the equivalence classes of relation x − y ≡ (0 mod 5) on set {0, 1, 2, … 20}.

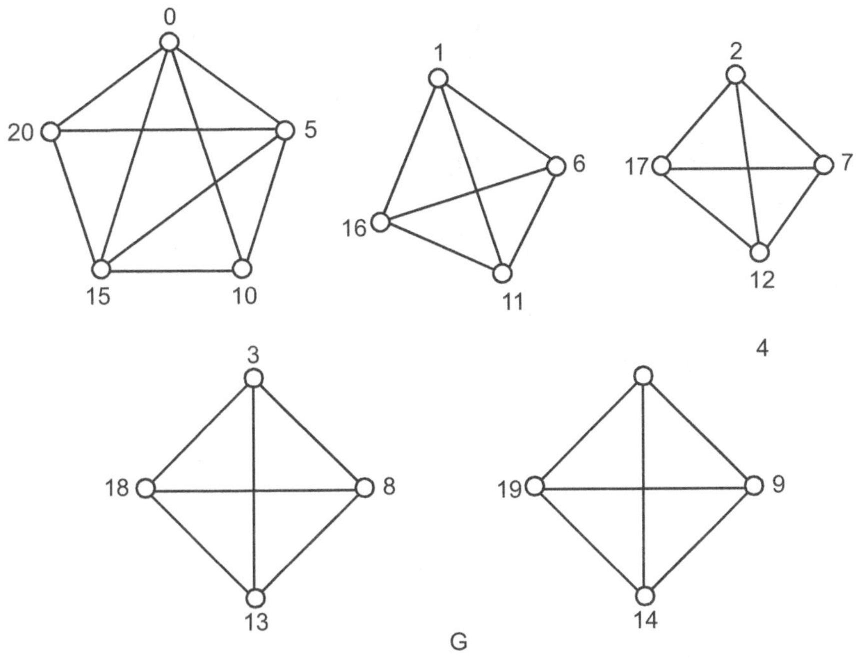

Fig. 2.41

Example 2.16 : *What is the maximum edge connectivity of a connected graph with 5 vertices and 8 edges. Draw two graphs G_1 and G_2 such that G_1 has maximum connectivity is achieved but G_2 it is not.*

Solution : Let G is connected graph with

$$n = \text{number of vertices} = 5$$

$$e = \text{number of edges} = 8$$

$$\therefore \quad \lambda(G) \leq \left\lfloor \frac{2e}{n} \right\rfloor = \left\lfloor \frac{16}{5} \right\rfloor = 3$$

∴ The maximum value of λ(G) (edge connectivity) is 3.

Now we will give the examples of graphs G_1 and G_2 as below.

Consider G_1 as

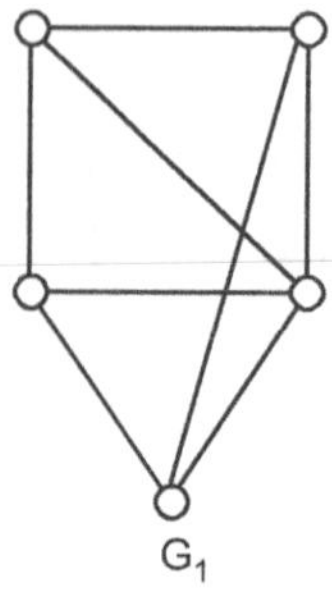

Fig. 2.42

Here removal of any two edges do not disconnect the graph G_1.

But removal of three edges incident on any vertex will disconnect G_1.

$\therefore \quad \lambda(G_1) = 3$

Consider graph G_2 as

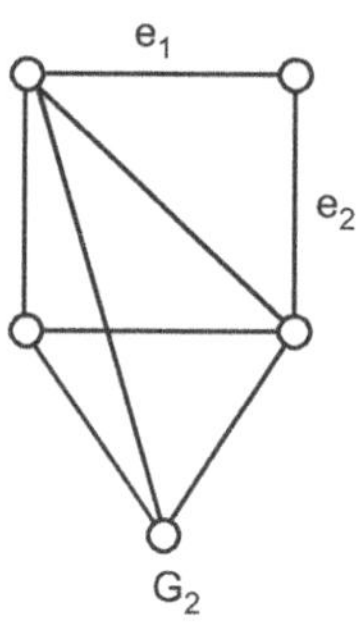

Fig. 2.43

Here removal of any edge do not disconnect G_2.

Also, here removal of e_1, e_2 disconnect G_2 producing components as below.

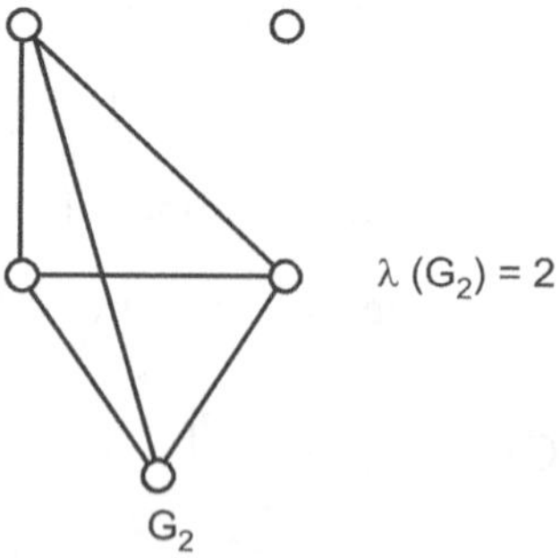

Fig. 2.44

$\therefore \quad \lambda(G_2) = 2$

Example 2.17 : *G is a connected graph with at least 3 vertices. Prove that if G has a bridge then G has a cut vertex.*

Solution : Let e = xy is bridge in G.

∴ G – e is disconnected graph.

∴ G – e has two components C_x and C_y containing x and y respectively.

Now G has more than two vertices.

∴ Let v ∈ G be a vertex other than x and y.

∴ $v \in C_x$ or $v \in C_y$

∴ x is cut vertex or y is cut vertex, because G – x has two components containing v and other containing y or G – y has two components containing v and other containing x.

Example 2.18 : *Find the vertex connectivity K(G) of the following graph.*

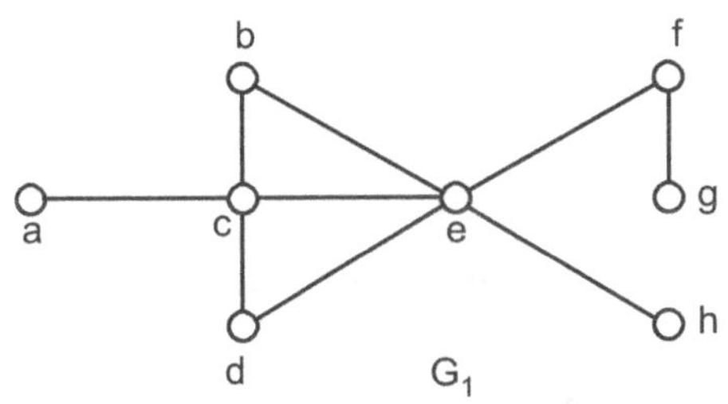

Fig. 2.45

Solution : Removal of single vertex e disconnected the graph G.

$$\therefore \quad K(G) = 1$$

Example 2.19 : *Find vertex connectivity K(G) of the following graph.*

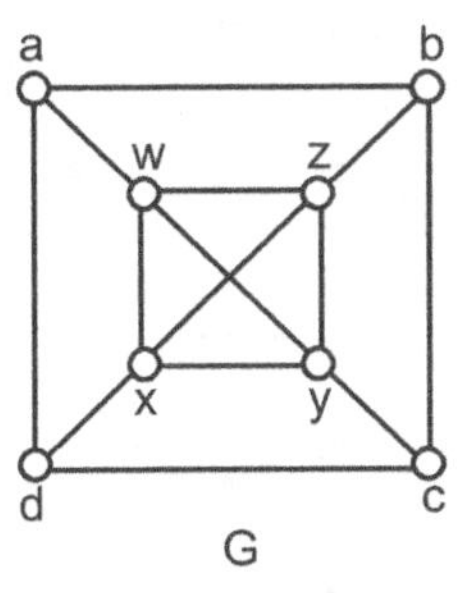

Fig. 2.46

Solution : Removal of any single vertex do not disconnect the graph G.

Also removal of any two vertices do not disconnect the graph G.

Removal of a, c, z disconnects the graph G

$\therefore$ $K(G) = 3.$

Example 2.20 : *Find the edge connectivity $\lambda(G)$ of the following graph.*

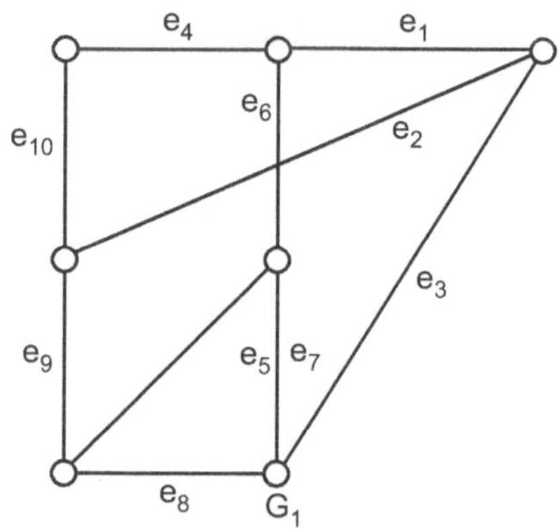

Fig. 2.47

Solution : Removal of any single edge do not disconnect the graph G_1.

Removal of any two edges do not disconnect the graph G_1.

But if we remove e_1, e_2, e_3 the graph is disconnected.

$\therefore$ $\lambda(G_1) = 3$

Example 2.21 : *Find the edge connectivity of graph G_2.*

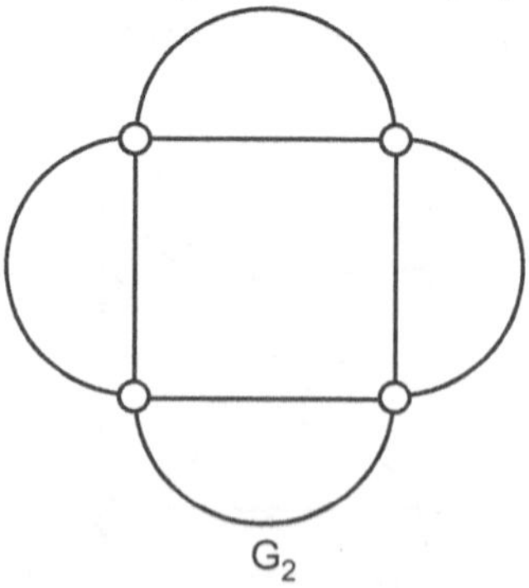

Fig. 2.48

Solution : Removal of any single edge, do not disconnect the graph G_2.

Removal of any two edges do not disconnect the graph G_2.

Removal of any three edges do not disconnect the graph G_2.

Now, if we remove any four edges incident on any vertex leaves a disconnected graph

$\therefore \quad \lambda(G_2) = 4$

Example 2.22 : *Prove that in a cubic graph, vertex connectivity equals the edge connectivity .*

Solution :

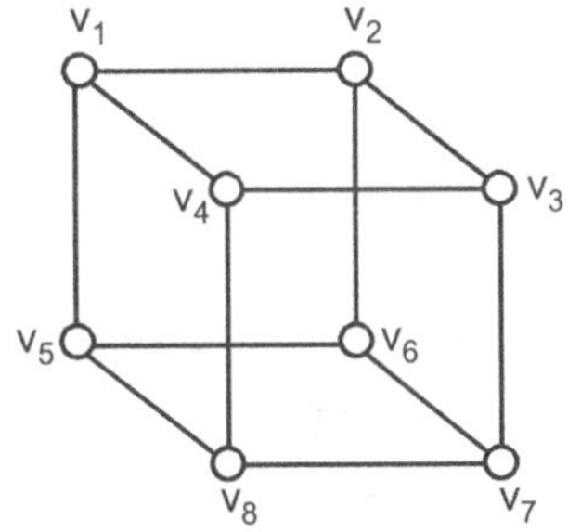

Fig. 2.49

Cubic graph is as shown in Fig. 2.49.

For any graph, we have

$$K(G) \leq \lambda(G) \leq (G)$$

But $\quad \delta(G) = 3$ (minimum vertex degree)

$\therefore \quad K(G) \leq \lambda(G) \leq 3 \quad \ldots (*)$

Now removal of any single vertex do not disconnect G.

Removal of any two vertices also do not disconnect G.

But removal of v_1, v_3, v_6 leaves G disconnected

$\therefore \quad K(G) = 3$

$\therefore$ From (*) $\quad K(G) = \lambda(G) = 3$

Example 2.23 : *Find number of cycles in the following graph.*

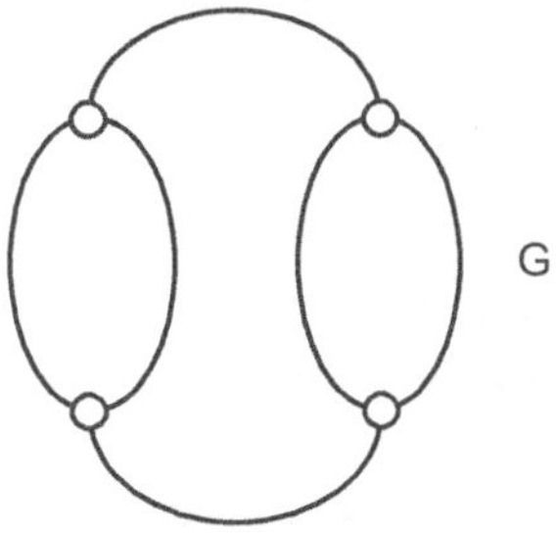

Fig. 2.50

Solution : Cycles of G are listed as below.

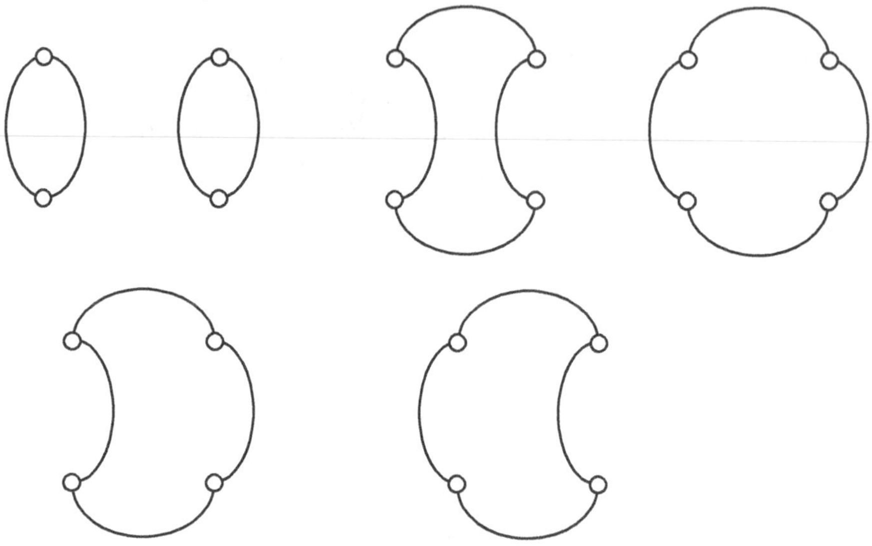

Fig. 2.51

Hence, there are 6 cycles in G.

Note that there are 4 vertices. Since, any cycle in G has atmost length equals to 4.

Example 2.24 : *What is the diameter of Peterson's graph ?*

Solution : Peterson's graph is a graph with vertex set as 2-subsets of {1, 2, 3, 4, 5} and we join any two vertices i.e. 2-subsets if they are disjoint.

Hence, Peterson graph as shown below.

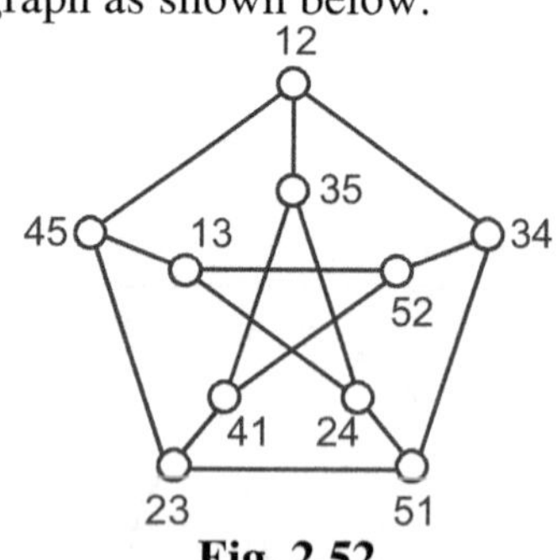

Fig. 2.52

Now we will find diameter of G.

For any two vertices u, v of G, we have

$$d(u, v) \leq 2$$

Also max $\{d(u, v)/u, v \in G\} = 2$

$\therefore$ Diameter of G is equal to 2.

Think Over It

1. Show that every connected graph with n vertices has at least n – 1 edges.
2. Show that, if a simple graph G has K connected components and these components have $n_1, n_2, \ldots, n_k$ vertices, respectively, then the number of edges of G does not exceed $\sum_{i=1}^{k} C(n_i, 2)$.
3. Show that a simple graph with n vertices and k connected components has at most $\frac{(n-k)(n-k+1)}{2}$ edges.
4. Show that a simple graph G with n vertices is connected if it has more than $\frac{(n-1)(n-2)}{2}$ edges.

Summary

1. Let G = (V, E) be an undirected graph.

   A **path** of length n from u to v in G is a sequence of n edges $e_1, \ldots, e_n$ of G such that $e_1 = \{x_1, x_2\}$, $e_2 = \{x_1, x_2\}$, …, $e_n = \{k_{n-1}, x_n\}$ where $x_0 = u$ and $x_n = v$. When the graph is simple, we denote this path by its vertex sequence $x_0, x_1, \ldots, x_n$.

   A path is a **circuit** if it begins and ends at the same vertex.

   A path or circuit is **simple** if it does not contain the same edge more than once.

   A circuit in a graph is also called as **cycle** in a graph.

2. Let G = (V, E) be a directed graph.

   A **path** of length n from u to v in G is a sequence of edges $e_1, e_2, \ldots, e_n$ of G such that $e_1 = (x_0, x_1)$, $e_2 = (x_1, x_2)$, …, $e_n = (x_{n-1}, x_n)$, where $x_0 = u$ and $x_n = v$. When there are no multiple edges in the directed graph, this path is denoted by its vertex sequence $x_0, x_1, \ldots, x_n$. A path of length greater than zero that begins and ends at the same vertex is called a **circuit** or **cycle**. A path or circuit is called **simple** if it does not contain the same edge more than once.

3. An undirected graph is called **connected** if there is a path between every pair of distinct vertices of the graph.
4. There is a simple path between every pair of distinct vertices of a connected undirected graph.
5. In a connected graph G, a **cut-set** is a set of edges whose removal from G leaves G disconnected, provided removal of no proper subset of these edges disconnects G.
6. A directed graph is **strongly connected** if there is a path from a to b and from b to a whenever a and b are vertices in the graph.
7. A directed graph is **weakly connected** if there is a path between every two vertices in the underlying undirected graph.
8. The maximal strongly connected subgraphs, are called the **strongly connected components** or **strong components** of G.
9. Let G be a graph with adjacency matrix A with respect to the ordering 1, 2, …, n. The number of different paths of length r from i to j, where $r \in \mathbb{N}$, equals the $(i, j)^{th}$ entry of A^r.

Exercise

[A] Say True or False : Justify !

1. Graph has cut vertex of degree 1.
2. Let v be cut vertex of simple graph G then $\overline{G} - v$ is connected.
3. Let G_n be graph whose vertices are the permutations of {1, 2, 3, … n} with two permutations $a_1, a_2 \ldots a_n$ and $b_1, b_2 \ldots b_n$ adjacent iff they differ by interchanging a pair of adjacent entries. Then G_n is connected.
4. If G is connected graph with atleast three vertices then G has two vertices x, y such that G – {x, y} is connected.
5. If u and v only two vertices of odd degree in a graph G then G has u – v path.
6. Let G be graph with vertex set {1, … 15} in which i and j are adjacent iff their greatest common factor exceeds 1, then diameter of G is 7.
7. The edge set of every closed trail can be partitioned into edge sets of cycle.
8. The longest trail which is not closed then its end points have odd degree.
9. Bipartite graph has unique partition, iff it is connected.
10. Complement of a simple disconnected graph is disconnected.

[B] Multiple Choice Questions : Choose the Correct Alternative

1. Let G(V, E) be simple graph with 5 components and $|V| = 10$ then $|E|$ less than or equal to
   (a) 15 (b) 14
   (c) 13 (d) 12
2. Let G(V, E) be a simple graph with 5 components and $|V| = 10$ then $|E|$ is greater than or equal to
   (a) 5 (b) 6
   (c) 7 (d) 8
3. Let G be a simple graph and K(G), λ(G), δ(G) denotes vertex connectivity, edge connectivity and the minimum vertex degree in G respectively, then
   (a) $K(G) \leq \lambda(G) \leq \delta(G)$ (b) $\lambda(G) \leq K(G) \leq \delta(G)$
   (c) $\delta(G) \leq \lambda(G) \leq K(G)$ (d) $K(G) \leq \delta(G) \leq \lambda(G)$
4. Let K_n be a complete graph on n vertices and $K_{m,n}$ be a complete bipartite graph on m + n vertices, then
   (a) $K(K_n) = n - 1,\ \lambda(K_{m,n}) = \min\{m, n\}$
   (b) $\lambda(K_n) = n - 1,\ K(K_{m,n}) = \max\{m, n\}$
   (c) $K(K_n) = 0,\ K(K_{m,n}) = m + n$
   (d) None of these
5. Dijkstra's algorithm can be used for
   (a) Path of minimum weight for source vertex to destination vertex in weighted graph
   (b) Path of maximum weight from source vertex to destination vertex in a weighted graph
   (c) Smallest path from source vertex to destination vertex in a graph
   (d) All of these
6. Which of the following graph has a bridge

(a) 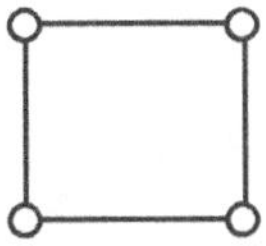 (b) 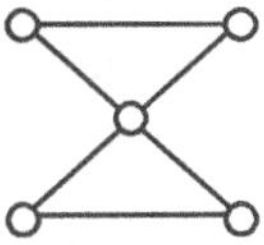

(c) 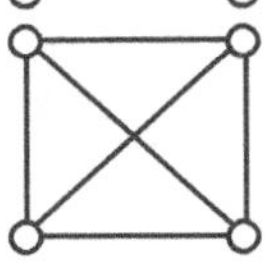 (d) 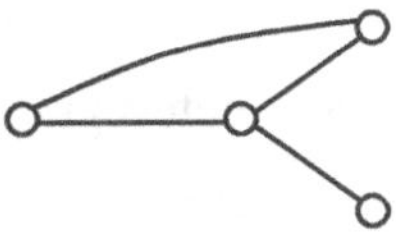

7. Which of the following graph has a cut vertex

(a) 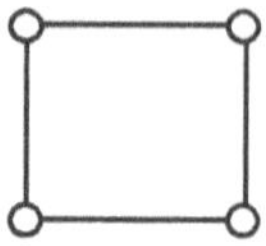

(b) 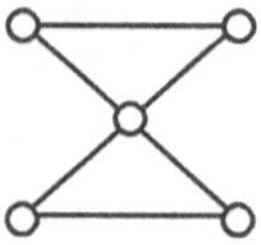

(c) 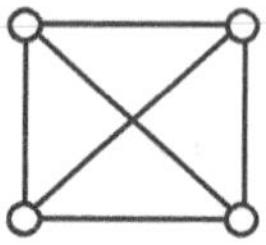

(d) 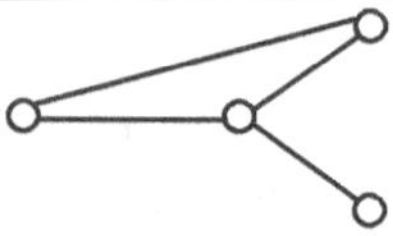

8. Consider a simple connected graph G with n vertices and n edges (n > 2) then which of the following is true ?
   (a) G has atleast one cycle
   (b) G has no cycles
   (c) The graph obtained by removing any edge from G is not connected
   (d) G has exactly one cycle

9. Let G be a graph with 100 vertices numbered 1 to 100. Two vertices i and j are adjacent iff $|i - j| = 8$ or $|i - j| = 12$. The number of components in G is
   (a) 8 (b) 12
   (c) 25 (d) 4

10. The minimum number of edges in a connected cyclic graph on n vertices are
   (a) n – 1 (b) n
   (c) n + 1 (d) None of these

[C] Theory Questions :

1. Define walk, tour, path cycle in a graph and give difference between them by giving examples.
2. Let G be a graph.
   Let d(u, v) = The minimum of lengths of u – v path $\forall$ u, v $\in$ V
   where, V = Set of vertices of G
   Prove that d is a metric function on V.
3. Show that maximum number of edges in a simple graph with n vertices and k components is $\frac{(n-k)(n-k+1)}{2}$.
4. Let G be a connected graph. Let r and d be radius and diameter of G. Prove that $r \leq d \leq 2r$.

5. Let G be a simple graph with n vertices and m edges. Let k = number of components in G. Show that $n - k \leq m$.
6. Define cut vertex and cut edge. Illustrate these definitions by examples.
7. Let G be a simple graph, show that $k(G) \leq \lambda(G) \leq \delta(G)$

   where, $k(G)$ = vertex connectivity of G

   $\lambda(G)$ = edge connectivity of G

   $\delta(G)$ = the minimum of degrees of vertices in G

[D] Numerical Problems :

1. Find the number of cycles in the following two graphs :

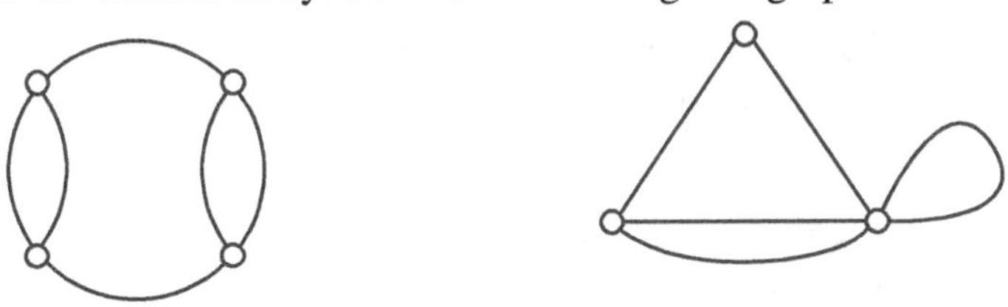

(a) (b)

Fig. 2.55

2. If an edge e is in a closed trail of a graph G then show that e is in cycle of G.
3. What is the diameter of Peterson's graph ?
4. x, y, z are different vertices in a graph G. Prove that if there is a path from x to y and also a path from y to z then there is a path from x to z.
5. Draw the graphs G_1^2 and G_2^2 where

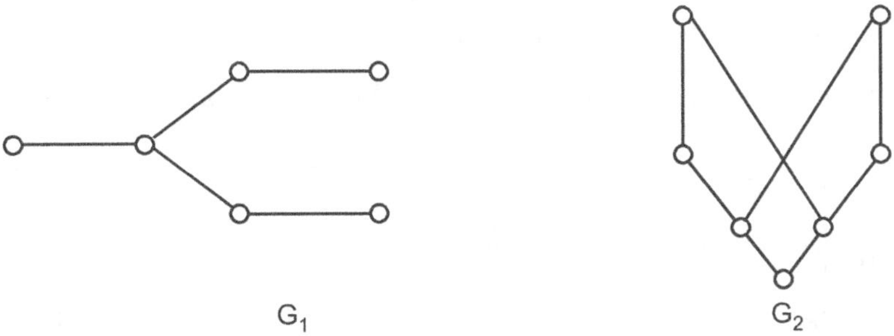

(a) (b)

Fig. 2.56

6. Find (a) the maximum number of edges in a simple disconnected graph with n vertices. (b) The maximum and minimum number of edges in a simple connected graph with n vertices. (c) The maximum number of edges in a simple bipartite graph with n vertices.
7. Let V = {0, 1, 2, ..., 20} be the vertex set of a graph G. An edge between x and y exists when x-y is divisible by 5. Draw a graph G. Explain why G is not connected. What the components of G represent ?
8. Give example of a connected graph such that the removal of any single edge results in a disconnected graph. Show that the number of edges in such a graph is exactly one less than the number of vertices.
9. A graph G has vertices and edges equal in number. Show that G must contain at least one cycle.
10. G is a graph with n vertices and m edges. If $m > {}^{n-1}C_2$ then show that G is connected. For n = 2, 3, 4, draw a disconnected graph satisfying the condition $m = {}^{n-1}C_2$.
11. Prove that in a connected graph G, any two longest paths have a vertex in common.
12. Find all the bridges in the graph.

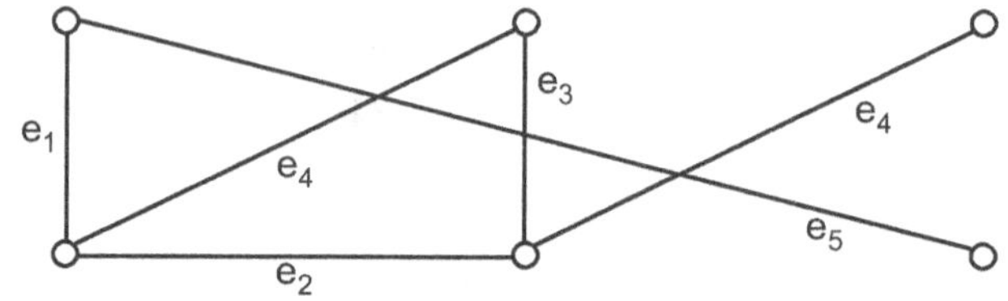

Fig. 2.57

13. What is the edge connectivity of K_n ?
14. Find the vertex connectivity of the following graphs G_1, G_2, G_3.

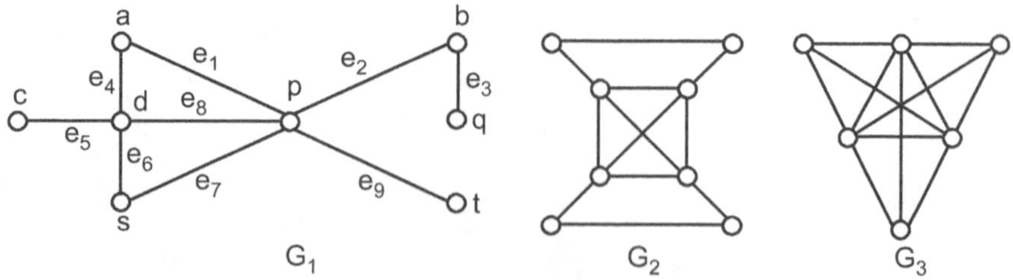

Fig. 2.58

15. Find the edge connectivity of the following graphs G_1 and G_2.

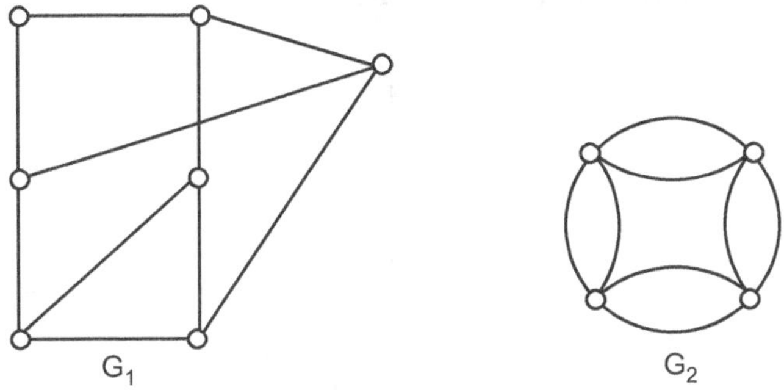

Fig. 2.59

16. A graph is called a cubic graph if it is 3-regular. Prove that a cubic graph as a cut vertex iff it has a bridge.

17. Prove that in a cubic graph, vertex connectivity equals the edge connectivity.

18. Find what maximum vertex connectivity and edge connectivity can be achieved with 8 vertices and 16 edges. Draw a graph showing that they are achieved.

19. In the weighted graph given below, apply Dijkstra's algorithm and find the shortest path and its weight from the vertex s to the vertex t.

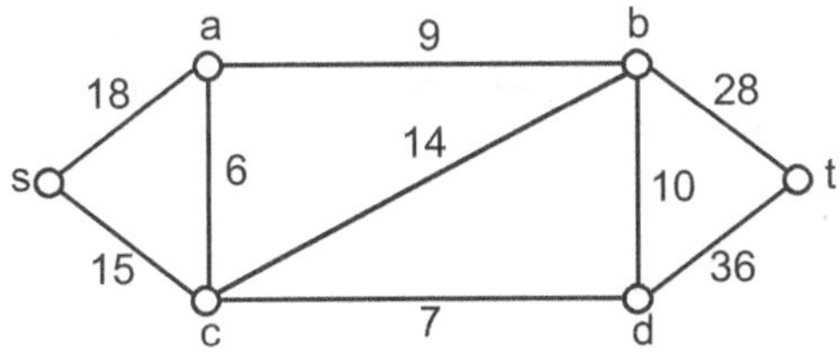

Fig. 2.60

20. Find the shortest path from a to z in the graph below.

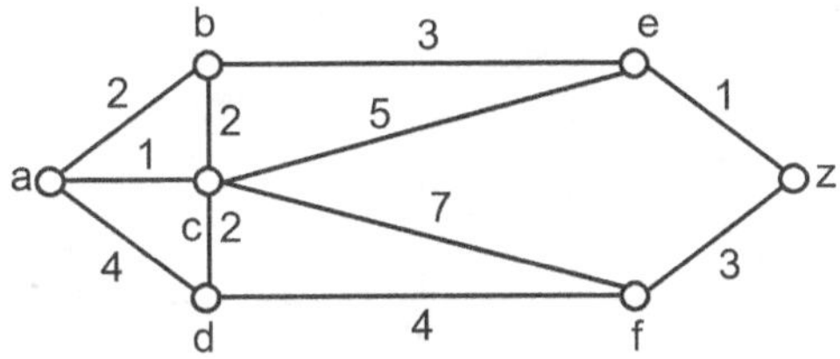

Fig. 2.61

21. Find by Dijkstra's algorithm the shortest path from the vertex a to the remaining vertices of the following graph.

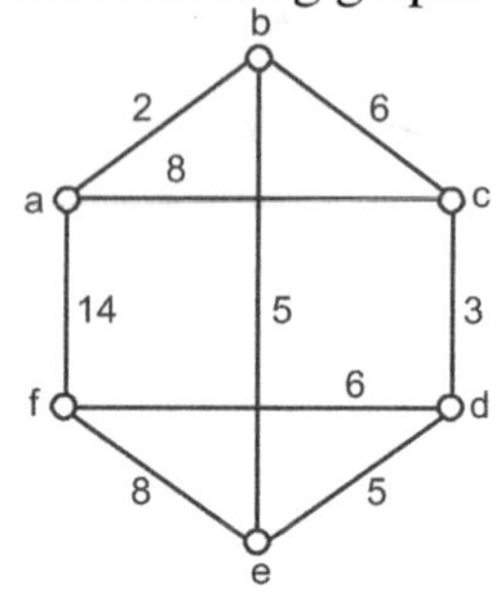

Fig. 2.62

22. Find the shortest path from the vertex a to all other vertices of the following graph.

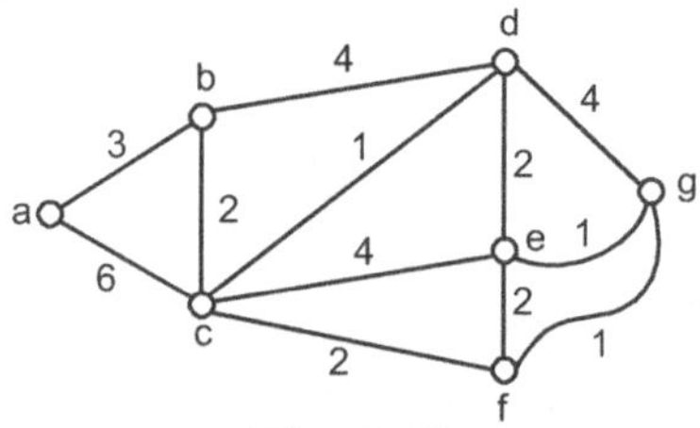

Fig. 2.63

23. Find the shortest path from the vertex a to the vertex z, by using Dijkstra's algorithm.

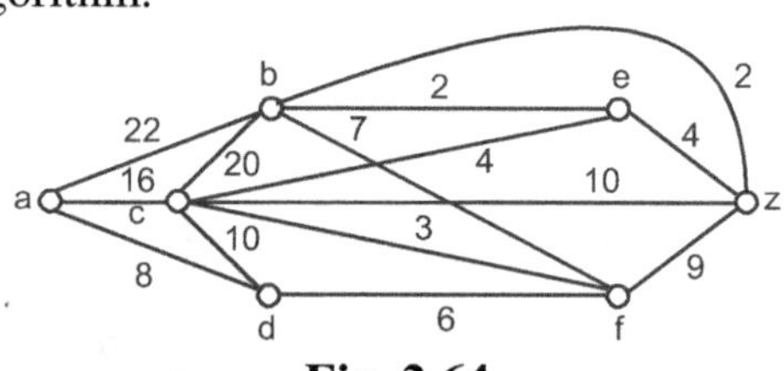

Fig. 2.64

24. Find the shortest path from the vertex h to the remaining vertices of the following graph.

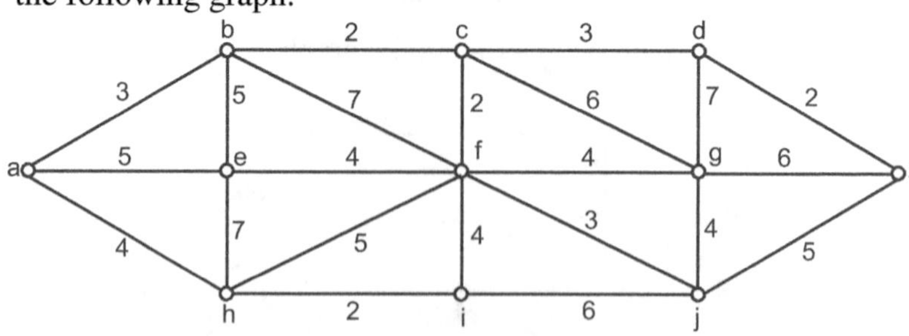

Fig. 2.65

25. How many connected components does each of the following graphs have ? For each graph find each of its connected components.

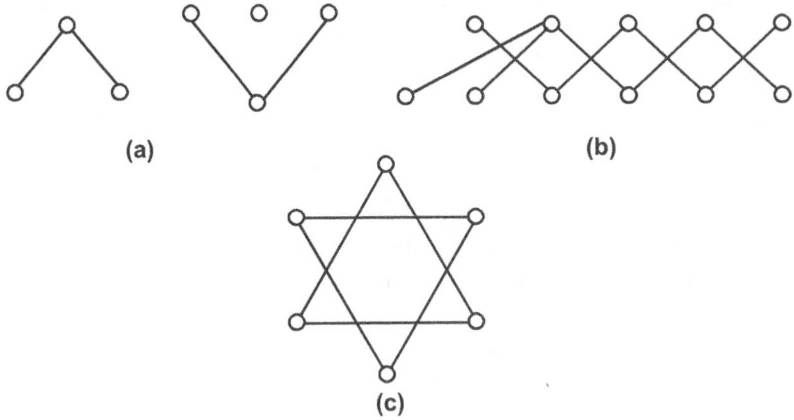

Fig. 2.66

26. Determine whether each of these graphs is strongly connected and if not, whether it is weakly connected.

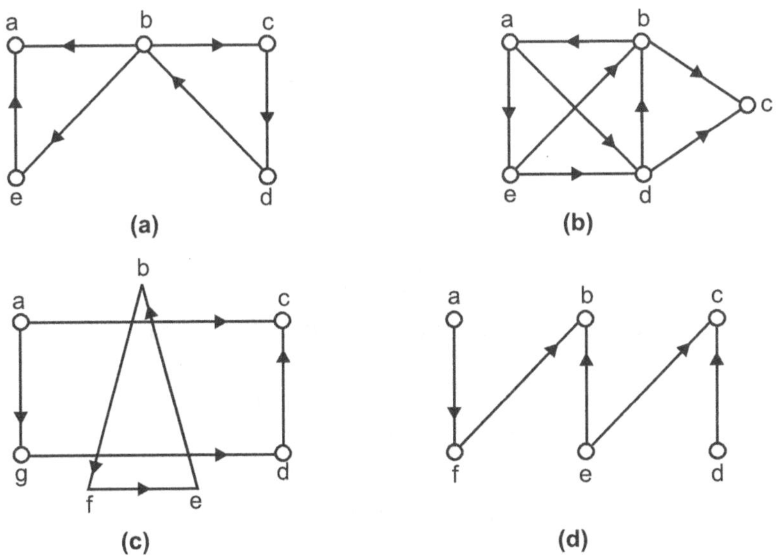

Fig. 2.67

27. Find the strongly connected components of each of the following graphs.

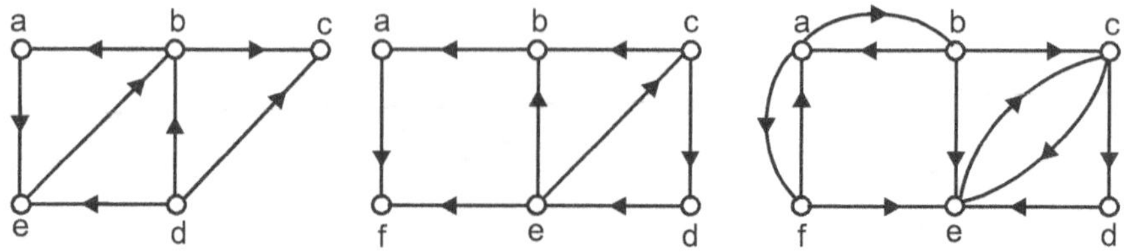

Fig. 2.68

28. Use paths either to show that these graphs are not isomorphic or to find an isomorphism between them.

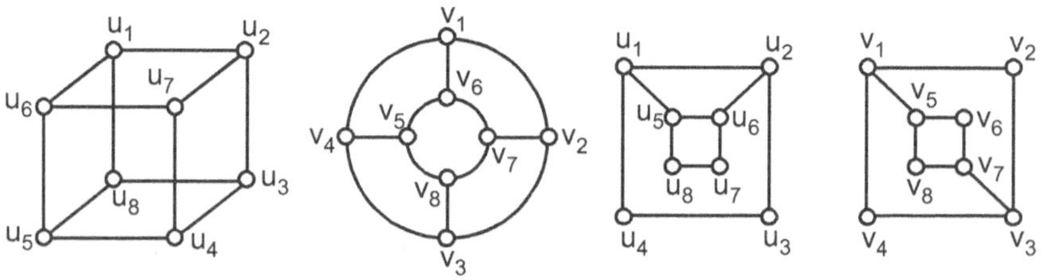

Fig. 2.69

29. Find the number of paths between c and d in the following graph of length 5.

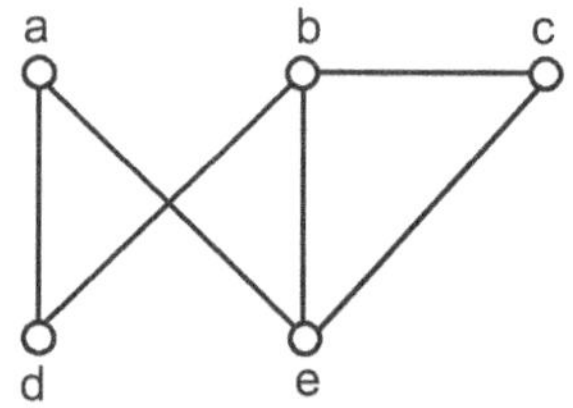

Fig. 2.70

30. Find the number of paths from a to e in the directed graph below of length G.

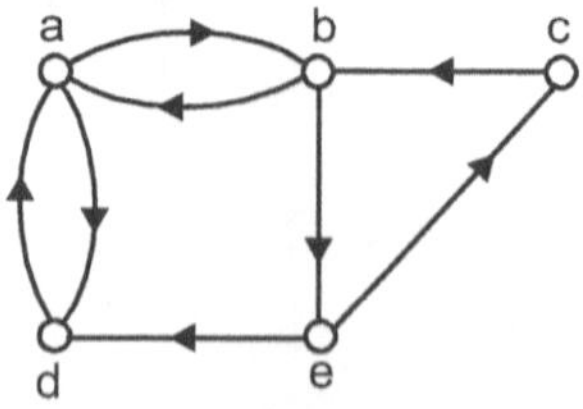

Fig. 2.71

Answers

[A] (1) False, (2) True, (3) True, (4) True, (5) True, (6) True, (7) True, (8) True, (9) True, (10) False

[B] (1) - (a), (2) - (a), (3) - (a), (4) - (a), (5) - (d), (6) - (d), (7) - (d), (8) - (a) (9) - (a), (10) - (b)

[C] 1. 6, 4

3. 2

5.

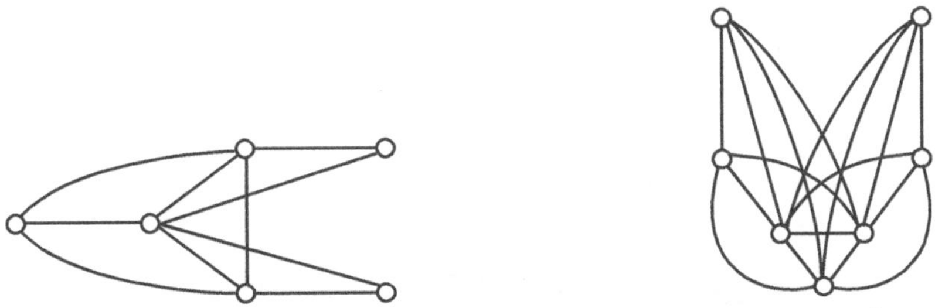

(a) G_1^2 **(b)** G_2^2

Fig. 2.72

6. (a) $\frac{(n-1)(n-2)}{2}$, (b) $\frac{n(n-1)}{2}$, n – 1, (c) $\frac{n^2}{4}$.

7.

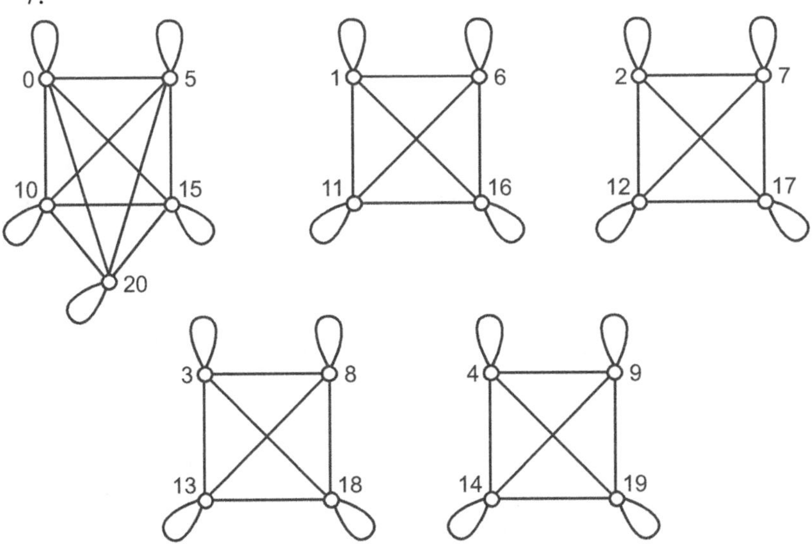

Fig. 2.73

Components are equivalence classes with respect to equivalence relation congruence modulo 5.

1. e_1, e_5, e_6
2. n – 1
3. 1, 2, 3
4. 2, 4
5. 4

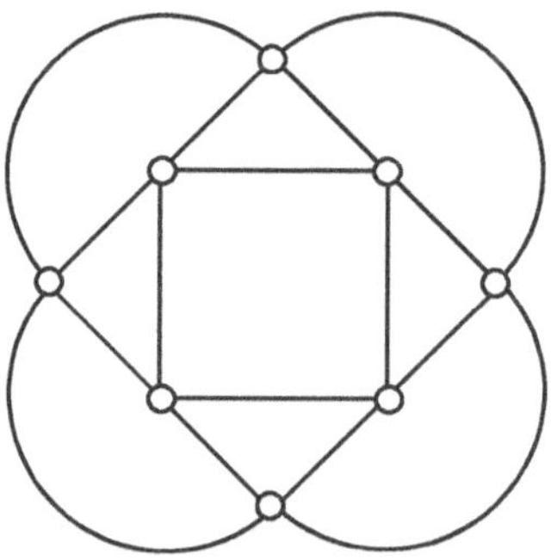

Fig. 2.74

1.

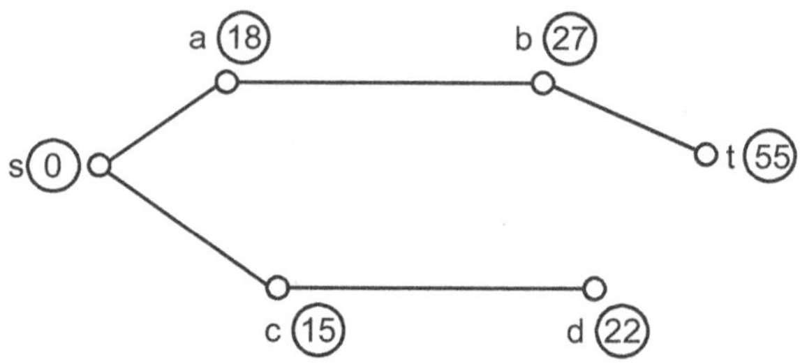

Fig. 2.75

2.

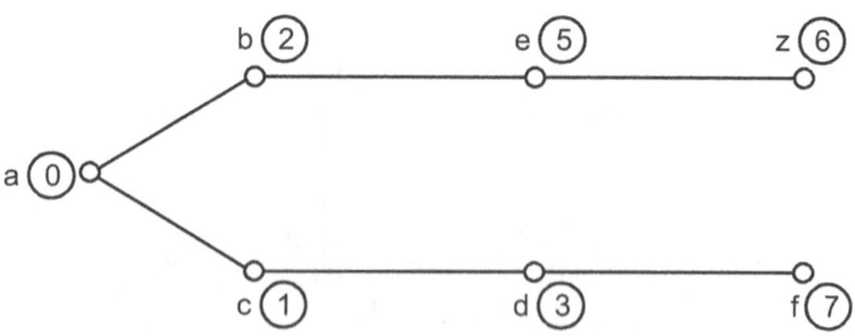

Fig. 2.76

3.

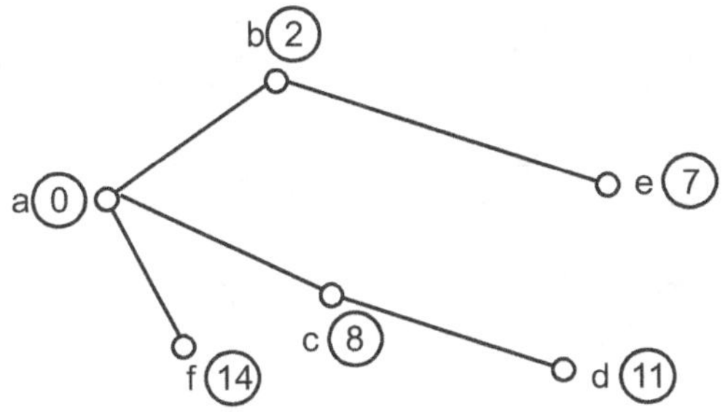

Fig. 2.77

4.

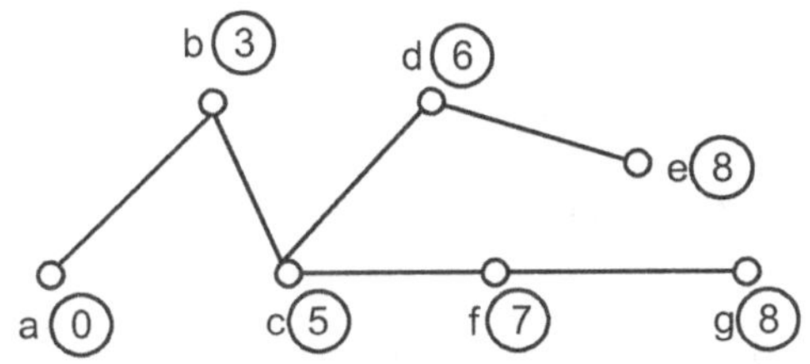

Fig. 2.78

5.

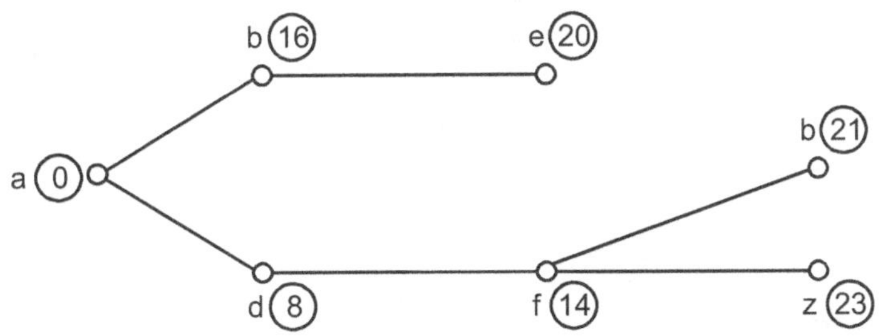

Fig. 2.79

6.

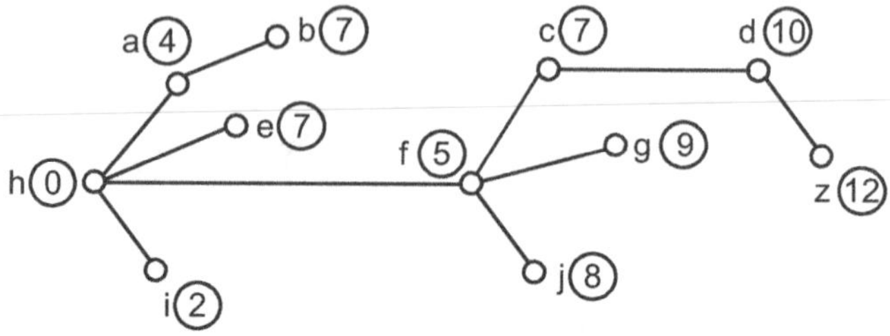

Fig. 2.80

✍✍✍

Chapter 3...

Eulerian and Hamiltonian Graphs

Sir William Rowman Hamilton

Hamilton entered Trinity College, Dublin at the age of 18 and in his first year he obtained on 'optime' in Classics, a distinction only awarded once in 20 years. In 1826 Hamilton received an 'optime' in both science and Classics, which was unheard of, while in his final year as an undergraduate he presented a memoir *Theory of Systems of Rays* to the Royal Irish Academy. It is in this paper that Hamilton introduced the characteristic function for optics.

On 4 November 1833 Hamilton read a paper to the Royal Irish Academy expressing complex numbers as algebraic couples, or ordered pair of real numbers. He used algebra in treating dynamics in *On a General Method in Dynamics* in 1834. In this paper Hamilton gave his first statement of the characteristic function applied to dynamics and wrote a second paper on the topic the following year.

On 16 October 1843 (a Monday) Hamilton was walking in along the Royal Canal with his wife to preside at a Council meeting of the Royal Irish Academy. Although his wife talked to him now and again Hamilton hardly heard, for the discovery of the qaternions, the first non-commutative algebra to be studied.

Hamilton defined a Hamiltonian graph.

3.1 Introduction

In this chapter, we will study two important types of graphs, namely Eulerian graph and Hamiltonian graph. Also we will study their applications to real life problems.

3.2 Konigsberg Seven Bridges Problem

Konigsberg was a city in Prussia situated on the banks of Pregel River, which served as the residence of the dukes of Prussia in the 16th century. (Today, the city is named Kaliningrad, and is a major industrial and commercial center of western Russia.) The river Pregel flowed through the town, creating an island, as in the following picture. Seven bridges spanned the various branches of the river, as shown.

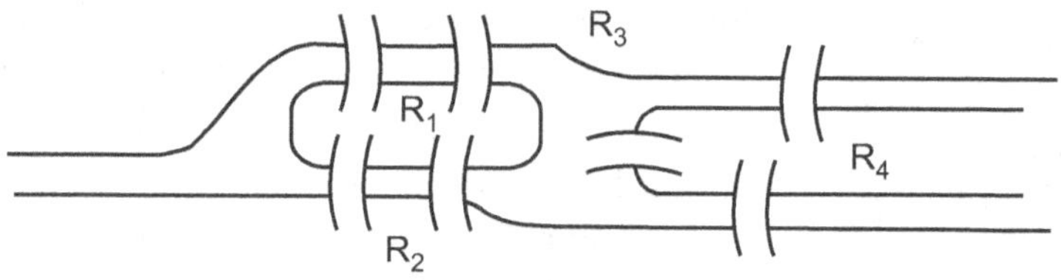

Fig. 3.1

The Bridges of Konigsberg :

A famous problem concerning Konigsberg was whether it was possible to take a walk through the town in such a way as to cross over every bridge once, and only once. An example of a failed attempt to take such a walking tour is shown below.

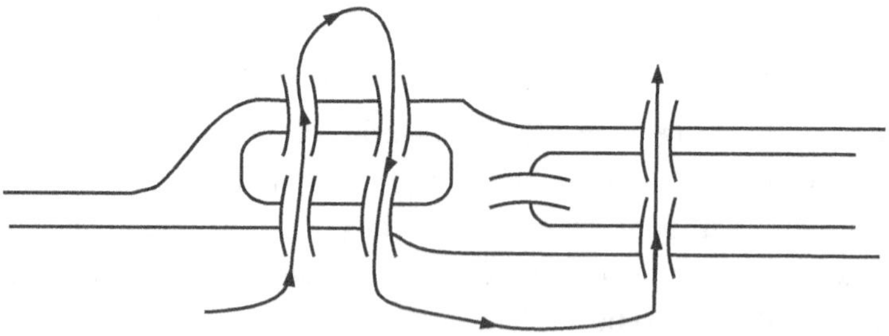

Fig. 3.2

OK, so this attempt didn't work. But might there be some other path that would cross every bridge exactly once ? This problem was first solved by the prolific Swiss mathematician Leonhard Euler, who invented the branch of mathematics now known as graph theory in the process of his solution.

Graphs :

Euler's approach was to regard the spots of land (there are 4 of them) as points to be visited, and the bridges as paths between those points. The mathematical essentials of the map of Konigsberg can then be reduced to the following diagram which is an example of a graph.

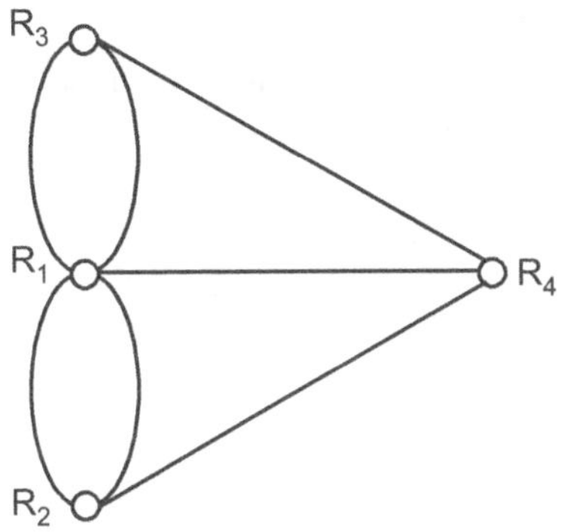

Fig. 3.3

The problem of the bridges of Konigsberg can then be reformulated as whether this graph can be traced without tracing any edge more than once.

Euler's Solution :

Euler's solution to the problem of the Konigsberg bridges involved the observation that when a vertex is "visited" in the middle of the process of tracing a graph, there must be an edge coming into the vertex, and another edge leaving it; and so the degree of the vertex must be an even number. This must be true for all but at most two of the vertices– the one you start at, and the one you end at, and so a connected graph is traversible if and only if it has at most two vertices of odd degree. (Note that the starting and ending vertices may be the same, in which case the degree of every vertex must be even.) Now a quick look at the graph above shows that there are more than two vertices of odd degree, and so the graph cannot be traced; that is the desired walking tour of Konigsberg is impossible.

3.3 Eulerian Graphs

Definition :

A trail in a graph which consist all edges in the graph is called as Eulerian trail in the graph.

A tour in a graph which consist all edges in the graph is called as Eulerian tour in the graph.

A graph is called as Eulerian if there exist Eulerian tour in the graph.
Definition: A graph is called as semi-Eulerian if there exist Eulerian trail in the graph.

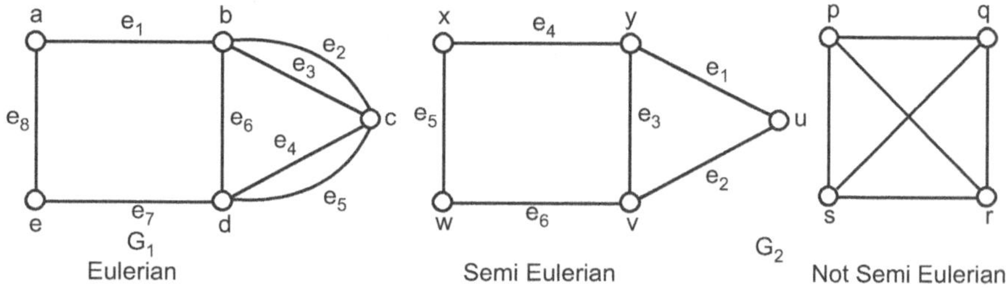

Fig. 3.4

In graph G_1,

$ae_1\ be_2\ ce_5\ de_6\ be_3\ ce_4\ de_7\ ee_8\ a$ is Eulerian tour

In graph G_2,

$ye_1\ ue_2\ ve_3\ ye_4\ xe_5\ we_6\ v$ is Eulerian trail.

In G_3, there is no Eulerian tour.

Theorem 1 **Characterisation of a Eulerian graph:**

Let G(V, E) be graph.

G is a Eulerian graph if G is connected and degree of each vertex is even.

Proof: Hypothesis: G is Eulerian graph.

Claim : G is connected and degree of each vertex is even.

Since G is Eulerian, there is Eulerian tour say $v_1e_1v_2e_2v_3 \ldots e_{k-1}v_ke_k \ldots e_{n-1}\ v_ne_nv_1$.

Since this walk covers all vertices (possibly with repetition) and all edges (without repetition), it contains x, y– walk and hence x, y path for any two vertices x and y in G.

Therefore, G is connected.

Also each occurrence $e_{k-1}v_ke_k$ contribute 2 degrees to $d(v_k)$, for each intermediate vertex v_k.

Also the occurence v_1e_1, and e_nv_1 contribute 2 degrees to $d(v_1)$.

Hence, degree of each vertex is even.

Conversely, Hypothesis : G is connected and degree of each vertex is even.

Claim : G is a Eulerian graph.

Since, the graph G is connected, it does not have isolated vertex.

We can construct an Eulerian trail as follows.

For this we will use induction on number of edges in G say m

Basic step: $m = 0$.

Since, G is connected, G contains single vertex.

Hence, there is Eulerian trail consisting of no edge.

Induction step : $m > 1$

Let any connected graph with degree of each vertex even and with less than m edges be Eulerian.

Let v_1 be any vertex in G. Since $d(v_1)$ is even, we can choose edge $e_1 = v_1v_2$. Also since $d(v_2)$ is even we can choose edge $e_2 = v_2v_3$. Continue in this way without repetition of edges. Since, the number of edges in a graph is finite we eventually reach at v_1 again. In this way, we get cycle $C : v_1e_1v_2e_2 \ldots. e_kv_1$.

Now degree of each v_i in C is even. We denote degree of v_i in C by $d_C(v_i)$.

Let E_l = set of edges in C.

Now $d_G(v) = d_C(v) + d_{G-E}(v)$ for each $v \in G$.

Hence, $d_{G-E}(v) = d_G(v) - d_C(v)$ = even – even = even.

Hence, G – E is connected graph with degree of each vertex even and having less than m edges. Hence, by induction hypothesis, G – E is Eulerian.

Let T is Eulerian trail in G – E.

Clearly traversing C and then T, we get $C \cup T$ as Eulerian tour in G.

Hence, G is a Eulerian graph.

3.4 Fleury's Algorithm - To Find Eulerian Tour in a Eulerian Graph

This algorithm finds a Eulerian tour if exist in a graph.

Input : An Eulerian graph G(V, E).

Idea : Start with any vertex v_0, we walk along the edges from it to cover all the edges in the graph. We delete any edge traversed to prevent repetition of edges. Traverse a bridge in the traversed edges deleted subgraph if there is no alternative to it, because its deletion will disconnect the graph and hence we cannot reach the starting vertex at the end.

Initialisation : Choose any vertex v_0 in the graph G and set $W_0 = v_0$.

Iteration : Let the trail $W_i = v_0e_1v_1 \ldots e_iv_i$ (say) has been chosen

Choose an edge $e_{i+1} \notin W_i$ from v_i to v_{i+1} (say), unless there is no alternative for a bridge of $G - \{e_1, e_2, e_3, \ldots e_i\}$.

Set $W_{i+1} = v_0e_1v_1 \ldots e_iv_ie_{i+1} v_{i+1}$.

Repeat the above steps for W_{i+1} and so on, until we cover all the edges in G.

3.5 Chinese Postman Problem (CPP)

Real life problem : A postman pick up letters at the post office, then he must deliver letters along each street on his route and finally must return to the post office with undelivered letters.

Postman wishes to cover his route with minimum distance as possible. How he covers all streets on his route?

Graph model: We construct a weighted graph G in which vertices are junction of streets. Edges are the streets. The weight assigned to each edge represents the length of street between the junctions.

Then we say that postman wishes to find the tour in the graph with minimum weight.

The weight of a tour is sum of weights of the edges in the tour.

If the given graph is Eulerian then any Euler tour of the graph is tour with minimum weight since it involves the each edge of the graph exactly once. We can find this Eulerian tour by Fleury's algorithm.

But if the given graph is not Eulerian then the postman cannot get such Eulerian tour.

The postman has to repeat some streets with minimum weight as possible. That is we have to duplicate the edges of G with minimum weights untill we get new graph which is Eulerian.

Duplication of an edge means putting the parallel edge to it having same weight as that of the edge .

If the graph G is not Eulerian then there are odd degree vertices in G. But by corollary of handshaking lemma they are even in number.

Now by Dijkstra's algorithm we can find shortest path between any pair of the odd degree vertices in the graph G, by pairing the odd degree vertices of minimum distances.

Duplicating all the edges in all of these shortest paths between paired vertices, we get the new graph G* from G.

Now Eulerian tour in G* is required tour with minimum weight.

3.6 Hamiltonian Graphs

Definition :

The path in a graph is called as Hamiltonian path if it contains all vertices of the graph.

The cycle in a graph is called as Hamiltonian cycle if it contains all vertices of the graph.

A graph is said to be Hamiltonian if there is a Hamiltonian cycle in the graph.

A graph is said to be semi-Halimtonian if there is a Hamiltonian path in the graph.

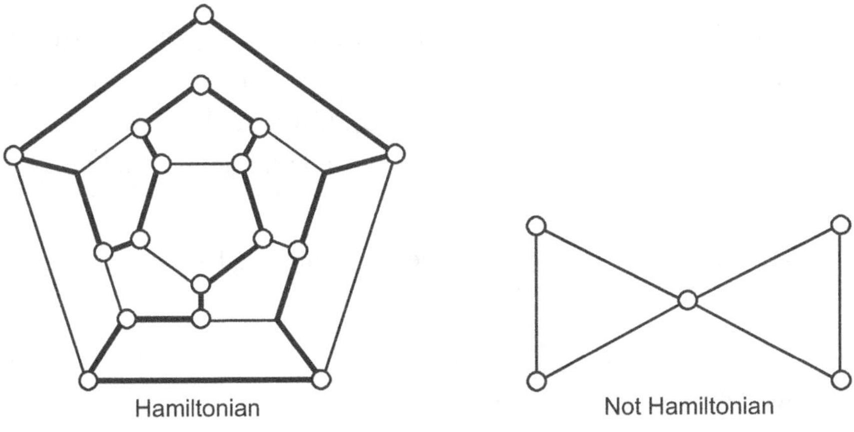

Fig. 3.5

3.7 Necessary and Sufficient Conditions for Hamiltonian Graphs

Theorem 2 [Necessary] If G is a Hamiltonian graph, then for any set $S \subseteq V$, the graph G – S has at most $|S|$ components. ■

Corollary : If G is a Hamiltonian graph then G has no cut vertex.

Theorem 3 [Sufficient : Dirac : 1952]

If G is a simple graph with at least three vertices and $d(v) \geq \frac{n}{2}$ for each vertex v in G, then G is Hamiltonian. Here n = number of vertices in G. ■

Corollary 1 : K_n is a Hamiltonian graph.

Corollary 2 : Every k regular graph with atmost 2k vertices is Hamiltonian. In particular $K_{n, n}$ is Hamiltonian.

Theorem 4 [Necessary and sufficient :]

Let G(V, E) be a simple graph with n vertices and let u and v be non-adjacent vertices in G such that $d(u) + d(v) \geq n$.

Let G + uv be a supergraph of G obtained by joining u and v by an edge.

Then G is Hamiltonian if G + uv is Hamiltonian. ■

Definition : Let G be a simple graph with n vertices. If there are two non-adjacent vertices u_1 and v_1 such that $d(u_1) + d(v_1) \geq n$ in G, join u_1 and v_1 by an edge to form a supergraph G_1. If there are two non-adjacent vertices u_2 and v_2 such that $d(u_2) + d(v_2) \geq n$ in G_1, join u_2 and v_2 by an edge to form a supergraph G_2.

Continue in this way, we get supergraph of G called as closure of G. It is denoted by C(G).

Corollary of last theorem : Let G be simple graph. G is Hamiltonian iff C(G) is Hamiltonian.

Consider graph G

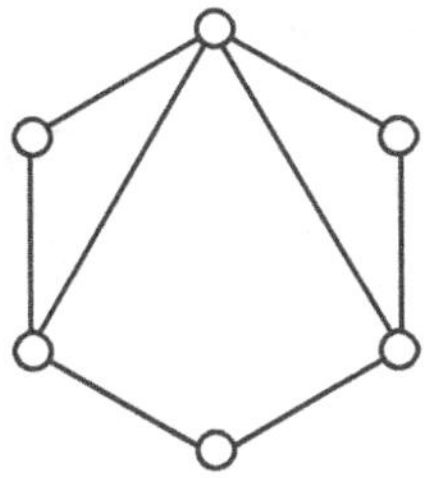

Fig. 3.6

Its closure is obtained as follows.

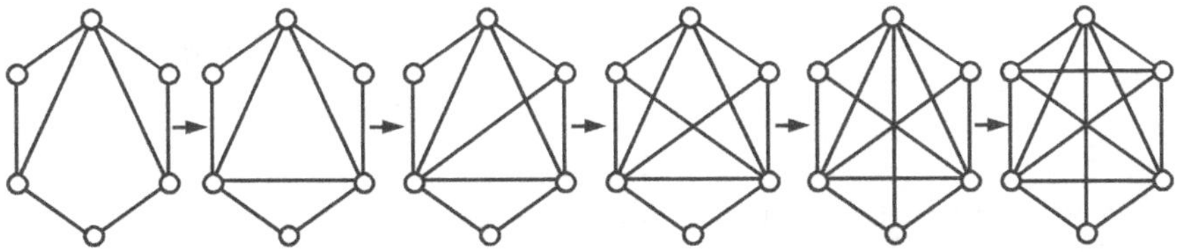

Fig. 3.7

3.8 Travelling Salesman Problem

Problem : Suppose a travelling salesman's territory includes several towns with roads connecting certain pairs of these towns. His job requires him to visit each town. Is it possible for him to plan a round trip by a car enabling him to visit each town exactly once and if such a trip is possible, can he plan one which minimizes the total distance travelled ?

Graph model : We can represent the salesman's territory by a weighted graph G where the vertices represents the towns and two vertices joined by an edge iff there is road connecting the corresponding towns and which does not pass through any other town. We assign each edge with weight representing the length of the corresponding road.

Then the question posed above becomes :

Is G a Hamiltonian graph ?

If Yes, then can we construct the Hamiltonian cycle of minimum weight in G?

Illustrative Examples

Example 3.1 : *Find an Euler tour in following Eulerian graph.*

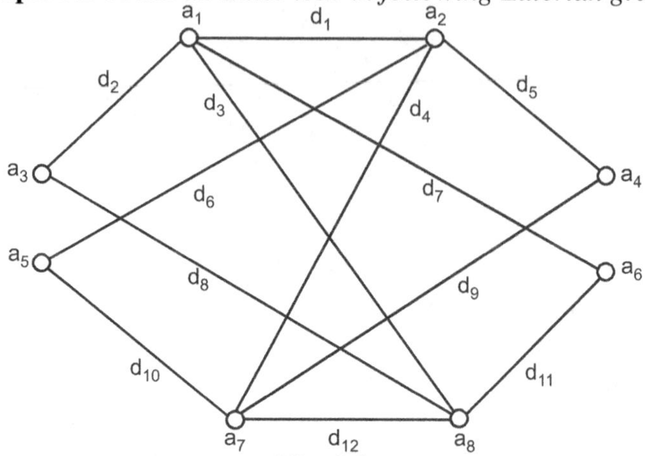

Fig. 3.8

Solution : Initialisation : $W_0 = a_1 \cdot G_0 = G$

Iteration (1) : Choose d_1, so that

$$W_1 = a_1d_1a_2, G_1 = G - d_1.$$

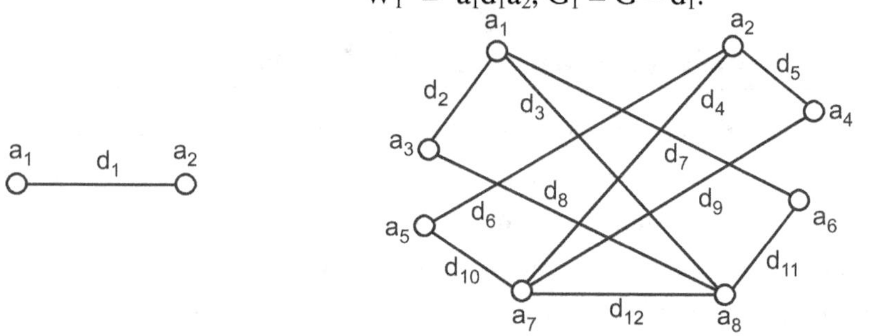

Fig. 3.9

Iteration (2) : Choose d_5. So that $W_2 = a_1d_1a_2d_5a_4$,

$G_2 = G - \{d_1, d_5\}$.

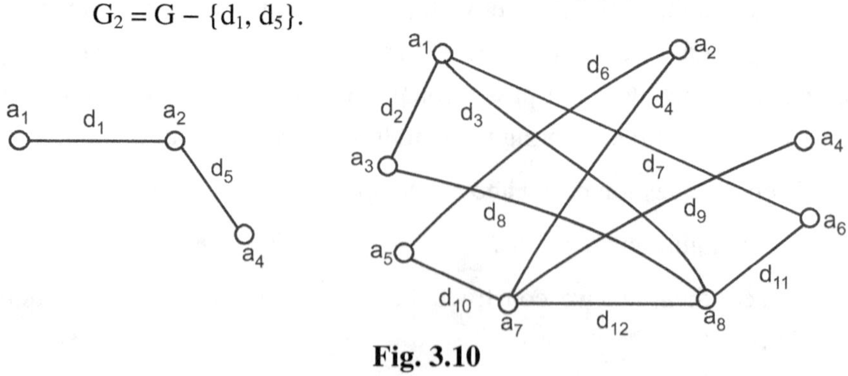

Fig. 3.10

Iteration (3) : Choose d_9 (although d_9 is a bridge in G_2, there is no alternative to it).

So that $W_3 = a_1d_1a_2d_5a_4d_9a_7$, $G_3 = G - \{d_1, d_5, d_9\}$ and so on, we get an Euler tour

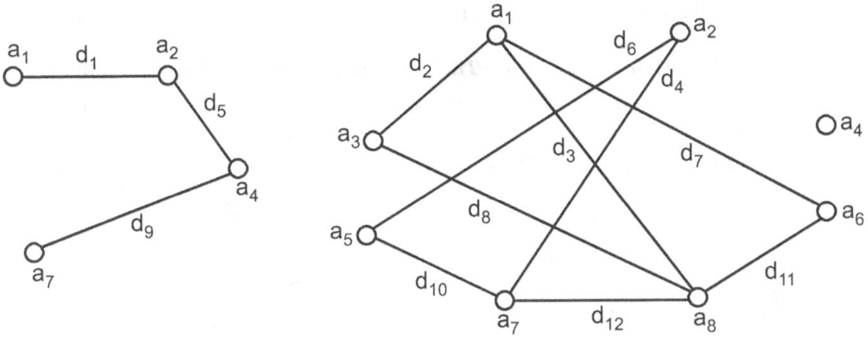

Fig. 3.11

W_{11} =

$a_1d_1a_2d_5a_4d_9a_7d_7a_2d_6a_5d_{10}a_7d_{12}a_8d_8a_3d_2a_1d_3a_8d_{11}a_6d_7a_1$

G_{11} is null graph.

Example 3.2 : *Which of the following graphs are Eulerian ?*

(i) K_n, $n \geq 3$

(ii) Q_n ,, $n \geq 3$

(iii) W_n ,, $n \geq 4$

Solution : (i) $d(v) = n - 1 \;\; \forall \;\; v \in K_n$

$\therefore$ K_n has each vertex degree even if n is odd.

$\therefore$ K_n is Eulerian if n is odd.

(From characterization of Eulerian graph)

(ii) Q_n is a graph with vertex set as set of n tuples of 0's and 1's and two vertices joined by an edge iff the differ in exactly one position e.g. Q_3 is as shown below.

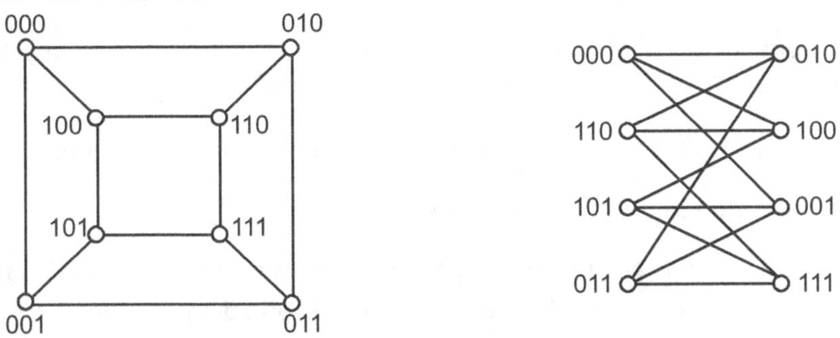

Fig. 3.12

Thus, each Q_n is bipartite graph with each partition contains equal number of vertices.

Also each vertex of Q_n has degree equals to n.

$\therefore$ Q_n is Eulerian iff n is even.

(iii) W_n is never a Eulerian graph. Since, each vertex except possibly center has degree equals to 3. Which is odd

We can draw a picture of W_5, W_6

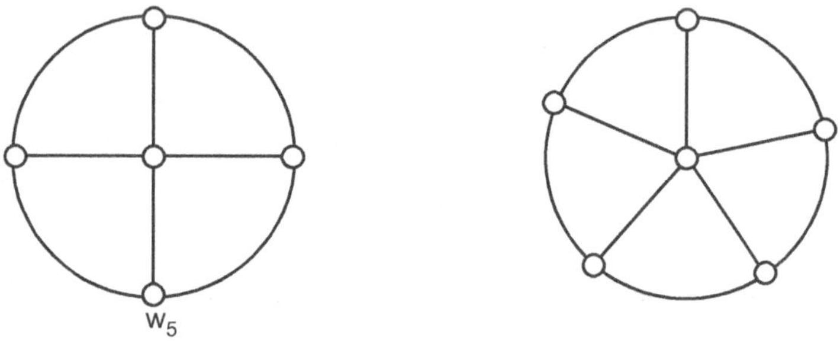

Fig. 3.13

Example 3.3 : *Show that a graph G is semi-Eulerian iff all vertices of G except possibly two has even degree.*

Solution : If G is a semi-Eulerian graph then there exists a Eulerian trail.

$$v_1e_1v_2e_2v_3 \ldots e_{n-1}\ v_n \quad \text{(Say)}$$

Here, each intermediate vertex has even degree because each occurrence of intermediate vertex contribute 2 to its degree.

$\therefore$ G has all vertices with even degree except possibly v_1 and v_n.

Conversely, if G has each vertex degree even except possibly two vertices x and y.

i.e. $d(v) = \text{even}\ \forall\ v \neq x,\ v \neq y$ in G and d(x), d(y) are odd in G.

Now add temporary edge e = xy in G.

$\therefore$ G + e has each vertex degree even, because in G + e, each vertex other than x, y has same degree as that of in G and d(x), d(y) in G + e are increased by 1 as that of in G.

∴ G + e is Eulerian graph.

∴ It has Eulerian tour.

$$t = xeye_1v_1e_2v_2 \ldots e_nv_ne_{n+1}\, x \text{ (Say)}$$

Removing temporary edge from t, we get

$ye_1v_1e_2 \ldots e_nv_ne_{n+1}x$ which is Eulerian trail in G.

∴ G is semi-Eulerian.

Example 3.4 : *Prove that W_n, wheel graph on n vertices for $n \geq 4$, is Hamiltonian graph.*

Solution : Consider W_n as shown in Fig. 3.14 below.

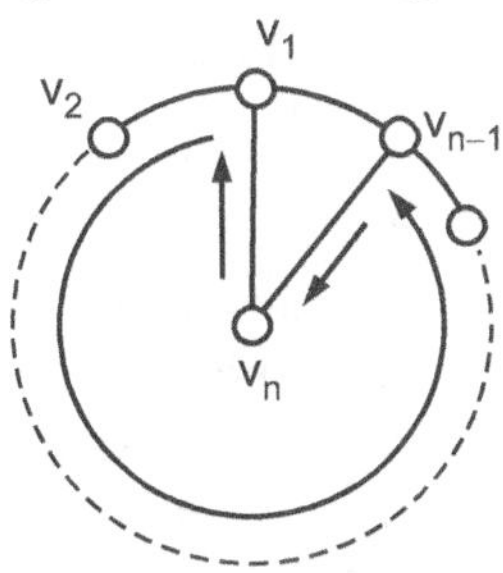

Fig. 3.14

Starting from v_n. We can complete Hamiltonian cycle as

$v_nv_1v_2 \ldots v_{n-1}\, v_n$

∴ W_n is Hamiltonian graph

Example 3.5 : *Prove that Q_n is Hamiltonian graph for $n \geq 2$.*

Solution : Since Q_n is bipartite graph with partition {X, Y} and $|X| = 2^{n-1}$, $|Y| = 2^{n-1}$.

Start with any vertex in X and meeting each vertex in Y and X alternately, we can complete Hamiltonian cycle with even length.

∴ Q_n is Hamiltonian graph.

Example 3.6 : *Prove that the complete graph K_n has $\frac{(n-1)!}{2}$ different Hamiltonian cycles.*

Solution : In K_n, each two vertices are adjacent.

∴ Let $\{v_1 v_2 \ldots v_n\}$ be vertex set of K_n. Each cyclic arrangement of $v_1, v_2 \ldots v_n$ corresponds to a Hamiltonian cycle.

Now there are $(n-1)!$ cyclic arrangements of $v_1, v_2 \ldots v_n$.

Now the two cyclic arrangements which are same upto anticlockwise and clockwise order gives same Hamiltonian cycle.

∴ Number of different Hamiltonian cycles are $\frac{(n-1)!}{2}$.

Examples 3.7 : *How many different Hamiltonian cycles does $K_{n,\,n}$ have ?*

Solution : Let $K_{n,\,n}$ has partition $\{X, Y\}$

$|X| = n, \ |Y| = n.$ Let $X = \{u_1, u_2 \ldots u_n\}$ $Y = \{v_1, v_2 \ldots v_n\}$

Putting the vertices in $K_{n,\,n}$ in cyclic arrangement with condition that vertices are in X and Y alternately.

Each such alternate, cyclic arrangement of vertices gives us, a Hamiltonian cycle. But the two such cyclic arrangements which are same upto anticlockwise and clockwise order gives same Hamiltonian cycle.

The vertices in a cycle which are in X arranged in $(n-1)!$ ways and which in Y in $n!$ ways.

∴ Number of different Hamiltonian cycles in $K_{n,\,n} = \frac{(n-1)!\,n!}{2}$.

Example 3.8 : *Show that the following graph is non-Hamiltonian.*

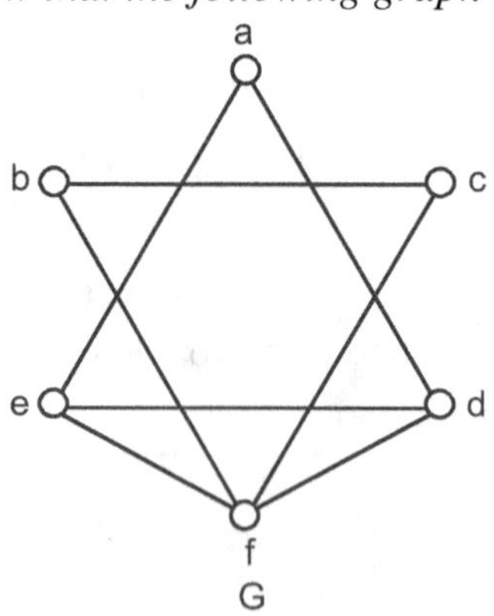

Fig. 3.15

Solution : If we delete f from G, we get two components in G.

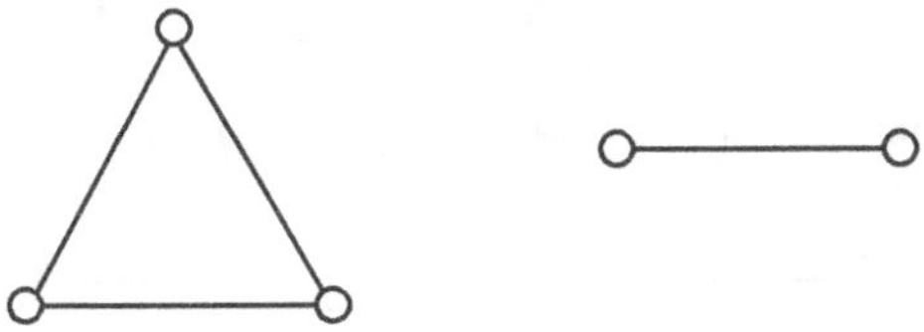

Fig. 3.16

∴ f is cut vertex in G.

∴ G is not Hamiltonian graph.

Example 3.9 : *Show that*

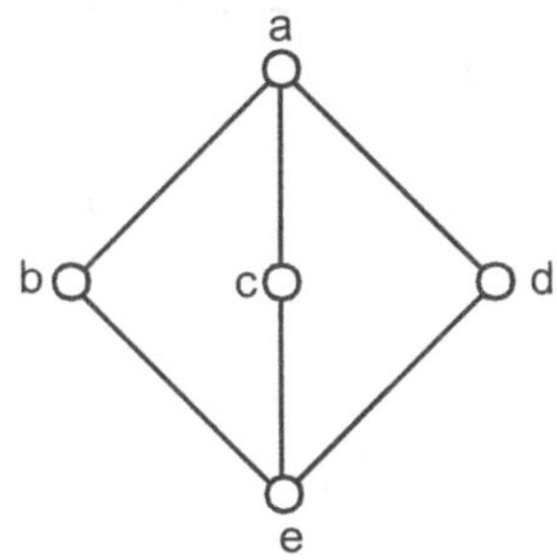

Fig. 3.17

is not Hamiltonian graph.

Solution : If we remove vertices a, e from the given graph, we get three components as shown below.

Fig. 3.18

∴ For $S = \{a, e\}$

(G – S) has more components than $|S|$.

∴ Given graph is not Hamiltonian graph.

Example 3.10 : *Give example of a graph which is Eulerian but not Hamiltonian.*

Solution : Consider the graph.

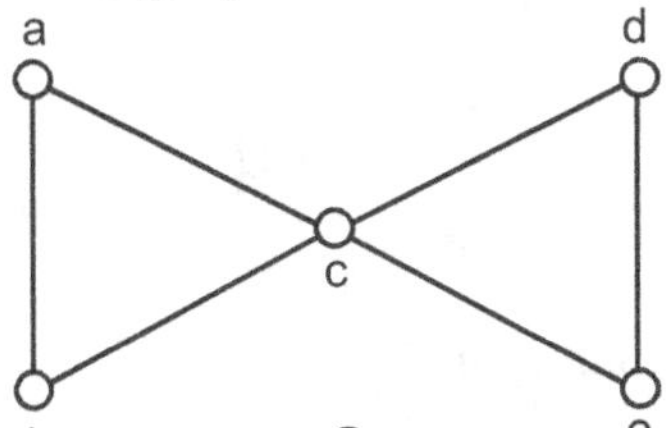

Fig. 3.19

Here c is cut vertex.

∴ G is not Hamiltonian and degree of each vertex is same.

∴ G is Eulerian.

Example 3.11 : *Give example of graph which is Hamiltonian but not Eulerian.*

Solution :

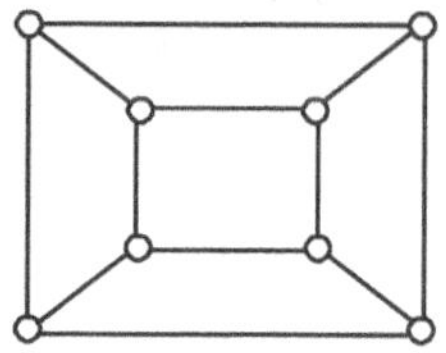

Fig. 3.20

Given graph is bipartite graph with partition sets have equal cardinality.

∴ G is Hamiltonian.

Now degree of each vertex is not even, therefore G is not Eulerian graph.

Example 3.12 : *Give example of graph which is Eulerian and Hamiltonian.*

Solution :

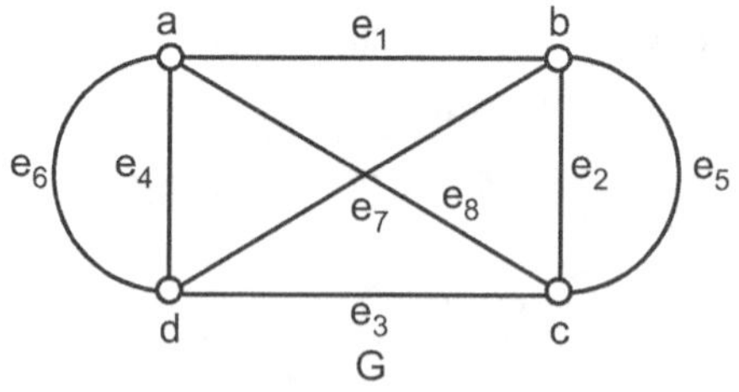

Fig. 3.21

Here $ae_1be_2ce_3de_4a$ is Hamiltonian cycle.

∴ G is a Hamiltonian graph.

Now degree of each vertex is even, therefore G is Eulerian also.

Example 3.13 : *Give an example of a graph which is neither Hamiltonian nor Eulerian.*

Solution :

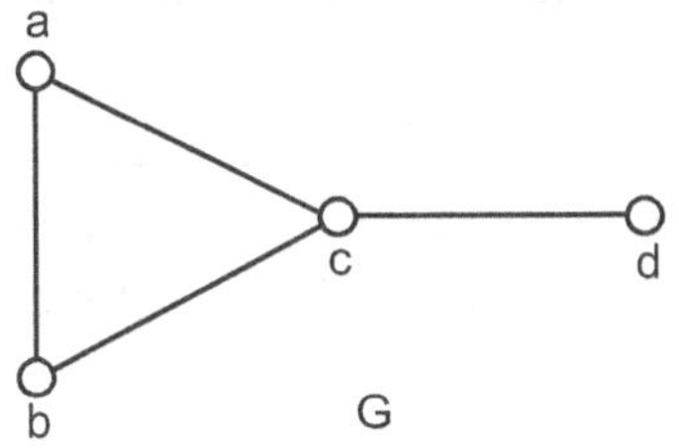

Fig. 3.22

Here c is cut vertex, therefore G is not Hamiltonian and degree of each vertex is not even, therefore G is not Eulerian also.

Think Over It

A knight is a chess piece that can move either two spaces horizontally and one space vertically or one space horizontally and two spaces vertically. That is, a knight on square (x, y) can move to any of the eight squares $(x \pm 2, y \pm 1)$, $(x \pm 1, y \pm 2)$. A knight's tour is a sequence of legal moves by a knight starting at some square and visiting each square exactly once. A knight's tour is called reentrant if there is a legal move that takes the knight from the last square of the tour back to where the tour began. We can model knight's tours using the graph that has a vertex for each square on the board, with an edge connecting two vertices if a knight can legally move between the squares represented by these vertices.

1. Draw the graph that represents the legal moves of a knight on a 3×3 chessboard.
2. Show that finding a knight's tour on an $m \times n$ chessboard is equivalent to finding a Hamilton path on the graph representing the legal moves of a knight on that board.
3. Show that finding a reentrant knight's tour on an $m \times n$ chessboard is equivalent to finding a Hamilton circuit on the corresponding graph.

4. Show that there is a knight's tour on 3×4 chessboard.
5. Show that there is no knight's tour on a 3×3 chessboard.
6. Show that there is no knight's tour on a 4×4 chessboard.

Summary

1. An **Euler circuit** in a graph G is a simple circuit containing every edge of G. An **Euler path** in G is a simple path containing every edge of G.
2. A connected multigraph with at least two vertices has an Euler circuit if and only if each of its vertices has even degree.
3. A connected multigraph has an Euler path but not an Euler circuit if and only if it has exactly two vertices of odd degree.
4. A simple path in a graph G that passes through every vertex exactly once is called a **Hamilton path** and a simple circuit in a graph G that passes through every vertex exactly once is called a **Hamilton circuit.** That is, the simple path $x_0, x_1, \ldots, x_{n-1}, x_n$ in the graph $G = (V_1 E)$ is a **Hamilton path** if $V = \{x_0, x_1, \ldots, x_n\}$ and $x_i \neq x_j$ for $0 \leq i < j \leq n$, and the simple circuit $x_0, x_1, \ldots, x_n$ (with $n > 0$) is a **Hamilton circuit** if $x_0, x_1, \ldots, x_{n-1}, x_n$ is Hamilton path.
5. **Dirac's Theorem :** If G is a simple graph with n vertices with $n \geq 3$ such that the degree of every vertex in G is at least $\frac{n}{2}$, then G has a Hamilton circuit.
6. **ORE's Theorem :** If G is a simple graph with n vertices with $n \geq 3$ such that $\deg(u) + \deg(v) \geq n$ for every pair of non-adjacent vertices u and v in G, then G has a Hamilton circuit.

Exercise

[A] Say True or False : Justify !

1. There is Eulerian graph which is not Hamiltonian.
2. There is Hamiltonian graph which is not Eulerian.
3. There is graph which is not Hamiltonian and Eulerian.
4. There is graph which is both Eulerian and Hamiltonian.
5. Every regular polyhedron (drawn on plane paper) is Hamiltonian graph.

6. Every semi-Eulerian graph is Eulerian.
7. K_n is Eulerian graph for any n.
8. Every cycle on n vertices has n edges and degree of each vertex is even.

[B] Multiple Choice Questions : Choose the Correct Alternative

1. Let G be Eulerian graph then
   (a) G is connected
   (b) G has one isolated vertex
   (c) Each vertex of G is of even degree
   (d) None of these
2. The graph 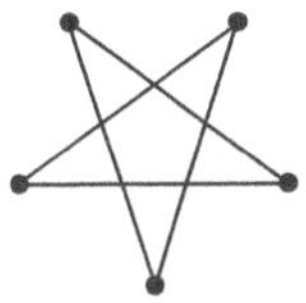 is
   (a) Eulerian but not Hamiltonian
   (b) Hamiltonian but not Eulerian
   (c) Both Eulerian and Hamiltonian
   (d) None of these
3. If Graph G is connected and consists of edge disjoint cycles then G is
   (a) Eulerian
   (b) Hamiltonian
   (c) Both Eulerian and Hamiltonian
   (d) None of these
4. The basic rule of Fleury's algorithm is
   (a) only travel across a bridge of the untravelled part of the graph if there is no alternative to it
   (b) only travel across a bridge of the original graph, if there is no other alternative
   (c) never travel across a bridge of the original graph
   (d) none of these
5. In a certain city, there is a river running through the middle of the city. There are six islands and nine bridges, as shown in the figure, the graph drawn representing this information, is
   (a) Eulerian (b) Hamiltonian
   (c) Not both (a) and (b) (d) None of these

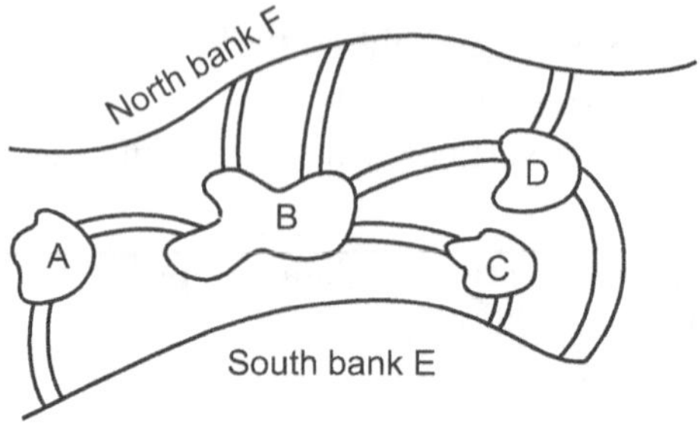

Fig. 3.23

6. The number of Hamiltonian circuits in K_{10} are
   (a) 5! (b) 4!
   (c) 10! (d) 9!
7. The Jacksons have relative in each state shown in the map below. Is it possible for the family to visit each state shown. While crossing each common state border exactly once ?

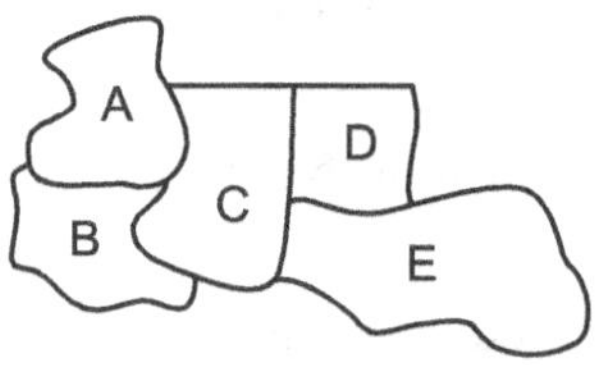

Fig. 3.24

   (a) Yes (b) No
   (c) Sometimes yes (d) Sometimes no
8. Which of the following graphs are Hamiltonian graphs ?
   (a) $K_{3, 2}$ (b) $K_{3, 3}$
   (c) $K_{3, 4}$ (d) None of these
9. If G and G^1 are two isomorphic graphs then
   (a) G is Eulerian $\Rightarrow G^1$ is Eulerian
   (b) G is Hamiltonian $\Rightarrow G^1$ is Hamiltonian
   (c) Both (a) and (b)
   (d) None of these

[C] Theory Questions :

1. Explain Konigsberg seven bridges problem in brief.
2. Prove that a graph G is Eulerian iff every vertex of graph G has even degree.

3. Give the steps of Fleury's algorithm to find Eulerian tour in a Eulerian graph.
4. Explain chinese postman problem in brief.
5. What is difference between Hamiltonian graph and semi-Hamiltonian graph ?
6. State the necessary and sufficient condition for graph G to be Hamiltonian. Explain this by giving an example.
7. Explain Travelling Salesman problem in brief.
8. Give necessary and sufficient condition for graph to be semi-Eulerian.

[D] Numerical Problems :

1. Show that Eulerian graph is expressed as union of disjoint cycles.
2. Apply Fleury's algorithm to find Eulerian tour in the graph.

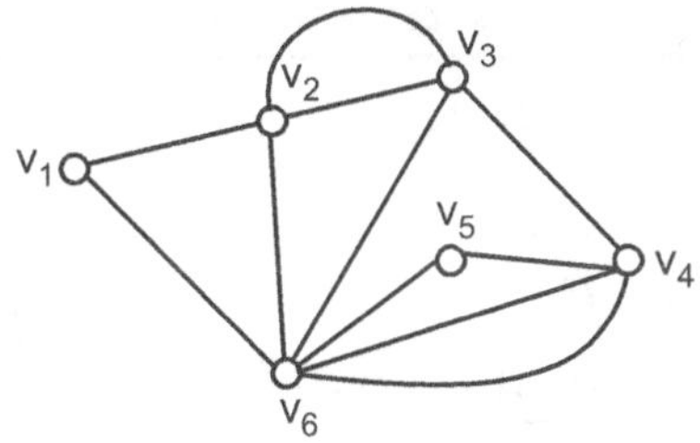

Fig. 3.25

3. Give example of graph in each of following case :
   (i) Hamiltonian and Eulerian
   (ii) Hamiltonian but not Eulerian
   (iii) Eulerian but not Hamiltonian
   (iv) Not Hamiltonian and not Eulerian
4. Convert the following graph into Eulerian graph by drawing some edges again

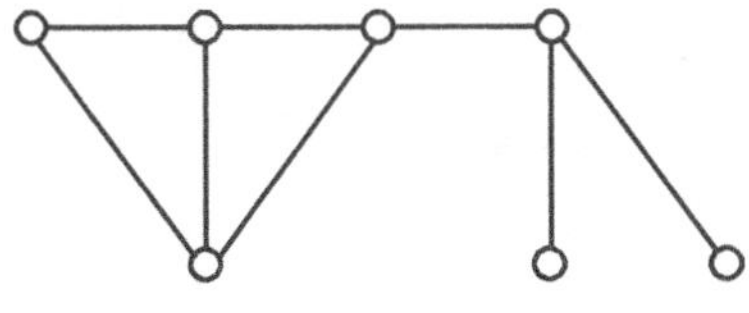

Fig. 3.26

5. Find number of Hamiltonian cycles in following graphs.

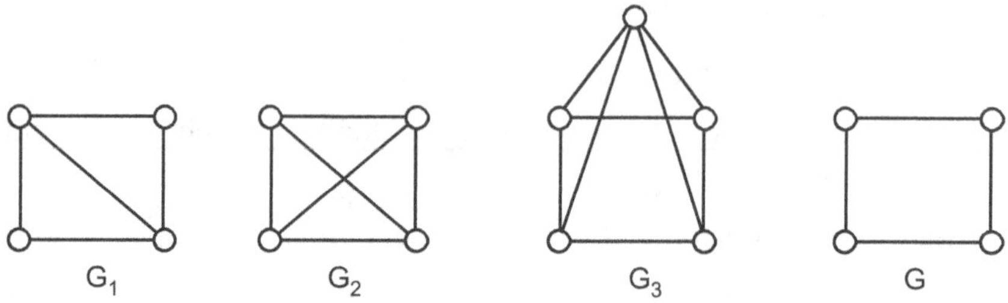

Fig. 3.27

6. Show that closure of graph Fig. 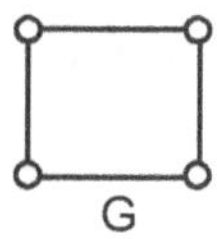

is K_4.

7. Show that semi-Eulerian graph contains exactly two vertices of old degree or not vertex of odd degree.

Answers

[A] (1) True (2) True (3) True (4) True (5) False (6) False (7) False (8) True

[B] (1) - (a) & (c) both, (2) - (c) (3) - (a) (4) - (a) (5) - (c) (6) - (d) (7) - (b) (8) - (b) (9) - (c)

[C] 2. $v_1 - v_2 - v_3 - v_2 - v_6 - v_3 - v_4 - v_5 - v_4 - v_6 - v_1$

4. 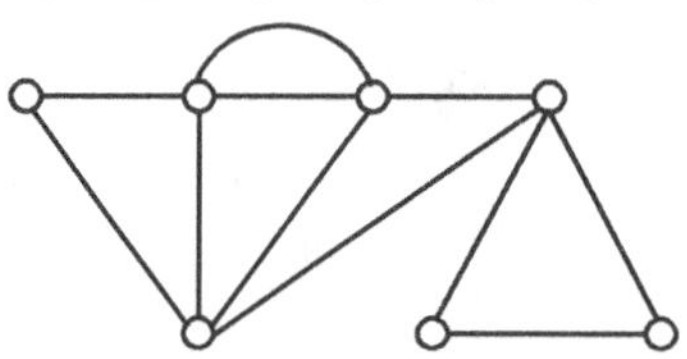

5. 1, 3, 3, 1

6. 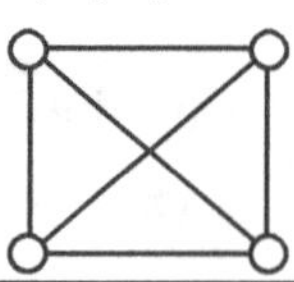

Chapter 4...

Trees

William Henry Kruskal

After graduating from Harvard with an S.B. in 1940, Kruskal remained there for a further year to take a Master's Degree in mathematics. With it looking increasingly likely that the United States would enter World War II, Kruskal then decided to take a job at the U.S. Naval Proving Ground in Dahlgren, Virginia, in 1941. There he worked on aviation ordinance as a civilian and it was through the work undertaken at the Proving Ground that he became interested in statistics. Kruskal married Norma Jane Evans on 23 August 1942.

He began working towards his doctorate with Henry Scheffe as his advisor but left to take up a position in Chicago in 1950 before completing the research for his thesis.

Kruskal was elected a fellow of the Institute of Mathematical Statistics, the American Statistical Association, the American Association for the Advancement of Science, and the American Academy of Arts and Sciences. He was president of the Institute of Mathematical Statistics in 1971, and of the American Statistical Association in 1982.

4.1 Introduction

In our everyday life, we come across with the graphs which look like trees; sometimes inverted. For example, if we consider the river together with its tributories and subtributories then the corresponding graph is as shown below.

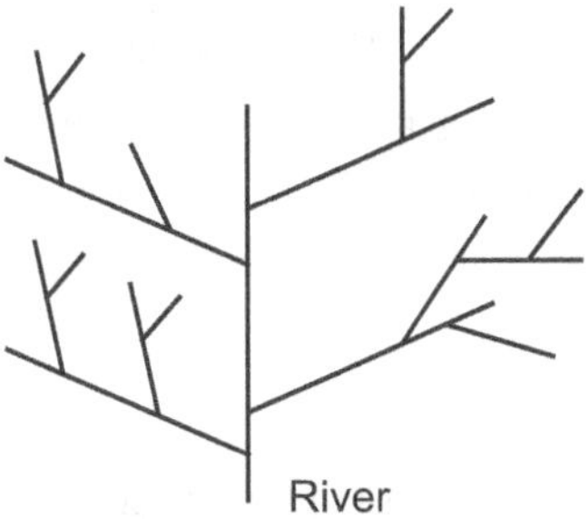

Fig. 4.1

The other examples of such graphs are family tree, postal index numbers and the star graph. All these graphs have the property that they are connected and moreover circuit free.

Definition : A connected circuit free graph is called a tree.

Following are the tree graphs with 1, 2, 3, 4, 5 vertices respectively.

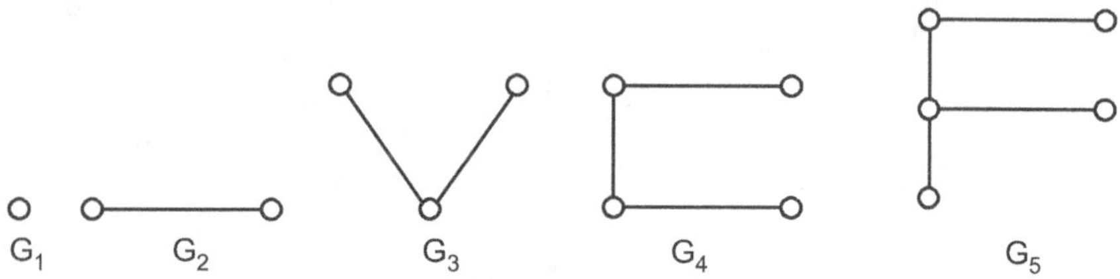

Fig. 4.2 : G_1, G_2, G_3, G_4, G_5

A tree can also be defined as follows.

Definition : A graph G in which there is exactly one path between every pair of vertices is called a tree.

We shall now first establish the equivalence of the above two definitions of a tree.

Theorem 1 The two definitions of a tree are equivalent.

Proof : First Part : Let the graph G be a tree according to the first definition. So G is connected and circuit free. Then the connectedness of G implies that there exists a path between every pair of vertices of G.

Now, if possible suppose that there are two different paths between two vertices u and v of G. But then union of these two paths create a circuit in G; which is a contradiction.

Thus, there is exactly one path between every pair of vertices of G and hence G is a tree according to the second definition.

Second Part : Let the graph G be a tree according to the second definition. Therefore, in G there is exactly one path between every pair of vertices of G.

The existence of a path between every pair of vertices of G implies that G is connected.

Now, we show that G contains no circuit. If possible suppose there is a circuit say Γ in G. If u and v be any two vertices of G belonging to the circuit Γ then there are two different paths joining u and v; which is a contradiction to the fact that there is exactly one path between any two vertices of G. Hence, G contains no circuit. Thus, G is a connected and circuit free. Therefore, G is a tree according to the first definition. ■

Theorem 2 A tree with n vertices has n – 1 edges.

Proof : Let the graph G be a tree with n vertices. We shall prove the required result by induction on n and for it we use the second principle of mathematical induction.

Clearly a tree with one vertex has zero number of edges and a tree with two vertices has one edge. Thus the result is true for n = 1 and n = 2. Assume that a tree with k vertices has k – 1 edges; k = 1, 2, 3, ..., n – 1. Now, consider a tree G with n vertices. Let e be any edge in G. By deleting this edge e from G, the resulting graph G - e is disconnected and it has two connected components say G_1 and G_2. The two connected graphs G_1 and G_2 are both circuit free because there is no any circuit in original graph G. Thus, G_1 and G_2 both are trees. Suppose G_1 has n_1 vertices and G_2 has n_2 vertices, where $n_1 + n_2 = n$. Then by the assumption, we see that G_1 has $n_1 - 1$ edges and G_2 has $n_2 - 1$ edges.

The total number of edges in G_1 and G_2 is $n_1 - 1 + n_2 - 1 = n_1 + n_2 - 2 = n - 2$. These n – 2 edges and the edge e which was removed from G add upto n – 1.

Thus, G has n – 1 edges. Hence proved.

The following theorem gives the converse of the above result. ■

Theorem 3 A connected graph G with n vertices and n – 1 edges is a tree.

Proof : Let G be a connected graph with n vertices and n – 1 edges. In order to show that G is a tree, we need to show that G is circuit free. If possible assume that there is a circuit say Γ in G. If e is any edge belonging to circuit Γ then after removing e, the graph G - e is still connected. Thus, G - e is a connected graph with n vertices and n – 2 edges. This is a contradiction because it is quite impossible to connect n vertices by using n – 2 edges. Hence, our assumption is wrong. Thus, G is connected and circuit free. Therefore, G is a tree. ■

Note : After combining the results proved in the above two theorems, we note that a connected graph with n vertices is a tree iff it has n – 1 edges.

Theorem 4 A graph with n vertices is a tree iff it is circuit free and has $n - 1$ edges.

Proof : First Part : Let the graph G be a tree with n vertices. Then by definition, G is circuit free and also we have proved that G has $n - 1$ edges.

Second Part : Let G be a graph with n vertices, $n - 1$ edges and without any circuit. Now, we show that G must be connected. Assume that G is disconnected. Then G consists of at least two connected components say G_1 and G_2; with vertices n_1 and n_2 respectively where $n_1 + n_2 = n$. G_1 is connected and circuit free. Therefore G_1 is a tree with n_1 vertices. Hence, G_1 has $n_1 - 1$ edges. Similarly, G_2 has $n_2 - 1$ edges. These edges of G_1 and G_2 give the total number of edges of G as

$$n_1 - 1 + n_2 - 1 = n_1 + n_2 - 2 = n - 2$$

which is less than $n - 1$. This is a contradiction. Hence, G is connected.

Now, G being connected and circuit free, it is a tree. ■

Theorem 5 A graph G is a tree if it is minimally connected.

Proof : First Part : Let the graph G be a tree with n vertices. Therefore, G has $n - 1$ edges. This number $n - 1$ is the minimum number of edges required to connected the n vertices. Hence, G is minimally connected.

Second Part : Suppose that the graph G is minimally connected. Then removal of any single edge from G leaves the remaining graph disconnected. This implies that any edge of G is not a part of any circuit. This means G contains no circuit. Thus, G is connected and circuit free. Therefore, G is a tree.

The pendant vertex in a tree is called a leaf.

Consider now the disconnected graph G consisting k connected components $G_1, G_2, \ldots, G_k$. If every G_i is itself a tree then the graph G is a collection of k trees. Such a graph G is called a forest.

Suppose in the forest, the trees $G_1, G_2, \ldots, G_k$ have $n_1, n_2, \ldots, n_k$ vertices respectively. Then there are $n_1 - 1, n_2 - 1, \ldots, n_k - 1$ edges. Thus, the total number of edges in the forest is

$$(n_1 - 1) + (n_2 - 1) + \ldots + (n_k - 1) = (n_1 + n_2 + \ldots + n_k) - k = n - k$$

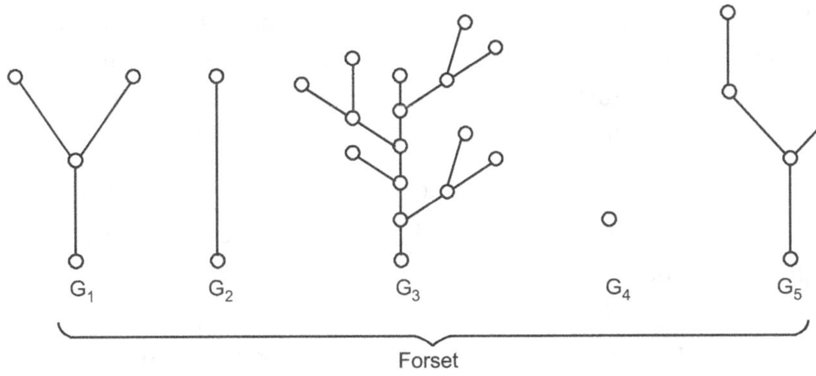

Fig. 4.3 ■

4.2 Centre of a Tree

Let the graph T be a tree and v be any fixed vertex in T. We find the distances from v to all the vertices of T. If the vertex u of T is farthest apart from v then the distance d(v, u) is called eccentricity of the vertex v and is denoted by E(v).

Thus E(v) = max {d(v, u); u is a vertex in T}.

In the following graph, the eccentricities of all the vertices are shown encircled against those vertices.

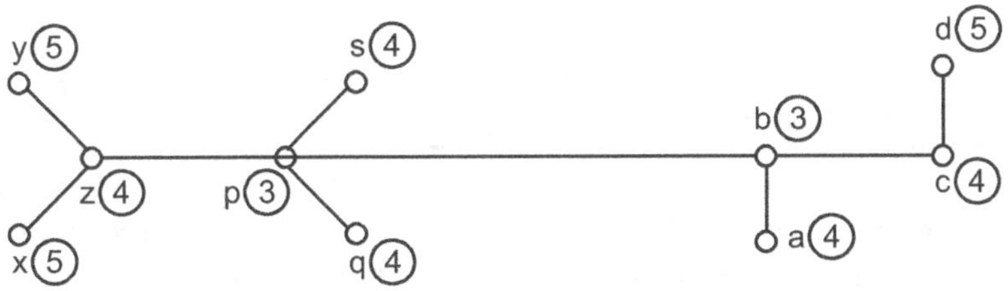

Fig. 4.4

It is very much easy to see that if v is any vertex of a tree T and u is a vertex of T which is farthest apart from v then u must be a pendant vertex. The maximum value of the eccentricity E i.e. E_{max} is diameter of a tree. In the above example, the diameter of a tree is 5.

A vertex whose eccentricity is the least is called a central vertex of a tree. The set of central vertices of a tree is called centre of a tree. Also the eccentricity of a central vertex is called the radius of a tree, denoted by r. Thus, $r = E_{min}$.

In the above example, there are two vertices having minimum eccentricity 3 viz. p and b. Therefore, centre of a tree is {p, b} and its radius is 3. This example shows that the diameter of a tree need not be equal to twice its radius.

Theorem 6 Every tree has a centre which consists of either a single vertex or two adjacent vertices. i.e. the centre of a tree is either k_1 or k_2; complete graph on 1 or 2 vertices.

Proof : If the tree consists of a single vertex or two vertices then obviously the theorem is true. Let T be any tree with more than two vertices. We know that a tree has at least two pendant vertices. Let T' be a tree obtained from T by removing all the pendant vertices of T. We shall show that the central vertices of T are the same as those of T'. For this we note that the maximum distance from the vertex v of T to the vertex u of T occurs when u is a pendant vertex. This implies that the eccentricity of a vertex v in T' is exactly one less than the eccentricity of v in T; and this is true for every vertex in T'. Therefore, the vertices of minimum eccentricity in T are exactly the vertices of minimum eccentricity in T'. Hence, T and T' have the same centre.

From T' we again remove all the pendant vertices and get a tree T''. Then centre of T' is exactly the centre of T''. By continuing in this way finally we reach to either a single vertex i.e. k_1 or two adjacent vertices i.e. k_2 which is the centre of original tree T. ■

4.3 Spanning Trees

Let G be a connected graph with n vertices and e edges. A subgraph of G which is a tree is called a *tree subgraph* of G. Some tree subgraphs of G will include all the vertices of G while the others may not.

Definition : A tree subgraph T of a connected graph G, containing all the vertices of G is called a *spanning tree* of G.

Consider the graph G given below.

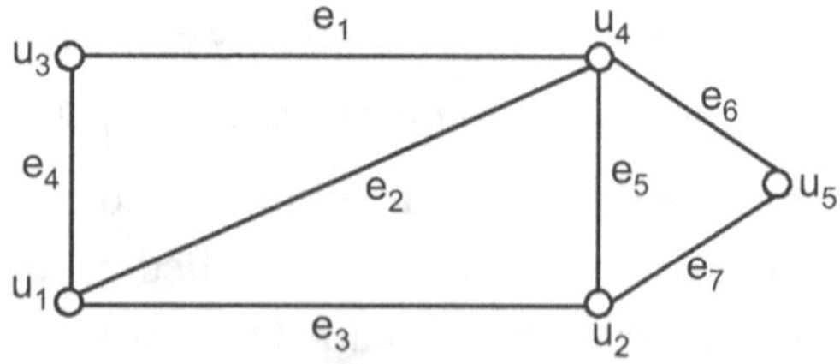

Fig. 4.5 : G

The two of its spanning trees T_1 and T_2 are shown below.

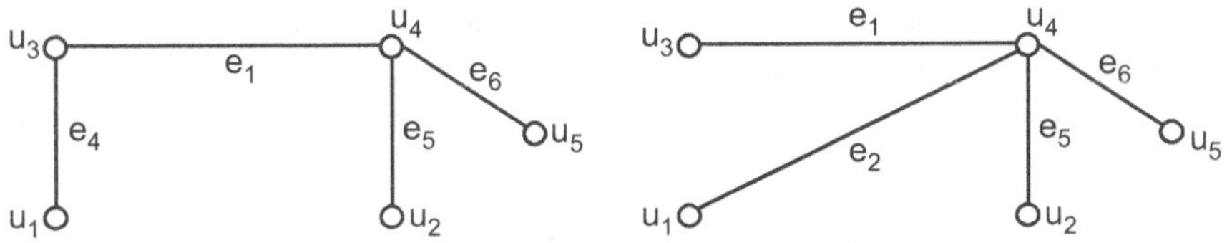

(a) T_1 **(b) T_2**

Fig. 4.6

There are some other spanning trees of G. Since, G has 5 vertices, any of its spanning tree has 5 vertices and hence 4 edges. The edges of G which are included in the spanning tree T are called branches of T while the remaining edges of G are called chords of T.

We note that the terms branch and chord are relative terms. A branch (chord) w.r.t. one spanning tree may be a chord (branch) w.r.t. another spanning tree.

In the above example, following the definition of a spanning tree we see that e_1, e_4, e_5, e_6 are branches and e_2, e_3, e_7 are chords w.r.t. spanning tree T_1. Also e_1, e_2, e_5, e_6 are the branches and e_3, e_4, e_7 are the chords w.r.t. spanning tree T_2.

Although the branches and chords change from one spanning tree of G to its another spanning tree, their number remains the same. This is because any spanning tree of G has n vertices and hence n – 1 edges. These fixed numbers of branches and chords in any spanning tree are referred to as the rank and nullity of the graph G respectively. Thus if G is a connected graph with n vertices and e edges then

Rank of G = Number of branches in any spanning tree = n – 1

and Nullity of G = Number of chords w.r.t. any spanning tree = e – (n – 1) = e – n + 1.

For the graph G, in the above example, we have n = 5 and e = 7.

$$\text{Therefore rank} = n - 1 = 5 - 1 = 4$$

$$\text{and nullity} = e - n + 1 = 7 - 5 + 1 = 3$$

We have following 16 spanning trees of G.

Fundamental circuit : Let G be a connected graph with n vertices and e edges and T be a spanning tree of G.

The branches w.r.t. T are the $n - 1$ edges $b_1, b_2, \ldots, b_{n-1}$ of G and the chords w.r.t. T are the $e - n + 1$ edges $c_1, c_2, \ldots, c_{e-n+1}$ of G. Suppose the chord c_1 has end vertices u and v in G and we add this chord c_1 to the spanning tree T. Then because there is already exactly one path between u and v in the spanning tree T, the addition of chord c_1 to T creates exactly one circuit. Such a circuit is called a fundamental circuit w.r.t. T created by the chord c_1. We note again that whenever we talk about fundamental circuit, first there must be some spanning tree of G with us. We also observe that the number of fundamental circuits is exactly equal to the number of chords i.e. $e - n + 1$ because each chord creates exactly one circuit.

Consider the graph G given below and its spanning tree T.

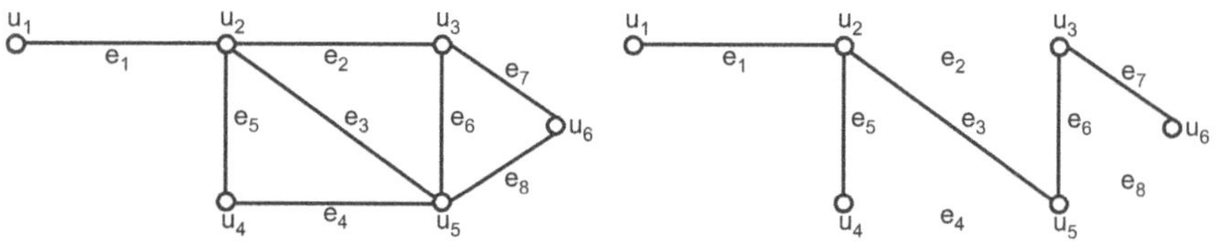

(a) G (b) T

Fig. 4.7

The chords w.r.t. spanning tree T are e_2, e_4, e_8.

The fundamental circuit created by the chord e_2 is

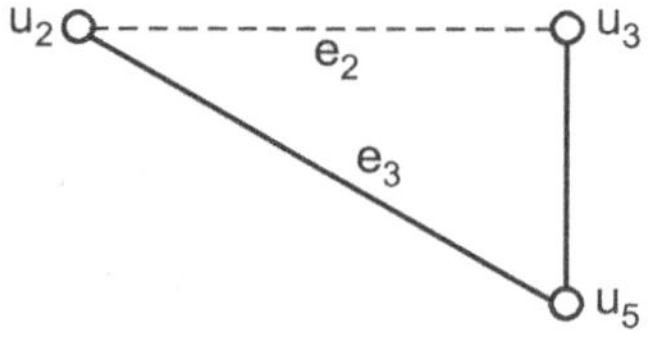

Fig. 4.7 (c)

The fundamental circuit created by the chord e_4 is

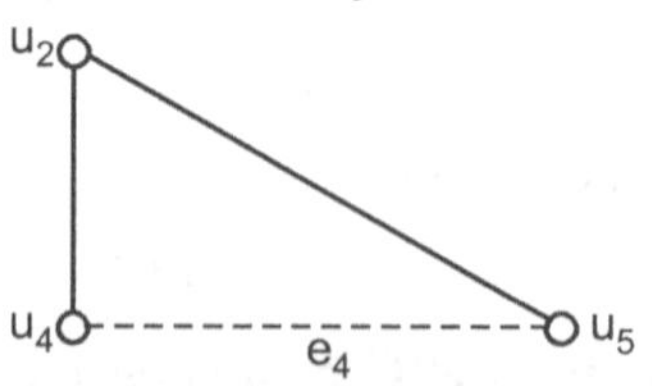

Fig. 4.8

Finally, the fundamental circuit created by the chord e_8 is

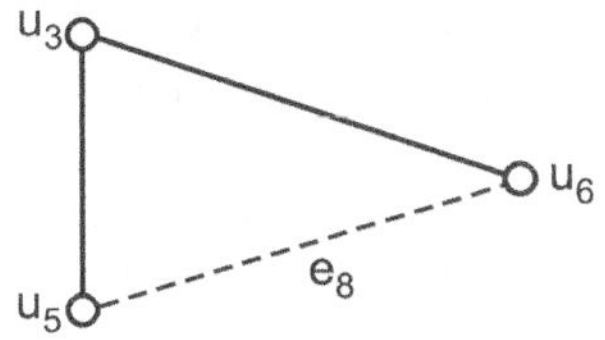

Fig. 4.9

It can be easily seen that the addition of two chords to the spanning tree may create more than two circuits but only two of them are fundamental circuits while the remainings are not.

Fundamental cut set : Let G be a connected graph. A minimal set S of edges in G whose removal from G leaves the disconnected graph into two connected components is called a cut set in G. The word minimal implies that the removal of any proper subset of S will not disconnect the graph G. It follows that in a tree every edge is a cut set.

In a connected graph, the pendant edge (an edge whose one end vertex is pendent vertex) is a cut set.

Now, consider the connected graph G below.

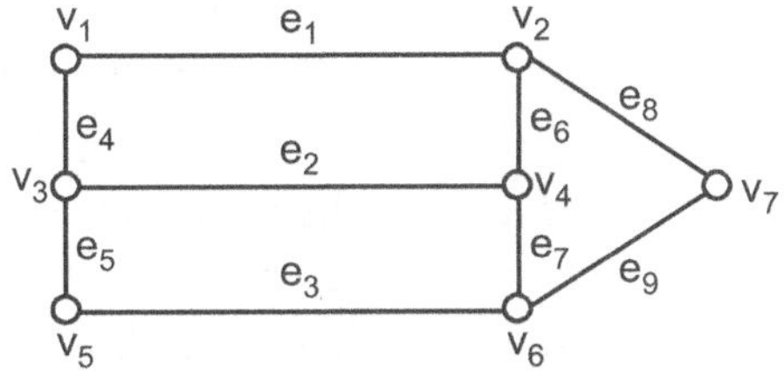

Fig. 4.10 : G

The set $\{e_1, e_2, e_3\}$ is a cut set. If it is removed from G then the remaining graph is

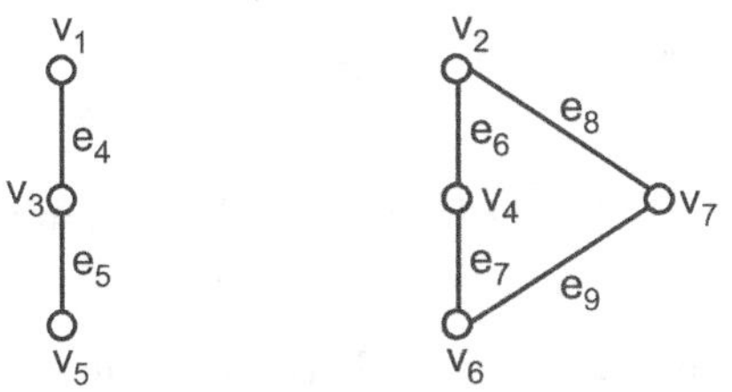

Fig. 4.11

This cut set makes a partition of vertices of the graph G into two subsets viz. $V_1 = \{v_1, v_3, v_5\}$ and $V_2 = \{v_2, v_4, v_6, v_7\}$. The cut set $\{e_3, e_7, e_8\}$ in G leads to the partition of vertices as $\{v_1, v_2, v_3, v_4, v_5\}$ and $\{v_6, v_7\}$.

Consider now the spanning tree T of the above graph G.

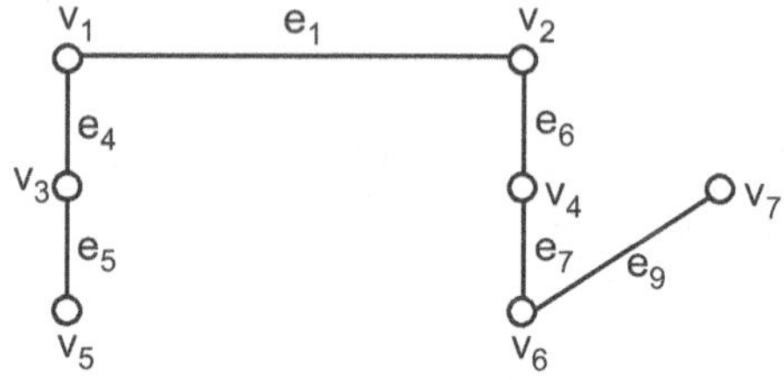

Fig. 4.12 : T

The branches w.r.t. this spanning tree T are $\{e_1, e_4, e_5, e_6, e_7, e_9\}$ and the chords are $\{e_2, e_3, e_8\}$.

We know that in a tree every edge is a cut set.

Consider the branch e_6 of above spanning tree T. After removing e_6 from T, the vertices are partitioned into two subsets $\{v_1, v_2, v_3, v_5\}$ and $\{v_4, v_6, v_7\}$. The cut set of G which leads to the above partition of vertices of G is the set $\{e_6, e_2, e_3, e_8\}$. This cut set includes exactly one branch of T and the remaining edges in it are chords w.r.t. T.

The partition of vertices corresponding to the branch e_1 is $\{v_1, v_3, v_5\}$ and $\{v_2, v_4, v_6, v_7\}$ and the cut set in G leading to this partition of vertices is $\{e_1, e_2, e_3\}$. As mentioned before, this cut set includes exactly one branch of T viz. e_1 while e_2 and e_3 are the chords w.r.t. T. Such cut sets including exactly one branch of the spanning tree T and the rest edges in it the chords in T, are called fundamental cut sets.

The number of fundamental cut sets is equal to the number of branches in any spanning tree of the given connected graph.

Theorem 7 Let G be a connected graph and T be any spanning tree of G. Then

(a) any circuit in G has at least one edge in common with the chord set (complement) of T.

(b) any cut-set of G contains at least one branch of T.

Proof : (a) G is a connected graph and T is a spanning tree of G.

Let Γ be any circuit in G. Assume that Γ does not include any chord of spanning tree T.

Then Γ is a circuit in the tree T. This is a contradiction because tree T cannot have any circuit. Hence, proved.

(b) G is a connected graph and T is a spanning tree of G.

Let S be any cut set of G. Then the removal of edges in S from G makes a partition of the vertices of G into two disjoint sets say V_1 and V_2. Assume that the cut set S does not include any branch of T but then the removal of edges in S does not effect the spanning tree T; and hence the vertices of G still remain connected together. This is a contradiction to the effect of cut set S.

Hence, S must include at least one branch of T. ■

Theorem 8 Every circuit in a connected graph G has even number of edges in common with every cut-set of G.

Proof : Let G be a connected graph and S be any cut-set of G. Then the removal of edges in S from G makes a partition of the vertices of G into two non-empty disjoint sets V_1 and V_2. Let Γ be any circuit in G.

If all the vertices in Γ are in V_1 only or in V_2 only then clearly Γ and S have no any edge in common and the theorem is true in these two cases.

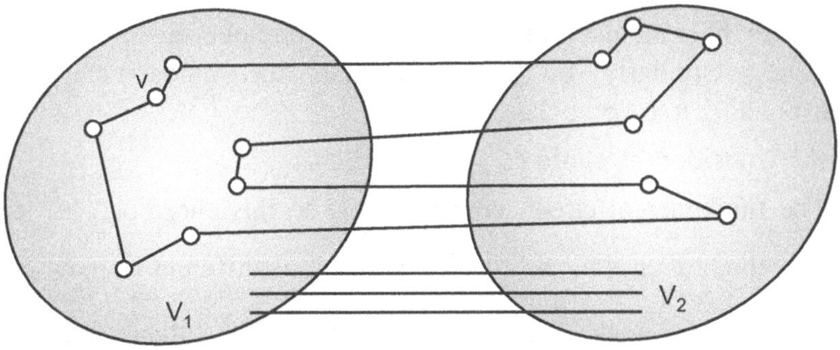

Fig. 4.13

Suppose that some vertices of Γ lie in V_1 and the remaining in V_2.

To trace the circuit Γ, we start with vertex v of Γ lying in V_1.

In this tracing of Γ if we go from V_1 to V_2 say r times then exactly same number of times
we go from V_2 to V_1 because finally we have to reach to the starting vertex.

Therefore, Γ and S have even number of edges in common. ■

Theorem 9 Let G be a connected graph and T its spanning tree. Let $\{b_1, c_1, c_2, \ldots, c_k\}$ be the fundamental cut-set corresponding to the branch b_1 of T. Then

(a) b_1 is contained in the fundamental circuit corresponding to every chord

$c_i : i = 1, 2, \ldots k$ and

(b) b_1 is not contained in any other fundamental circuit.

Proof : (a) $S = \{b_1, c_1, c_2, \ldots, c_k\}$ is a fundamental cut set corresponding to the branch b_1 of T.

Let Γ be the fundamental circuit corresponding to the chord c_1. Therefore, Γ has edges : one chord c_1 and some branches $b_1^{'}, b_2^{'}, \ldots, b_r^{'}$ say. We know that the cut set S and circuit Γ must have even number of edges in common.

The edge c_1 is already common to S and Γ, and c_1 is different from $c_2, c_3, \ldots, c_k$. Therefore, the only possibility is that b_1 is some $b_i^{'}$ so that S and Γ have two edges in common.

Hence, b_1 is included in the fundamental circuit corresponding to the chord c_1. Similarly b_1 is included in the fundamental circuit corresponding to $c_2, c_3, \ldots, c_k$.

(b) Consider the chord c_{k+1} other than $c_2, c_3, \ldots, c_k$.

The fundamental circuit corresponding to this chord c_{k+1} has edges c_{k+1} and the branches $b_1^{''}, b_2^{''}, \ldots, b_s^{''}$. Now c_{k+1} is different from $c_1, c_2, \ldots, c_k$. If $b_1 = b_t^{''}$ for some t then the cut set S and the fundamental circuit created by c_{k+1} have one edge in common, which is impossible.

Therefore, b_1 is different from $b_1^{''}, b_2^{''}, \ldots, b_s^{''}$. Hence, b_1 is not included in any other fundamental circuit. ■

Theorem 10 Let G be a connected graph and T is spanning tree. Let $\{c_1, b_1, b_2, \ldots, b_k\}$ be the fundamental circuit corresponding to the chord c_1 of T. Then

(a) c_1 is contained in the fundamental cut set corresponding to every branch $b_i : i = 1, 2, \ldots, k$ and

(b) c_1 is not contained in any other fundamental cut set.

Proof : (a) $\Gamma : c_1, b_1, b_2, \ldots, b_k$ is a fundamental circuit corresponding to the chord c_1 of T.

Let S be the fundamental cut set corresponding to the branch b_1. Then S has edges : one branch b_1 and some chords $c_1', c_2', \ldots, c_r'$ say. We know that the cut set S and the circuit Γ must have even number of edges in common.

The edge b_1 is already common to S and Γ, and b_1 is different from $b_2, b_3, \ldots, b_k$.

Therefore, the only possibility is that c_1 is some c_i so that S and Γ have two edges in common.

Hence, c_1 is included in the fundamental cut set corresponding to the branch b_1. Similarly, c_1 is included in the fundamental cut set corresponding to $b_2, b_3, \ldots, b_k$.

(b) Consider the branch b_{k+1} other than $b_1, b_2, \ldots b_k$.

The fundamental cutset corresponding to this branch b_{k+1} has edges b_{k+1} and the chords $c_1'', c_2'', \ldots, c_s''$. Now b_{k+1} is different from $b_1, b_2 \ldots, b_k$. If $c_1 = c_t''$ for some t then the circuit Γ and the fundamental cut set corresponding to b_{k+1} have one edge in common; which is impossible. Therefore c_1 is not included in any other fundamental cutset. ■

4.4 Binary Trees

A special class of trees known as binary rooted trees is of very much importance in binary search procedure in computer studies. A tree in which exactly one vertex is distinguishable from all their vertices is called a rooted tree and that particular vertex is called the root of that tree. The word binary suggests that as the tree grows out of the root, there are exactly two branches coming out of any vertex v, unless v is a pendant vertex. This means in a binary tree, the degree of the starting vertex i.e. root is 2, then the intermediate vertices will have degree 3 each and finally there are some pendant vertices (leaves).

Definition : A tree in which exactly one vertex is of degree 2 and the remaining vertices are of degree 3 or 1, is called a binary rooted tree.

A vertex of degree 2 is distinguishable from all other vertices; hence it is a root of the tree. Below we show two binary trees, both having 11 vertices.

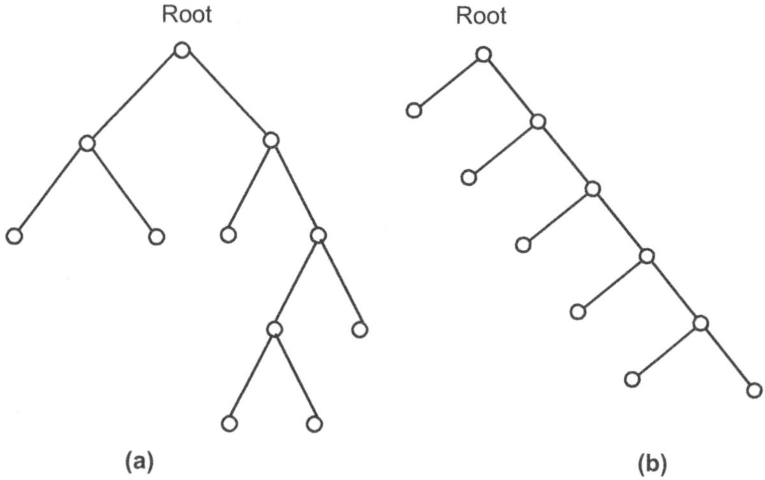

Fig. 4.14

We have the following elementary results about any binary tree.

Result 1 : Let T be a binary tree with n vertices. One vertex i.e. root has degree 2 and the remaining n – 1 vertices are of odd degree 3 or 1. We know that in any graph, the vertices of odd degree are even in number.

So n – 1 is even; hence n is odd. Thus, a binary tree has odd number of vertices.

Result 2 : Let T be a binary tree with n vertices out of which p vertices are pendant vertices. Hence, the intermediate vertices i.e. the vertices of degree 3 are n – p – 1 in number.

Then the total degree 2(n – 1) = 2n – 2 is given by

$$2n - 2 = 2 \times 1 + 3(n - p - 1) + 1 \times p$$

$$\therefore \quad 2n - 2 = 2 + 3n - 3p - 3 + p$$

$$\therefore \quad 2p = n + 1$$

$$\therefore \quad p = \frac{n+1}{2}$$

Thus, in a binary tree of n vertices, the pendant vertices are $\frac{n+1}{2}$ in number.

Result 3 : The intermediate vertices of degree 3 together with the root (degree 2) are $n - p = n - \left(\frac{n+1}{2}\right) = \frac{n-1}{2} = \frac{n+1}{2} - 1$ in number. They are called internal vertices. Thus, in a binary tree, the numbers of internal vertices are one less than the number of pendant vertices.

Height of a binary tree : In a binary tree we say that the vertex v is at level r if v is at a distance r from the root. In particular, the root itself is at level 0.

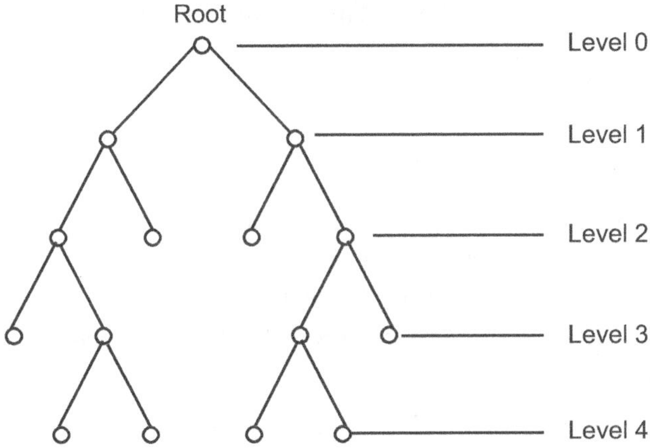

Fig. 4.15

The maximum value l_{max} of the level in a binary tree is called height of that tree. In the above binary tree with 15 vertices, there is one vertex viz. root at level 0, there are two vertices at level 1 and 4 vertices at level 2.

We see that we have put only 4 vertices at level 3; although the maximum capacity of the level 3 is $2^3 = 8$.

In general, at level k in a binary tree, the maximum 2^k vertices can be accommodated. Thus, in a binary tree, at any level $k > 0$, the minimum number of vertices can be put is 2 and the maximum number of vertices 2^k. The height of the binary tree shown above is 4 because $l_{max} = 4$.

The height of a binary tree with n vertices will be maximum if we put minimum number of vertices at each level i.e. one vertex at level 0 and only 2 vertices at each next level. Further, the height will be minimum if the maximum number of vertices are put at each level i.e. 2^k vertices at level k, meaning that the capacity of each level is fully utilised.

We shall now find the maximum and the minimum height of a binary tree with n vertices.

Maximum height : Let T be a binary tree with n vertices; n being odd.

Out of n vertices, one vertex i.e. root is put at level 0. Remaining n – 1 vertices which are even in number, are so arranged that there will be only 2 vertices at each level. This implies that the maximum value of the level is $l_{max} = \frac{n-1}{2}$.

Thus, the maximum height of a binary tree with n vertices is $\frac{n-1}{2}$.

Minimum height : If we want a binary tree with minimum height then we put maximum number of vertices at each level thereby utilising the capacity of each level fully. While doing so we note that the capacity of the last level k may not be utilised fully because there are no enough vertices. Hence, we have,

$$2^0 + 2^1 + 2^2 + 2^3 + \ldots + 2^k \geq n$$

$$\therefore \quad 1 + 2 + 2^2 + \ldots + 2^k \geq n$$

$$\therefore \quad 2^{k+1} - 1 \geq n$$

$$\therefore \quad 2^{k+1} \geq n + 1$$

$$\therefore \quad k + 1 \geq \log_2 (n + 1)$$

$$\therefore \quad k \geq \log_2 (n + 1) - 1$$

Thus, k is the smallest integer just greater than or equal to $\log_2 (n + 1)$. Thus, minimum height = k = $[\log_2 (n + 1) - 1]$ = Smallest integer greater than or equal to $\log_2 (n + 1) - 1$.

As for example, consider a binary tree with 25 vertices; n = 25. Maximum height of the tree = $\frac{n-1}{2} = \frac{25-1}{2}$ = 12 and the minimum height is

$$[\log_2(n+1) - 1] = [\log_2 26 - 1] = [4.abcd - 1]$$
$$= [3.abcd] = 4$$

These trees are shown as follows :

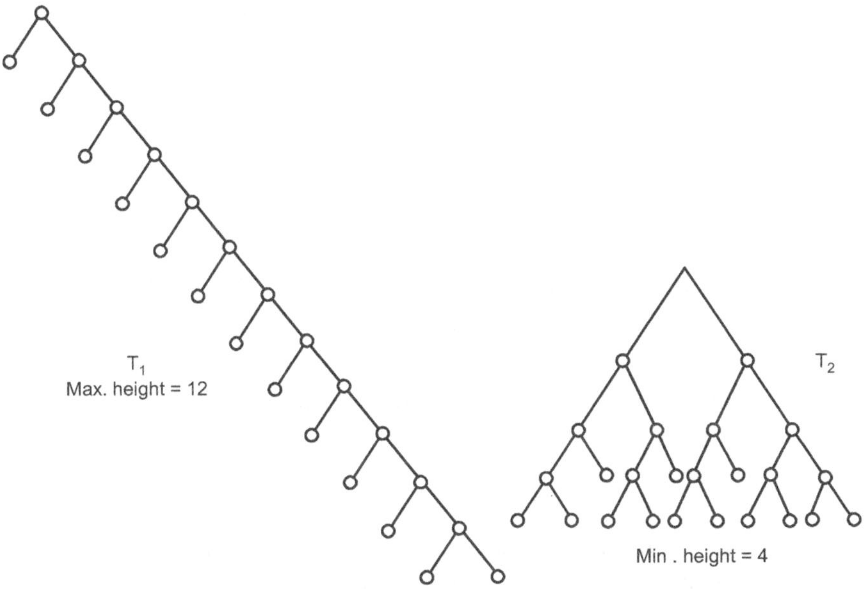

(a) (b)

Fig. 4.16

Maximum height = 12, Minimum height = 4.

A binary rooted tree of height h is said to be balanced if each pendant vertex i.e. leaf is at level h or h – 1.

We see that out of the two trees above, T_2 is balanced because each of its pendant vertex is at level 4 or 3.

The tree T_1 is not balanced.

4.5 Shortest Spanning Tree

Let G be a weighted connected graph. Each edge in G is assigned a weight which is a non-negative real number. If T is a spanning tree of G then the sum of the weights of branches of T is called the weight of T.

The different spanning trees of G will have in general different weights. A graph G and two of its spanning trees are shown below.

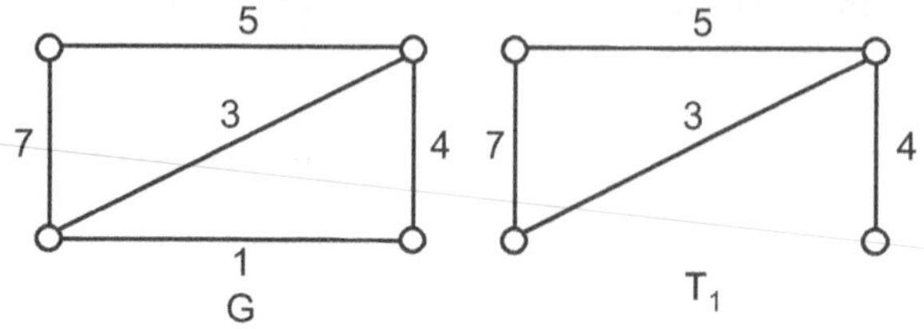

Fig. 4.17

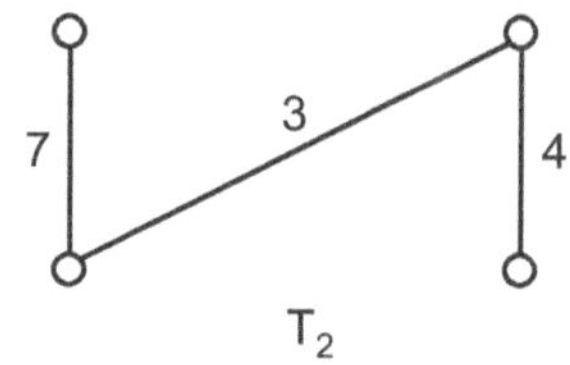

Fig. 4.18

The weight of T_1 is w (T_1) = 7 + 5 + 4 = 16 and that of T_2 is w (T_2) = 7 + 3 + 4 = 14. In practical situations, we are interested in that spanning tree whose weight is the smallest.

A spanning tree with minimum weight is called the shortest spanning tree or minimal spanning tree.

A connected weighted graph can have two or more shortest spanning trees.

As an application, suppose that an electricity board is interested in connecting seven of its junctions by six high tension cables. If the costs of putting the cables between any two junctions are estimated then the connecting network of cables which leads to the cost as small as possible will be accepted. This network is then infact the shortest spanning tree.

To find the shortest spanning tree of a given weighted connected graph, we use Kruskal's Algorithm.

Kruskal's Algorithm : Let G be a weighted connected graph. First we arrange the edges of G in non-decreasing order of their weights. We choose the first edge with the minimum weight and which is not a loop. At every successive step, we choose the next edge (from remaining edges) with minimum weight which is not a loop and which creates no circuit with the previously chosen edges. If the graph G has n vertices then we stop the procedure after n – 1 edges have been chosen.

We now prove that this algorithm actually produces a shortest spanning tree of a given connected weighted graph.

Theorem 11 Let G be a connected weighted graph and T be a subgraph of G obtained by Kruskal's algorithm. Then T is a shortest spanning tree of G.

Proof : T is a subgraph of connected weighted graph G obtained by Kruskal's algorithm. We prove the theorem in two parts.

First part : In this part we show that T is a spanning tree of G.

Clearly from the construction of T, it follows that there is no any circuit in T.

It remains to show that T includes all the n vertices of G.

Assume that T has m vertices and k connected components. Then the number of edges in T is m – k.

$\therefore \quad n - 1 = m - k$

$\therefore \quad n - m = 1 - k \quad \ldots (1)$

Now, $\quad n - m \geq 0$ and $1 - k \leq 0$ since $k \geq 1$

Hence the equality in (1) holds only when n = m and k = 1.

This proves that T includes all the n vertices of G.

Therefore, T is a spanning tree of G.

Second part : In this part, we show that T is a shortest spanning tree. Assume that there is a spanning tree S of G whose weight is less than that of T i.e. w (S) < w (T).

Consider the ordered sequence $e_1, e_2, e_3, \ldots, e_{n-1}$ of n – 1 edges as per Kruskal's algorithm.

Let e_k be the first edge in this sequence which is not in S i.e. $e_1, e_2, \ldots, e_{k-1}$ are in S but e_k is not in S. Let us add this edge e_k to S thereby giving a subgraph H of G.

This subgraph H has n vertices and n – 1 + 1 = n edges. Hence, there is a circuit say Γ in H. This circuit Γ in H must contain e_k because otherwise Γ would be in circuit free graph S. Further, the circuit Γ must contain an edge e which is in S but not in T, because otherwise Γ would be in circuit free graph T.

We now remove this edge e from H. Therefore H – e has n vertices and n – 1 edges; hence it is a spanning tree of G. Now since e is not in T and e_k is the first edge of T which is not in S, it follows from the algorithm that w $(e_k) \leq$ w (e). Thus, the spanning tree H – e is obtained from S by addition of an edge e_k with smaller weight and removal of an edge e with larger weight.

Therefore w (H – e) ≤ w (S).

We continue the same procedure on H – e now and its successors, every time getting a spanning tree of weight smaller than that of S.

Finally, we get a spanning tree T and we have w (T) ≤ w (S). This is a contradiction to the assumption. Hence, T is a shortest spanning tree of G. ■

4.6 Prim's Algorithm

Procedure : Prim's (G : weighted connected graph with n vertices)

T = a minimum - weight edge

for i = 1 to n – 2

begin e : = an edge of minimum weight incident to a vertex in T and not forming a simple circuit in T if added to T.

T : = T with e added

end {T is a minimum spanning tree of G}.

Note that the choice of an edge to add at a stage of the algorithm is not determined when there is more than one edge with the same weight that satisfies the appropriate criteria. We need to order the edges to make the choices deterministic. Also note that there may be more than one minimum spanning tree for a given connected weighted simple graph.

Example : Use Prim's algorithm to design a minimum-cost communications network connecting all the computers represented by the graph in the following figure.

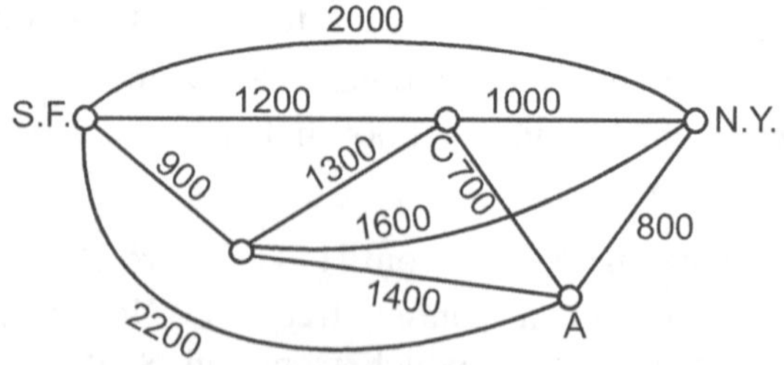

Fig. 4.19

Solution :

Choice	Edge	Cost
1	C to A	700
2	A to N.Y.	800
3	C to S.F.	1200
4	S.F. to D	900
		3600

Example : Use Prim's algorithm to find a minimum spanning tree in the graph shown in the following figure.

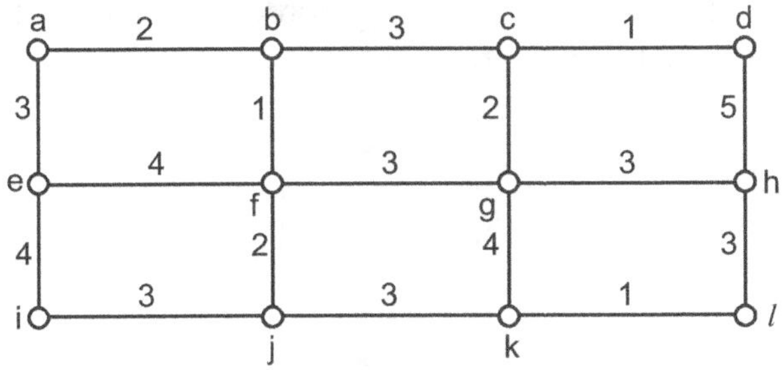

Fig. 4.20

Solution :

Choice	Edge	Cost
1	{b, f}	1
2	{a, b}	2
3	{f, j}	2
4	{a, e}	3
5	{i, j}	3
6	{f, g}	3
7	{c, g}	2
8	{c, d}	1
9	{g, h}	3
10	{h, *l*}	3
11	{k, *l*}	1
		24

4.7 Traversal Algorithms

Procedure for systematically visiting every vertex of an ordered rooted tree are called traversal algorithms. We will describe three of the most commonly used such algorithms, preorder traversal, in order traversal, and postorder traversal.

Definition : Let T be an ordered rooted tree with root r. If T consists only of r_l then r is the preorder traversal of T, otherwise, suppose that $T_1, T_2, \ldots, T_n$ are the subtrees at r from left to right in T. The preorder traversal begins by visiting r. It continues by traversing T_1 in preorder, then T_2 in preorder, and so on, until T_n is traversed in preorder.

Example : In which order does a preorder traversal visit the vertices in the ordered rooted tree T shown in the following figure.

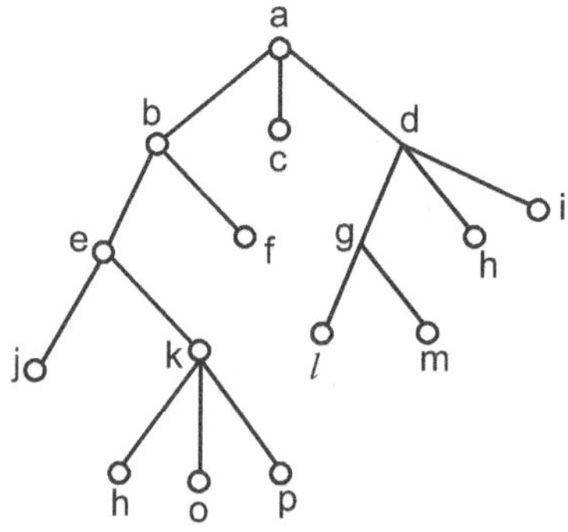

Fig. 4.21 (a)

Solution : We traverse T in preorder by first listing the root a, followed by the preorder list of the subtree with root b, the preorder list of the subtree with root c and the preorder list of the subtree with root d. The preorder list of the subtree with root b begins by listing b, then the vertices of the subtree with root e in preorder, and then the subtree with root f in preorder. The preorder list of the subtree with root d begins by listing d, followed by the preorder list of the subtree with root g, followed by the subtree with root h, followed by the subtree with root i. The preorder list of the subtree with root e begins by listing e, followed by the preorder listing of the subtree with root j, followed by the preorder listing of the subtree with root k. The preorder listing of the subtree with root g is g followed by *l*, followed by m. The preorder listing of the subtree with root k is, k, n, o, p. Consequently, the preorder traversal of T is a, b, e, j, k, n, o, p, f, c, d, g, *l*, m, h, i.

Definition : Let T be an ordered rooted tree with root r. If T consists only of r, then r is the inorder traversal of T. Otherwise, suppose that $T_1, T_2, \ldots, T_n$ are the subtree at r from left to right. The inorder traversal begins by traversing T_1 in inorder, then visiting r. It continues by traversing T_2 in inorder, then T_3 in inorder, …, and finally T_n in inorder.

Example : In which order does an inorder traversal visit the vertices of the ordered rooted tree T in the previous figure.

Solution : The inorder traversal begins with an inorder traversal of the subtree with root b, the root a, the inorder listing of the subtree with root c, which is just c, and the inorder listing of the subtree with root d. The inorder listing of the subtree with root b begins with the inorder listing of the subtree with root e, the root b, and f. The inorder listing of the subtree with root d begins with the inorder listing of the subtree with root g, followed by the root d, followed by h, followed by i. The inorder listing of the subtree with root e is j, followed by the root e, followed by the inorder listing of the subtree with root k. The inorder listing of the subtree with root g is *l*, m, g. The inorder listing of the subtree with root k is n, k, o, p. Consequently, the inorder listing of the ordered rooted tree is j, e, n, k, o, p, b, f, a, c, *l*, g, m, d, h, i.

Definition : Let T be an ordered rooted tree with root r. If T consists only of r, then r is the postorder traversal of T. Otherwise, suppose that $T_1, T_2, \ldots, T_n$ are the subtrees at r from left to right. The postorder traversal begins by traversing T_1 in postorder, then T_2 in postorder, …, then T_n in postorder and ends by visiting r.

Example : In which order does a postorder traversal visit the vertices of the ordered rooted tree T shown in previous figure.

Solution : The postorder traversal begins with the postorder traversal of the subtree with root b, the postorder traversal of the subtree with root c, which is just c, the postorder traversal of the subtree withroot d, followed by the root a. The postorder traversal of the subtree with root b begins with the postorder traversal of the subtree with root e, followed by f, followed by the root b. The postorder traversal of the rooted tree with root d begins with the postorder traversal of the subtree with root g, followed by h, followed by i, followed by the root d. The postorder traversal of the subtree with root e begins with j, followed by the postorder traversal of the subtree with root k, followed by the root e. The postorder traversal of the subtree with root g is *l*, m, g. The postorder traversal of the subtree with root k is n, o, p, k. Therefore, the postorder traversal of T is j, n, o, p, k, e, f, b, c, *l*, m, g, h, i, d, a.

Infix, Prefix, and Postfix Notation :

We can represent complicated expressions, such as compound propositions, combinations of sets, and arithmetic expression using ordered rooted trees. For instance, consider the representation of an arithmetic expression involving the operators + (addition), – (subtraction), × (multiplication), / (division), and ↑ (exponential). We will use parenthesis to indicate the order of the operations. An ordered rooted tree can be used to represent such expressions, where the internal vertices represent operations, and the leaves represent the variables or numbers. Each operation operates on its left and right subtrees (in that order).

Example : What is the ordered rooted tree that represents the expression (x + 4) ↑ 2) + (x – 4) / 3) ?

Solution : First, a subtree for the expression x + y is constructed. Then this is incorporated as part of the larger subtree representing (x + y) ↑ 2. Also, a subtree for (x – 4) is constructed and then this is incorporated into a subtree representing (x – 4) / 3. Finally the subtrees representing (x + y) ↑ 2 and (x – 4) / 3 are combined to form the ordered rooted tree representing ((x + y) ↑ 2) + ((x – 4 / 3).

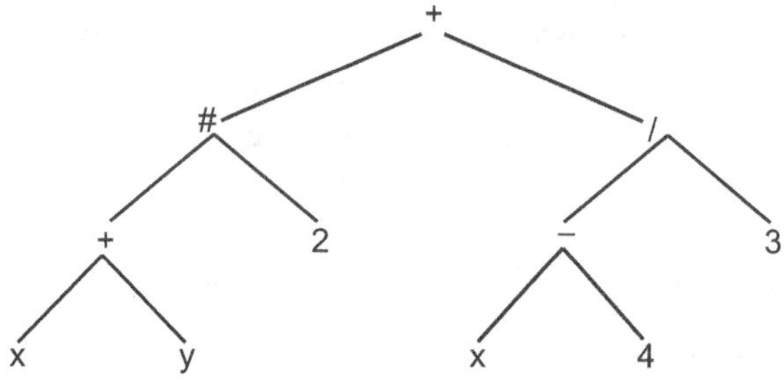

Fig. 4.21 (b)

A binary tree representing ((x + y) ↑ 2) + ((x – 4) / 3).

Example : Rooted tree representing (x + y) / (x + 3).

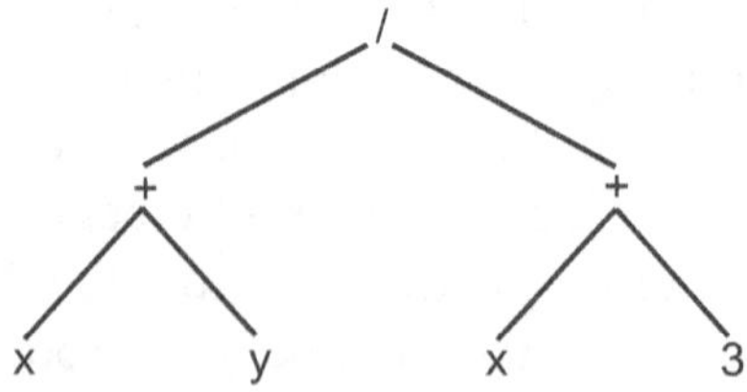

Fig. 4.22

Example : Rooted tree representing x + (y / (x + 3)).

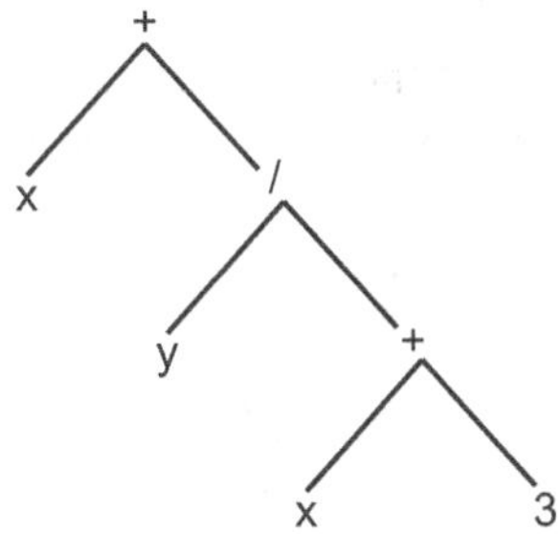

Fig. 4.23

Note :

1. To make expressions unambiguous it is necessary to include parenthesis in the inorder traversal whenever we encounter an operation. The fully parenthesized expression obtained in this way is said to be in **infix** form.
2. We obtain the **prefix** form of an expression when we traverse its rooted tree in preorder. Expressions written in prefix form are said to be in **polish notation.**

Example : What is the prefix form for ((x + y) ↑ 2) + ((x – 4) / 3) ?

Solution : By traversing the binary tree that represents it shown in the following figure.

This produces : + ↑ + xyz / – x43

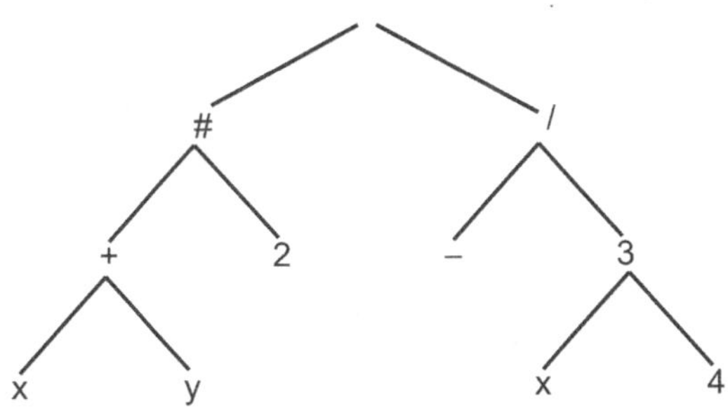

Fig. 4.24

Example : What is the postfix form of the expression

((x + y) ↑ 2) + ((x – 4) / 3) ?

Solution : By carrying out a postorder traversal of the binary tree for this expression shown in the above figure. This produces the post fix expression :

xy + 2↑ x4 – 3 / +.

Example : What is the value of the postfix expression

$723 \times - 4 \uparrow 93\ l + ?$

Solution : By starting at the left and carrying out operations when two operands are followed by an operator are shown in the following figure.

Evaluating a prefix expression :

$+ \ - \ * \ 2 \ 3 \ 5 \ / \ \uparrow \ 2 \ 3 \ 4$

$2 \uparrow 3 = 8$

$+ \ - \ * \ 2 \ 3 \ 5 \ / \ 8 \ 4$

$8/4 = 2$

$+ \ - \ * \ 2 \ 3 \ 5 \ 2$

$2 * 3 = 6$

$+ \ - \ 6 \ 5 \ 2$

$6 - 5 = 1$

$+ \ 1 \ 2$

$1 + 2 = 3$

Evaluating a postfix expression

$7 \ 2 \ 3 \ * \ - \ 4 \ \neq \ 9 \ 3 \ / \ +$

$7 \ 6 \ - \ 4 \ \neq \ 9 \ 3 \ l \ +$

$7 - 6 = 1$

$1 \ 4 \ \neq \ 9 \ 3 \ / \ +$

$1^4 = 1$

$1 \ 9 \ 3 \ l \ +$

$9 / 3 = 3$

$1 \ 3 \ +$

$1 + 3 = 4$

Illustrative Examples

Example 4.1 : *Let G be a tree with two or more vertices. If p : u_0, u_1, u_2 ... u_n is longest path in G then show that u_0 and u_n are of degree 1.*

Solution : Let G be a tree with two or more vertices.

Let p : u_0, u_1, u_2 ... u_n be longest path in G. We have to show that d (u_0) = d (u_n) = 1. Assume that d(u_0) > 1. The edge e joining u_0 and u_1 contributes degree 1 at u_0. Therefore, by assumption there is another edge e' which is incident on u_0. Let v be the other end vertex of e'. Now we show that v is different from u_0, u_1, u_2, ... u_n.

If v = u_0 then e' forms a loop at u_0 which is impossible.

If v = u_i for some i; $1 \leq i \leq n$ then u_0, u_1, u_2 ... u_i e'u_0 is a circuit in G.

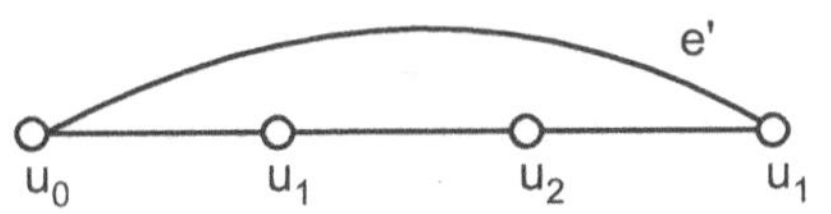

Fig. 4.25

This is also impossible. Thus, v is different from u_0, u_1, u_2 ... u_n.

Now consider the path v u_0 , u_1, u_2 ... u_n. It has length n + 1 which is greater than n, the length of the longest path in G. This is a contradiction. Hence, our assumption d(u_0) > 1 must be wrong. So d(u_0) = 1. Similarly, d(u_n) = 1. Below we see some other equivalent characterizations of a tree.

Example 4.2 : *Prove that a tree with two or more vertices has at least two pendant vertices.*

Solution : Let G be a tree with n vertices where $n \geq 2$. Then G has n – 1 edges. Therefore, total degree of G is 2(n – 1) = 2n – 2. By connectedness each of the n vertices must have minimum 1 degree. After assigning 1 degree to each vertex, there remains (2n – 2) – n = n – 2 degrees to be distributed among n vertices. The assignment of n – 2 degrees among n vertices implies that there will be at least two vertices say u and v not getting any degree in the second round of distribution. These vertices have degree 1 each assigned in the first round of distribution and they are pendant vertices in G. Hence proved.

Example 4.3 : *A vertex v is of maximum degree k in a tree T. Then prove that T contains at least k vertices of degree 1.*

Solution : Let the graph T be a tree and v be the vertex in T whose degree is maximum i.e. $d_{max} = d(v) = k$. Therefore, there are k edges incident on v and suppose that the other end vertices of these k edges are $v_1, v_2, \ldots, v_k$. If these k + 1 vertices give a complete list of vertices of T then the result is proved because in this case there are k vertices of degree 1.

Now, we note that there is no any other edge incident on v. Let $u_1, u_2, \ldots, u_r$ be the vertices of T other than above k + 1 vertices. Any one of them is not joined to the vertex v. By connectedness of T at least one u_i must be joined to v_j by an edge; so that v_j has now degree greater than 1.

But if we consider the path $v_j\, u_i\, u_m\, u_p \ldots$ then at the end of this path there is again at least one vertex of degree 1 and there can be more such vertices also. Therefore, in T there are at least k vertices of degree 1.

Example 4.4 : *Find eccentricity of each vertex in the following tree. Hence find centre of the tree.*

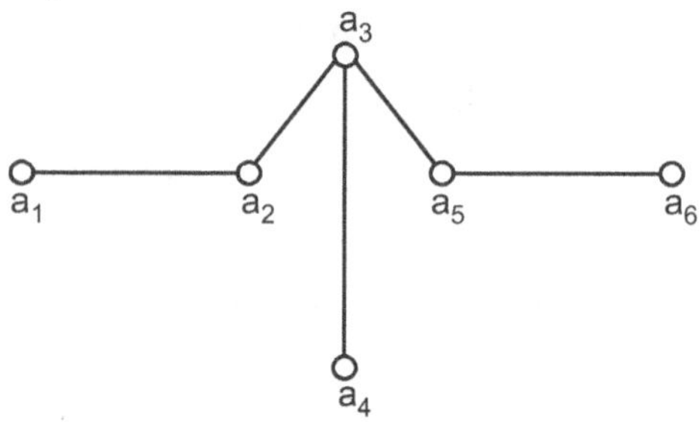

Fig. 4.26 (a)

Solution : The eccentricity of a vertex v in a tree is the distance of a vertex u from v such that u is fartest apart from v.

Given tree is

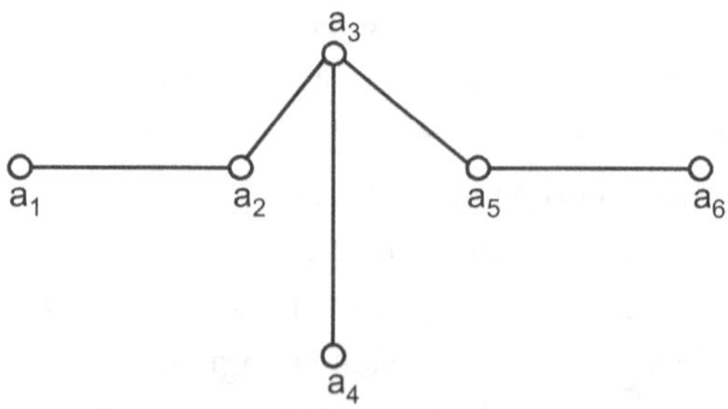

Fig. 4.26 (b)

We have $E(a_1) = 4$, $E(a_2) = 3$, $E(a_3) = 2$, $E(a_4) = 3$, $E(a_5) = 3$, $E(a_6) = 4$.

The eccentricity is minimum at the vertex a_3; $E(a_3) = 2$.

$\therefore$ a_3 is centre of the tree.

Example 4.5 : *The degrees of the vertices of a certain tree T of order 13 are 1, 2, 5. The tree T has exactly 3 vertices of degree 2. Find the number of end vertices of tree T.*

Solution : The number of vertices in a tree T is 13. Therefore, number of edges is $13 - 1 = 12$.

Each edge contributes 2 degrees.

$\therefore$ Total degree $= 2 \times 12 = 24$.

There are 3 vertices are of degree 2. Suppose x vertices are of degree 1. Then $13 - (x + 3) = 10 - x$ vertices are of degree 5 each.

$$\therefore \quad \text{Total degree} = 3 \times 2 + (x)(1) + (10 - x)(5)$$

$$\therefore \quad \text{Total degree} = 4x + 56$$

$$24 = -4x + 56$$

$$\therefore \quad 4x = 56 - 24 = 32$$

$$\therefore \quad x = 8$$

The number of end vertices is 8.

Example 4.6 : *Find the centre of the following tree :*

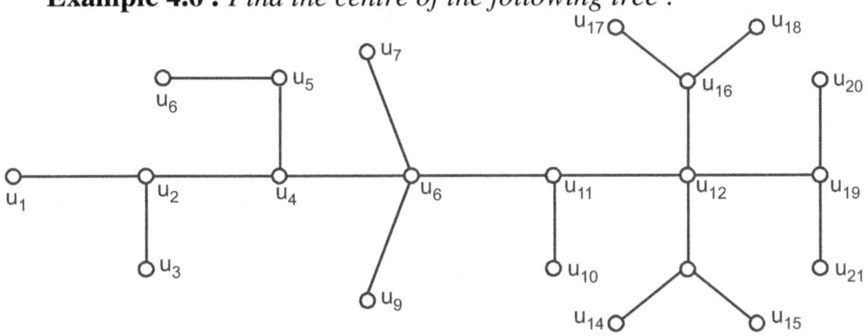

Fig. 4.27 : T

Solution : The removal of pendant vertices u_1, u_3, u_6, u_7, u_9, u_{10}, u_{14}, u_{15}, u_{17}, u_{18}, u_{20}, u_{21} from T we get a tree T'.

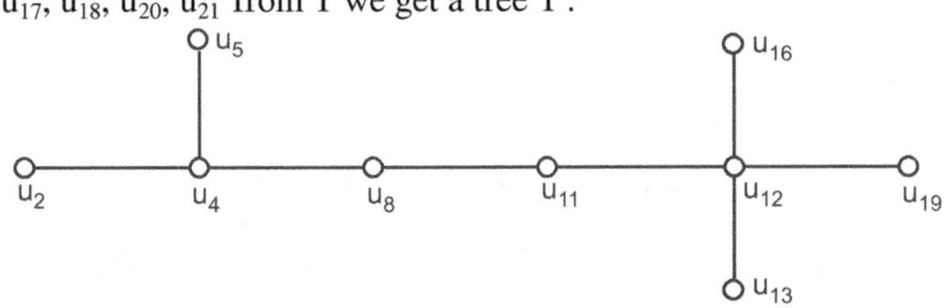

Fig. 4.28 : T'

The removal of pendant vertices u_2, u_5, u_{13}, u_{16}, u_{19} from T' we get a tree T".

Fig. 4.29 : T"

The removal of pendant vertices u_4, u_{12} from T", we get a tree T'".

Fig. 4.30 : T'"

Thus, centre of a given tree T is

Fig. 4.31

which is k_2. A tree whose centre consists of a single vertex i.e. k_1 is called a unicentral tree and a tree whose centre consists of two adjacent vertices i.e. k_2 is called a bicentral tree.

The tree given in the above example is a bicentral tree.

Example 4.7 : *Prove that the nullity of a graph does not change when*

(a) a vertex is inserted in the middle of an edge.

(b) a vertex of degree 2 is removed by merging two edges incident on it.

Solution : (a) Let G be a connected graph with n vertices and e edges.

Therefore, the nullity of G is $e - n + 1$. Consider the edge e_i of G whose end vertices are v_j and v_k. We now insert a vertex v^* in the middle of edge e_i so that in the new graph the number of vertices is $n + 1$. Also the single edge e_i in the original graph is converted into two edges; one from v_j to v^* and the other from v^* to v_k. Thus, in the new graph, the number of edges is $e + 1$.

Nullity of new graph $= (e + 1) - (n + 1) + 1 = e - n + 1 =$ nullity of G.

(b) Let G be a connected graph with n vertices and e edges so that the nullity of G is $e - n + 1$. Let v be a vertex of degree 2 in G. Suppose the two edges incident on v are e_1 with end vertices u, v and e_2 with end vertices v, w.

We now remove the vertex v from G by merging the two edges e_1 and e_2 together so that in the new graph there is a single edge joining u and w.

Thus, in the new graph, the number of vertices is n – 1 and the number of edges is e – 1.

Therefore, the nullity of new graph = (e – 1) – (n – 1) + 1 = e – n + 1 = nullity of G.

Example 4.8 : *Find all the spanning trees of the graph given below.*

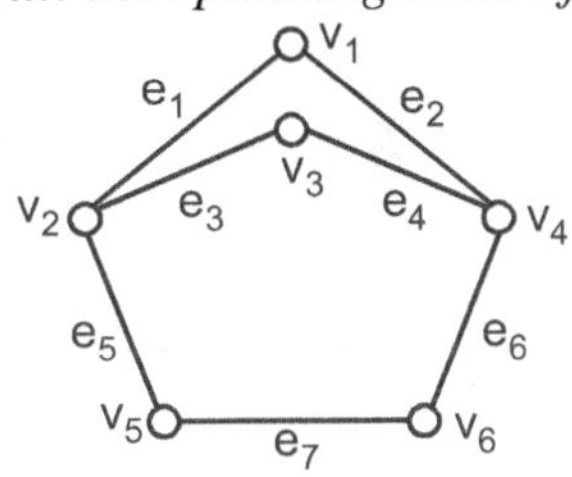

Fig. 4.32 : G

Solution : The number of vertices in the graph G is n = 6 and the number of edges are e = 7. Any spanning tree of G has n – 1 = 6 – 1 = 5 branches. This suggests that out of 7 edges, we delete 2 edges in such a way that the remaining graph is a tree on 6 vertices.

We have following 16 spanning trees of G.

Deletion of two edges	Spanning tree	Deletion of two edges	Spanning tree
e_1, e_3	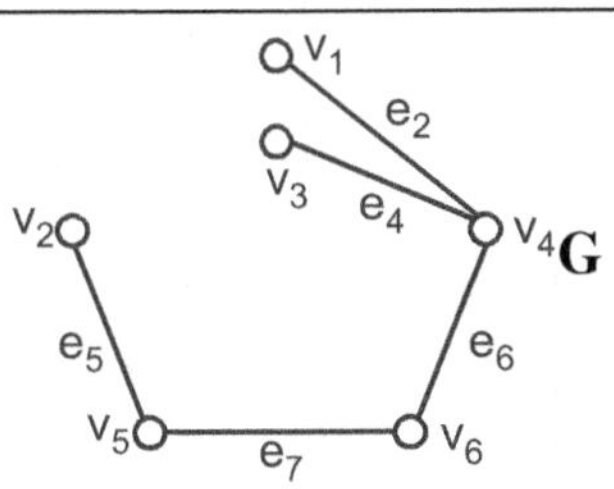	e_1, e_4	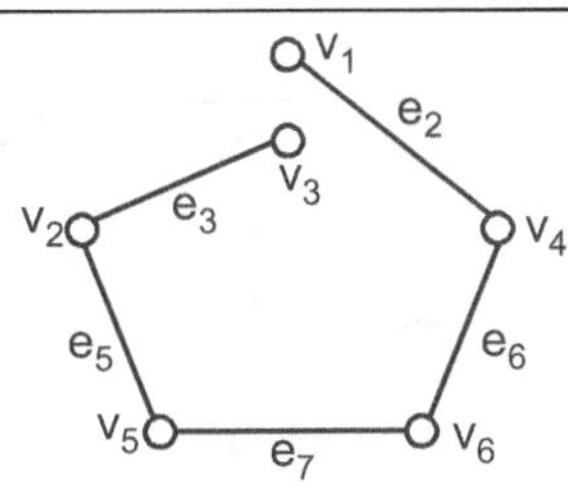
e_1, e_5	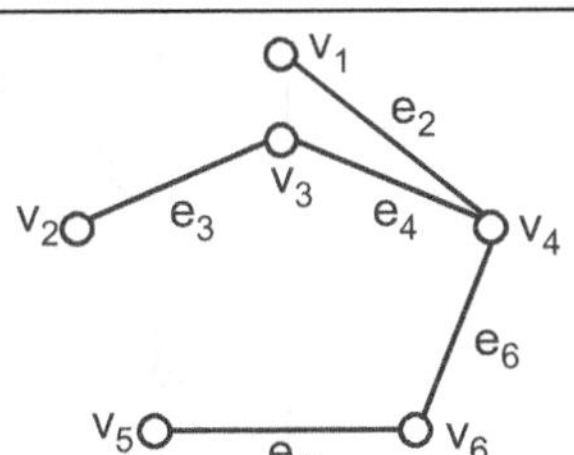	e_1, e_6	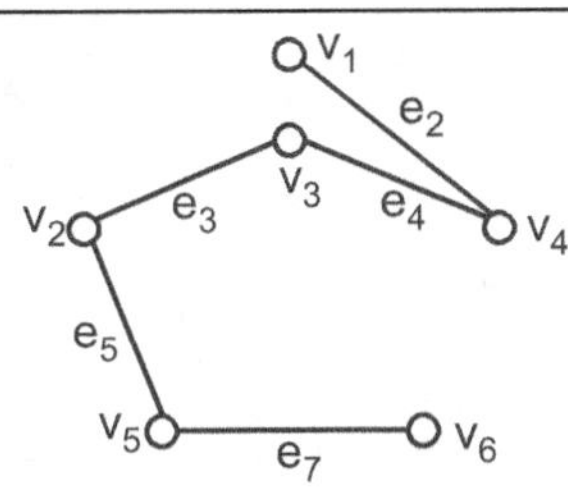

e_1, e_7	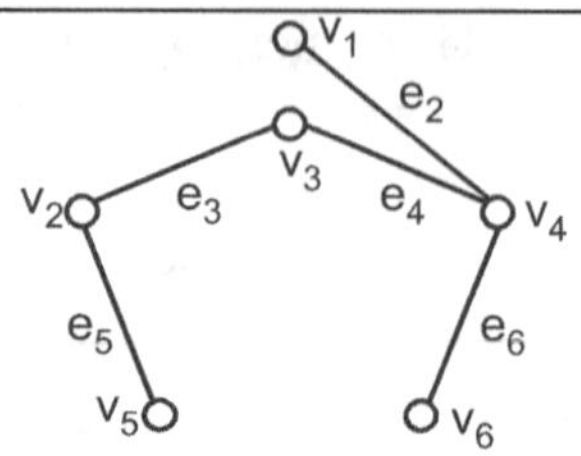	e_2, e_3	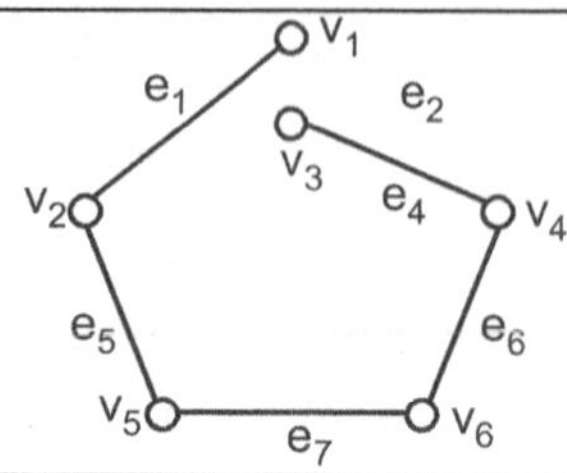
e_2, e_4	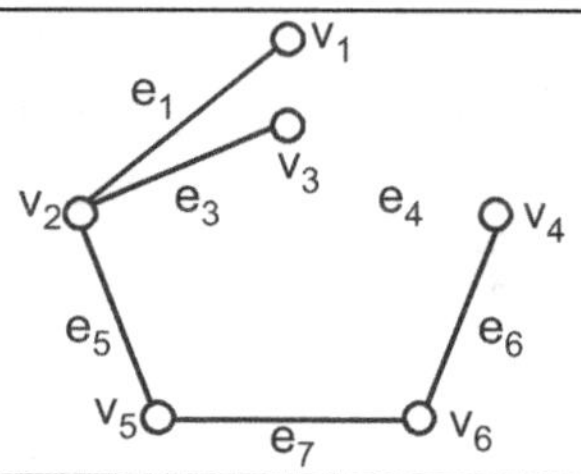	e_2, e_5	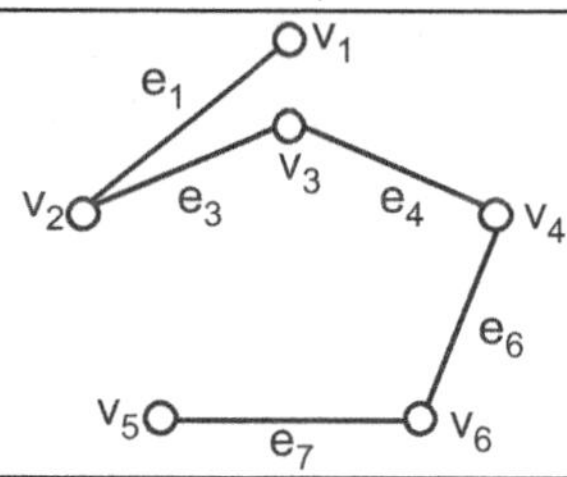
e_2, e_6	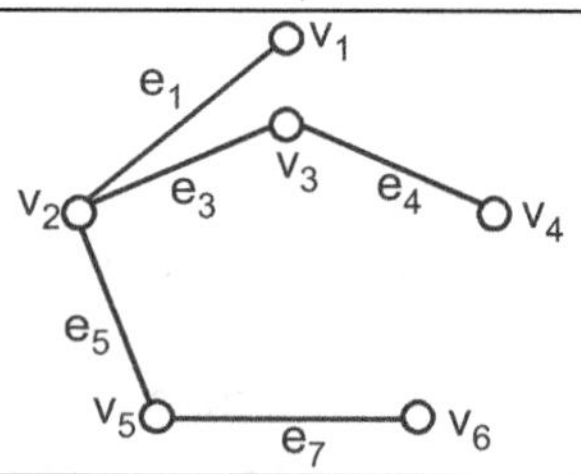	e_2, e_7	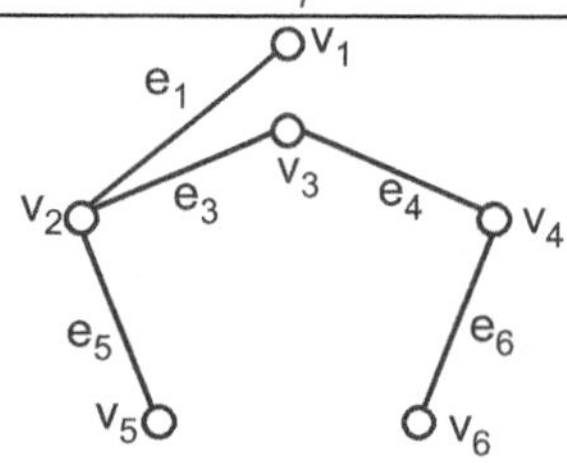
e_3, e_5	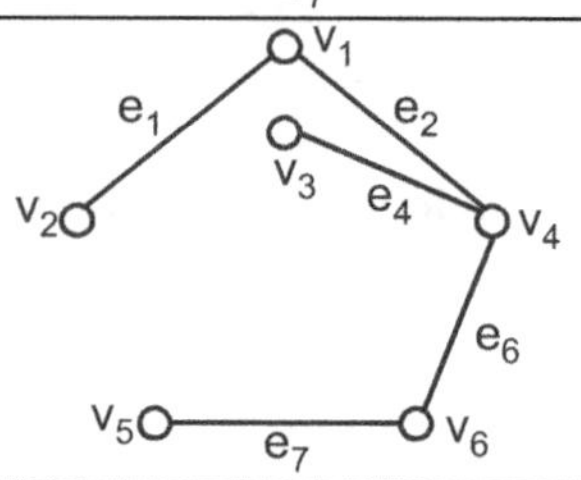	e_3, e_6	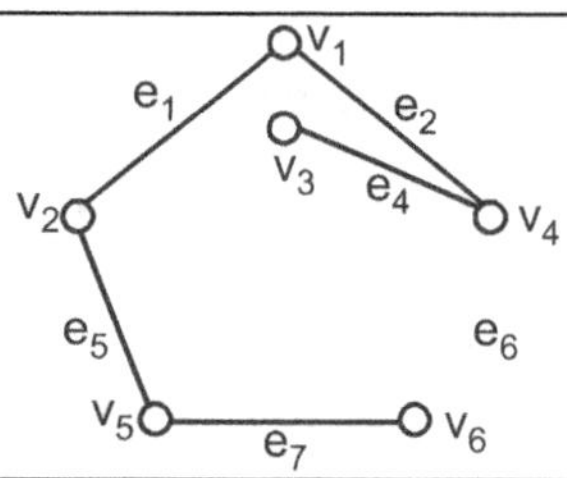
e_3, e_7	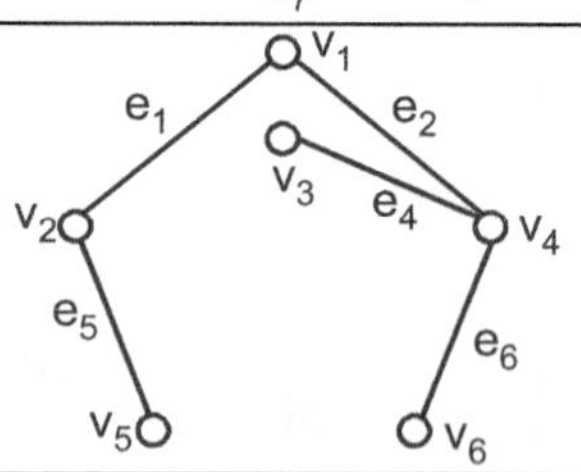	e_4, e_5	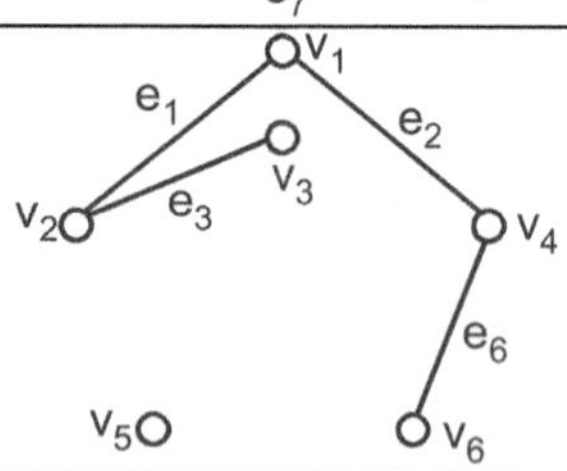
e_4, e_6	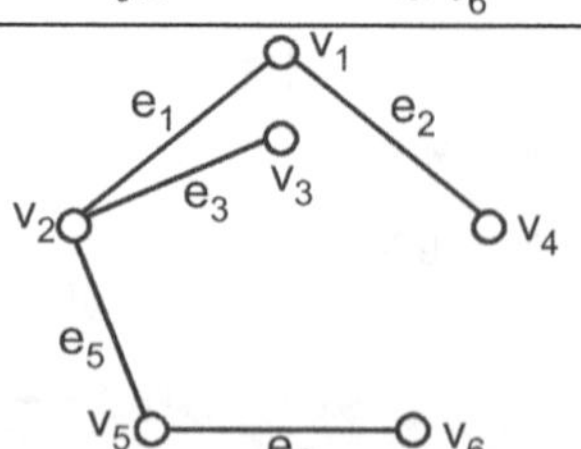	e_4, e_7	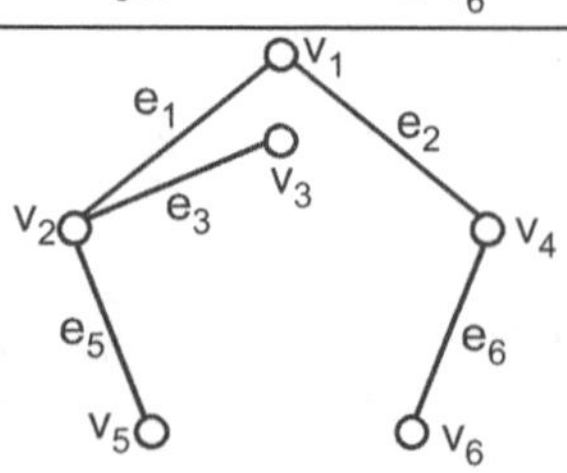

Note : We note in the above example that out of ${}^7C_2 = 21$ pairs, the 5 pairs cannot be deleted. These five pairs are

(1) e_1, e_2 (2) e_3, e_4 (3) e_5, e_6 (4) e_5, e_7 (5) e_6, e_7.

if any one of these pairs of edges is deleted then the remaining graph will not be a tree.

Example 4.9 : *Draw any two non-isomorphic spanning subgraphs of the following graph.*

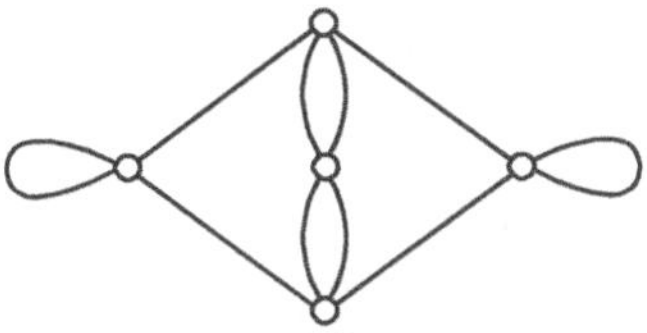

(a)

Fig. 4.433

Solution :

(b) **(c)**

Fig. 4.34

G_1 and G_2 are spanning subgraphs of a given graph.

G_1 and G_2 are not isomorphic because in G_1 there are 3 pendant vertices whereas in G_2 there are two pendant vertices.

Example 4.10 : *Consider the connected graph G and its spanning tree T. List all fundamental circuits (cycles) and cut sets of G with respect to T.*

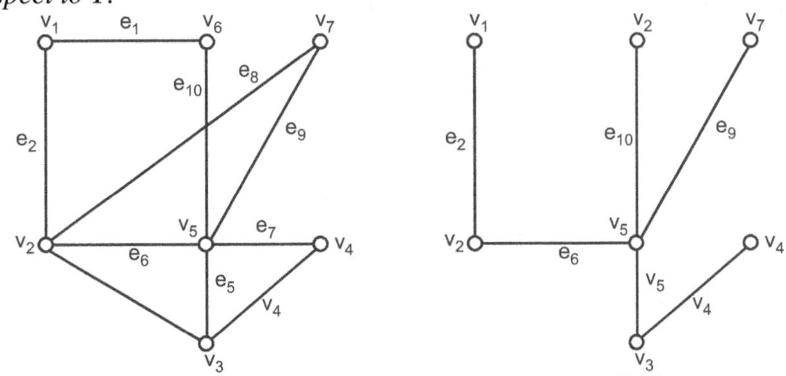

Fig. 4.35

Solution :

Chord	Fundamental circuit	Chord	Fundamental circuit
e_1	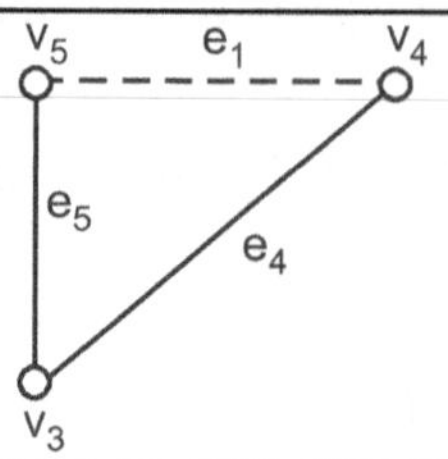	e_3	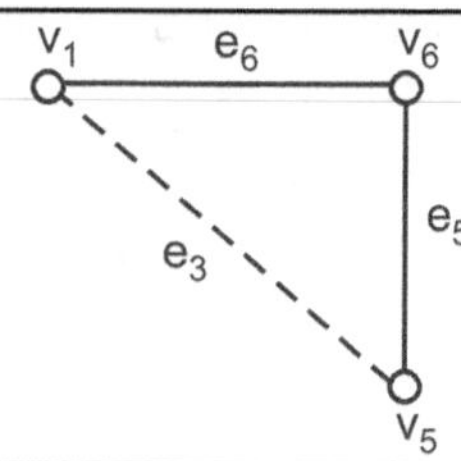
e_7		e_8	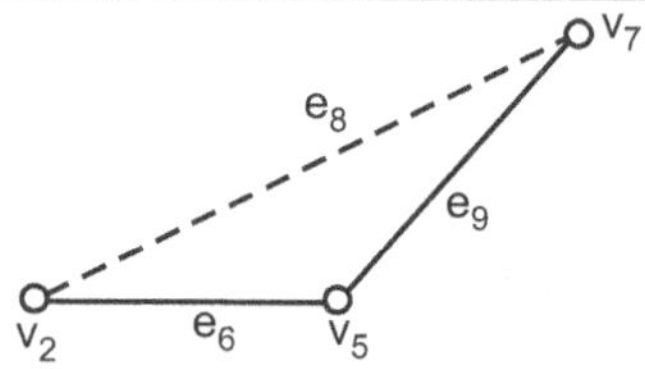

Fig. 4.36

We see that w.r.t. spanning tree T, the branches are $\{e_2, e_4, e_5, e_6, e_9, e_{10}\}$ and the chords are $\{e_1, e_3, e_7, e_8\}$.

The four fundamental circuits are created by the four chords (See Fig. 4.36).

There are 6 fundamental cut sets w.r.t. T associated with 6 branches of T.

Branch	Vertex partition	Fundamental cut set
e_2	$\{v_1\}, \{v_2, v_3, v_4, v_5, v_6, v_7\}$	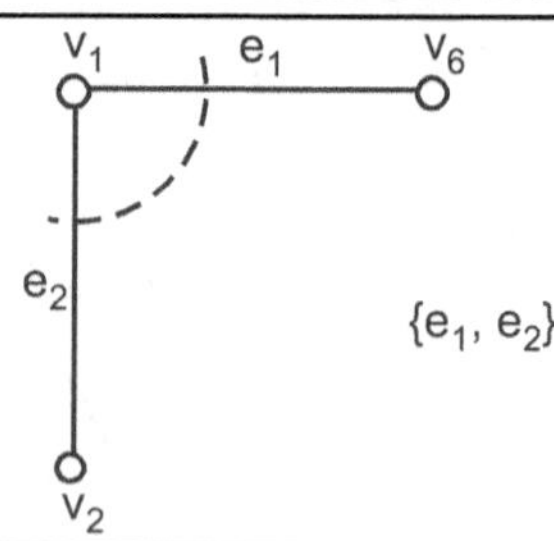
e_4	$\{v_4\}, \{v_1, v_2, v_3, v_5, v_6, v_7\}$	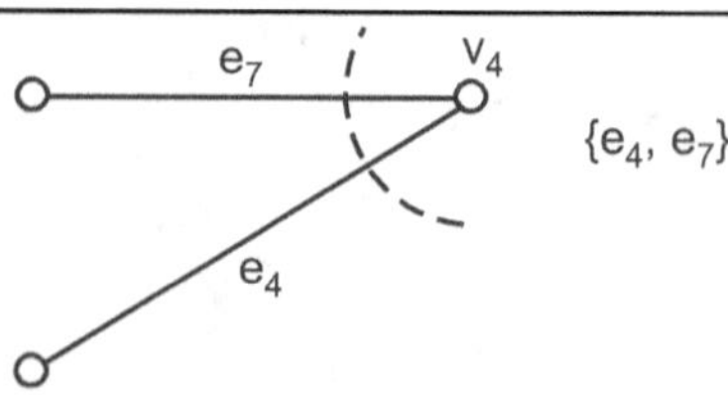

e_5	$\{v_3, v_4\}, \{v_1, v_2, v_5, v_6, v_7\}$	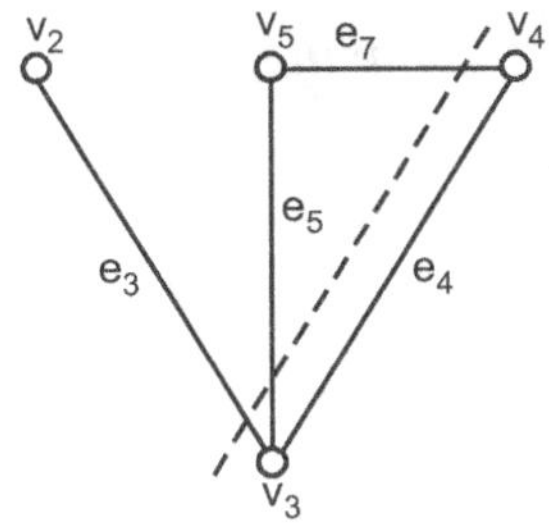 $\{e_3, e_5, e_7\}$
e_6	$\{v_1, v_2\}, \{v_3, v_4, v_5, v_6, v_7\}$	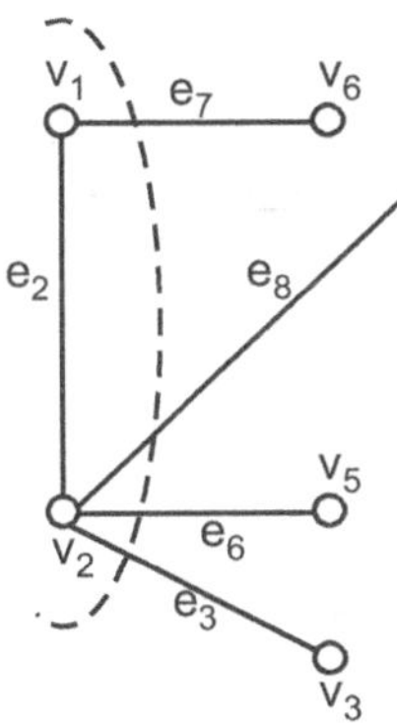 $\{e_1, e_8, e_5, e_3\}$
e_9	$\{v_7\}, \{v_1, v_2, v_3, v_4, v_5, v_6\}$	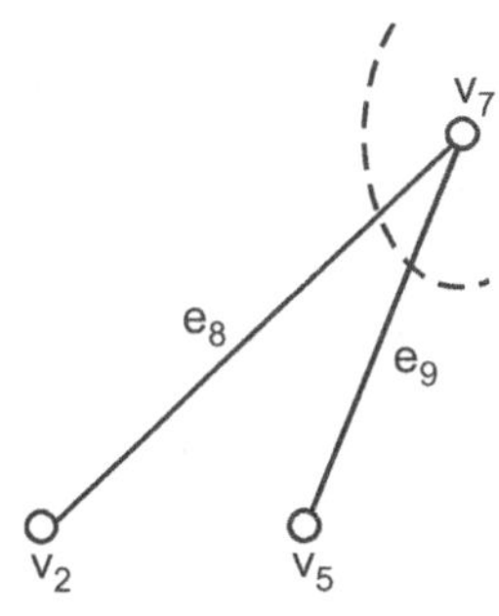 $\{e_8, e_9\}$
e_{10}	$\{v_6\}, \{v_1, v_2, v_3, v_4, v_5, v_7\}$	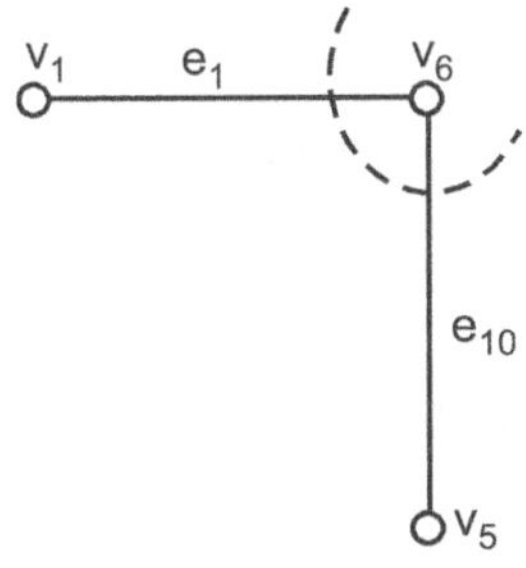 $\{e_1, e_{10})$

Example 4.11 : *For the following graph G, find all fundamental cutsets w.r.t. spanning tree T.*

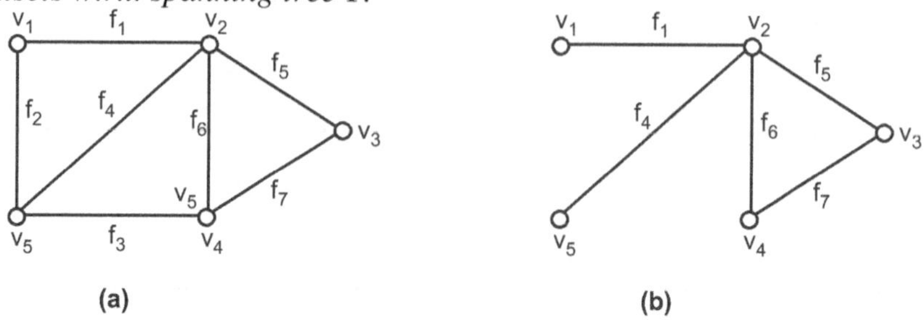

Fig. 4.37

Solution :

Branch	Vertex partition	Fundamental cut set
f_1	$\{v_1\}, \{v_2, v_3, v_4, v_5\}$	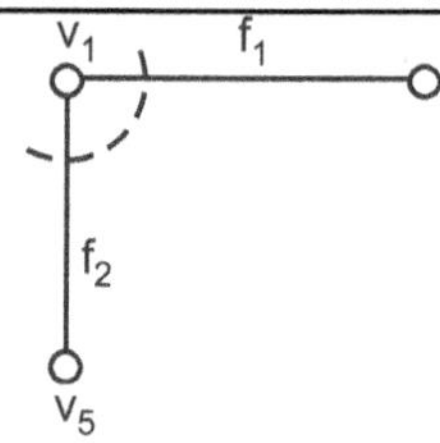 $\{f_1, f_2\}$
f_4	$\{v_5\}, \{v_1, v_2, v_3, v_4\}$	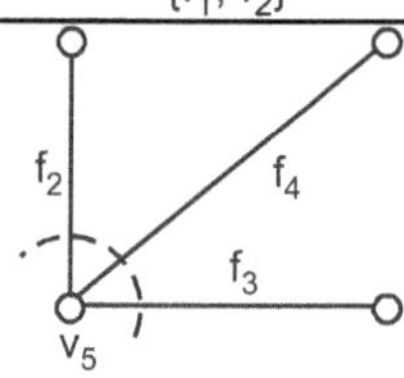 $\{f_1, f_2, f_3\}$
f_6	$\{v_1, v_2, v_5\}, \{v_3, v_4\}$	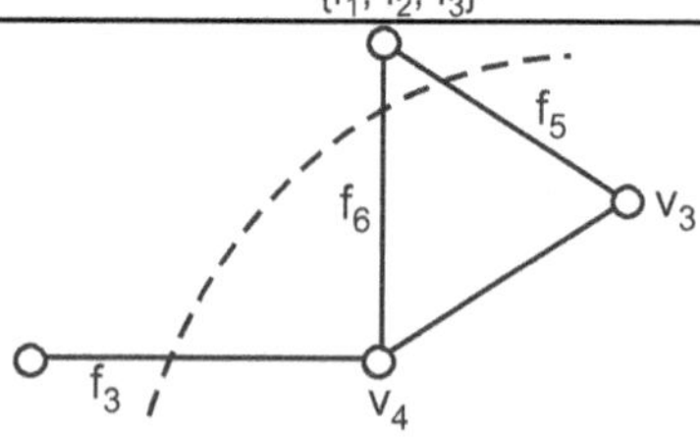 $\{f_3, f_6, f_5\}$
f_7	$\{v_3\} \{v_1, v_2, v_4, v_5\}$	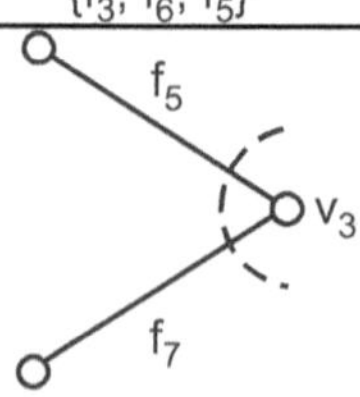 $\{f_5, f_7\}$

Example 4.12 : *Find maximum and minimum height of a binary tree with 13 vertices. Draw such trees.*

Solution : Let T be a binary tree with n vertices.

The maximum height of tree is

$$\frac{n-1}{2} = \frac{13-1}{2} = 6 \text{ and the minimum height is}$$

$$\lceil \log_2 (n+1) - 1 \rceil = \lceil \log_2 14 - 1 \rceil$$

$$= \lceil 3 \cdot abcd - 1 \rceil = \lceil 2 \cdot abcd \rceil = 3$$

Such trees are as shown below

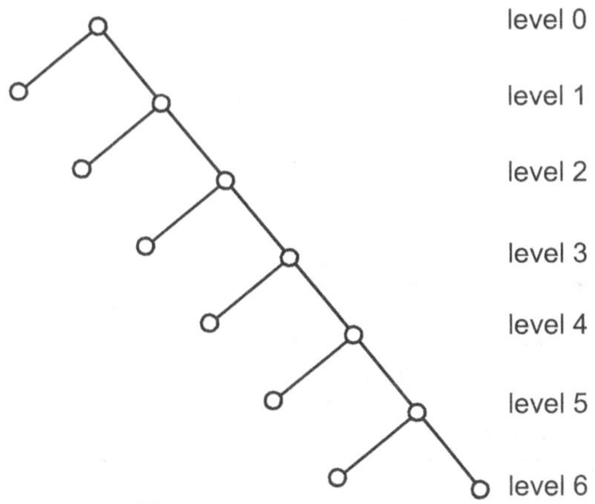

Maximum tree

(a)

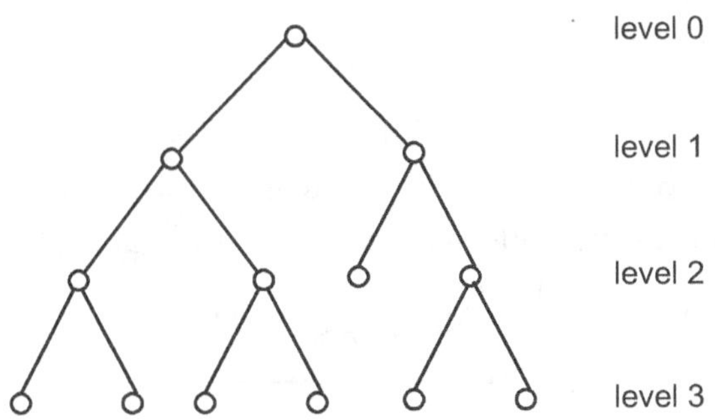

Minimum tree

(b)

Fig. 4.38

Example 4.13 : *By using Kruskal's algorithm, find the shortest spanning tree of the graph given below :*

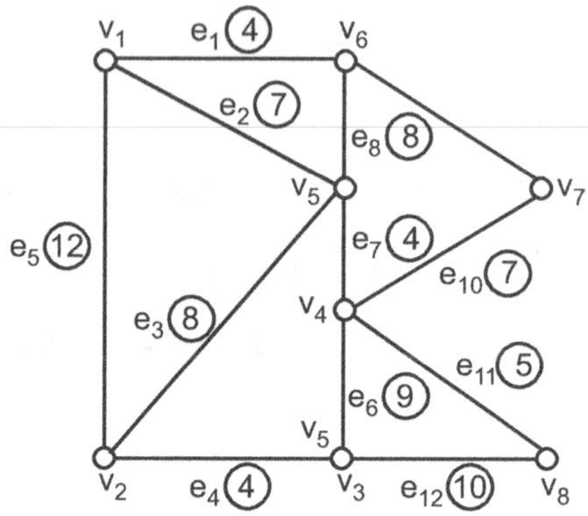

Fig. 4.39

Solution : For the given graph the edges and their weights are as follows :

Edge	e_1	e_2	e_3	e_4	e_5	e_6	e_7	e_8	e_9	e_{10}	e_{11}	e_{12}
Weight	4	7	8	4	12	9	4	8	7	7	5	10

We arrange the edges in non-decreasing order of their weights.

Edge	e_1	e_4	e_7	e_{11}	e_2	e_9	e_{10}	e_3	e_8	e_6	e_{12}	e_5
Weight	4	4	4	5	7	7	7	8	8	9	10	12

First step : We select the edge e_1 which is not a loop; the subgraph of G is

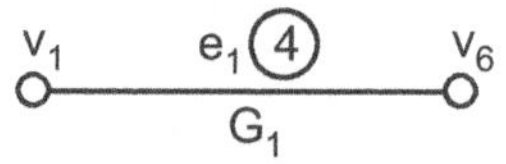

Fig. 4.40

Second step : Next edge selected is e_4 which does not create a circuit with previously selected edge. The subgraph of G is shown in Fig. 4.41.

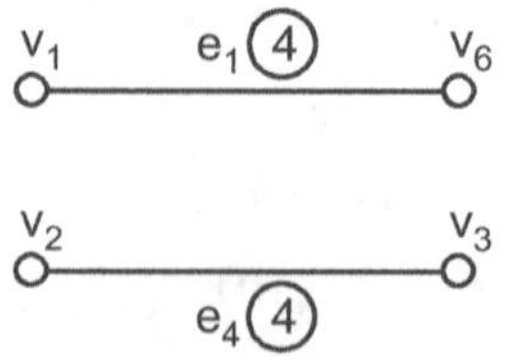

Fig. 4.41

Third step : Next edge for selection is e_7 and it does not create a circuit with G_2.

The subgraph of G is shown in Fig. 4.42.

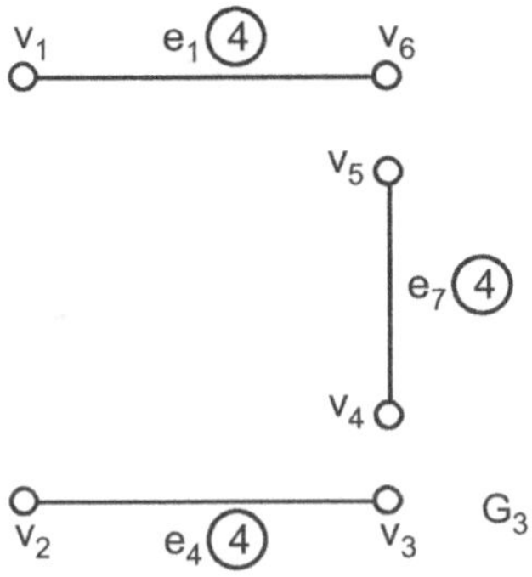

Fig. 4.42

Fourth step : Next number for selection is e_{11} which does not create a circuit with G_3. The subgraph of G is shown in Fig. 4.43.

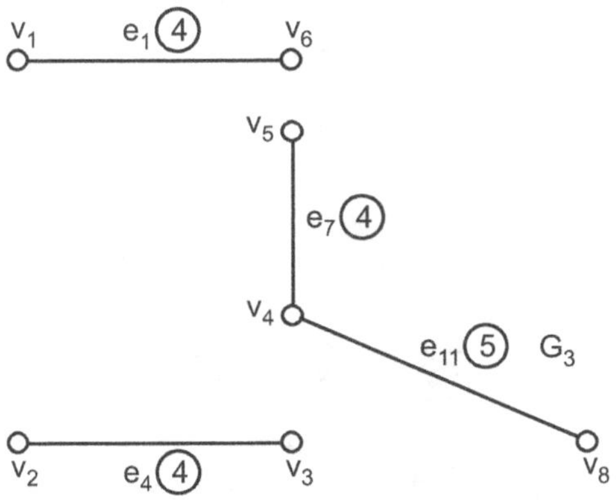

Fig. 4.43

Fifth step : Next number for selection is e_2 and it does not create a circuit with G_4. The subgraph of G is shown in Fig. 4.44.

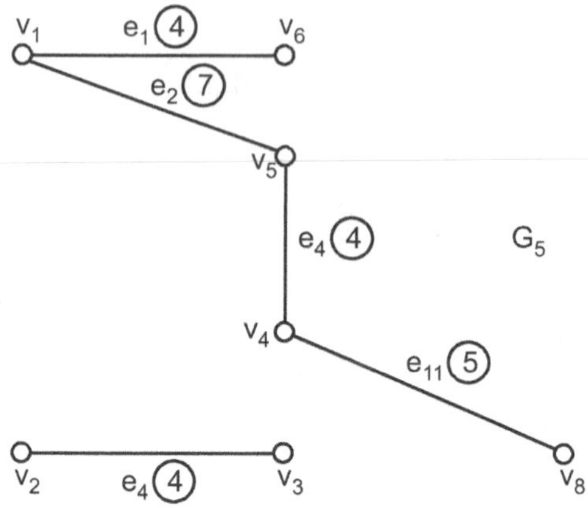

Fig. 4.44

Sixth step : Next number for selection is e_9 which does not create a circuit with G_5. The subgraph of G is shown Fig. 4.45.

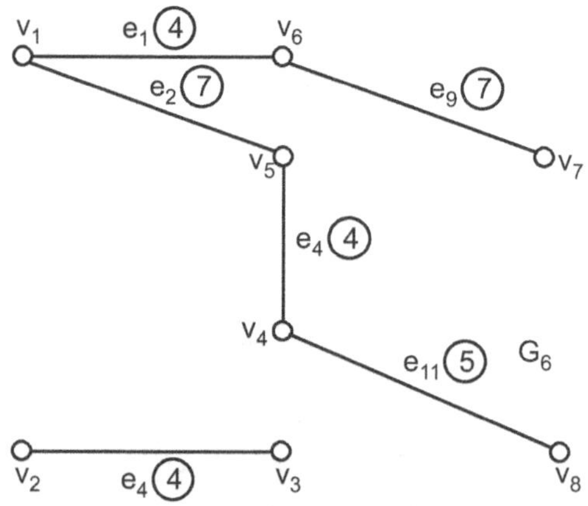

Fig. 4.45

Now, we note that if the next edge e_{10} is selected which joins v_4 and v_7 then a circuit is created viz. v_1, v_6, v_7, v_4, v_5, v_1. Therefore, we do not select the edge e_{10}.

Seventh step : Next edge for selection is e_3 which does not create a circuit with G_6. The subgraph of G is shown in Fig. 4.46.

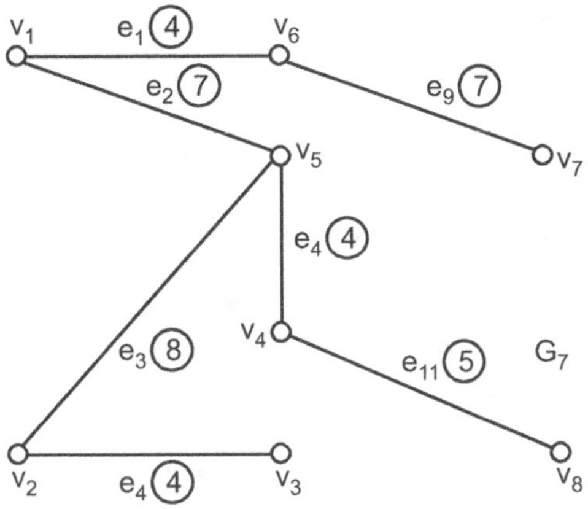

Fig. 4.46

The given graph G has 8 vertices and we have selected 7 edges. Algorithm stops here. G_7 is a shortest spanning tree. The weight of this shortest spanning tree is

$$4 + 4 + 4 + 5 + 7 + 7 + 8 = 39.$$

Example 4.14 : *Find eccentricity of every vertex for the graph. Also find center and radius.*

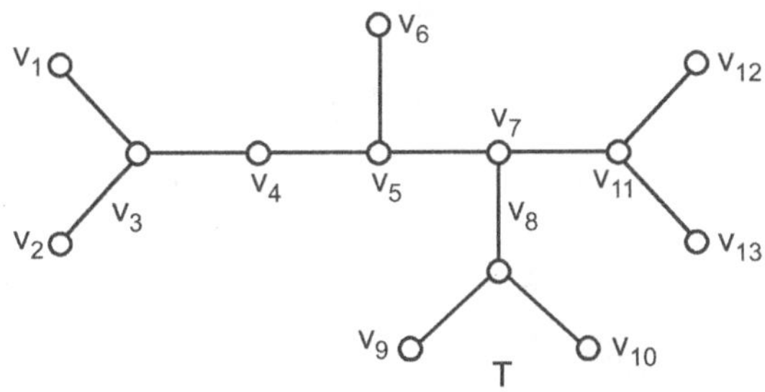

Fig. 4.47

Solution : $e(v_1) = \max \{d(v_1, v_i)/i = 1, 2, \ldots 13\} = d(v_1, v_{12}) = 6$

$e(v_2) = \max \{d(v_2, v_i)/i = 1, 2, 3, \ldots 13\} = d(v_2, v_{12}) = 6$

Secondly, $e(v_3) = 5$, $e(v_4) = 4$, $e(v_5) = 3 = 4$, $e(v_6) = 4$, $e(v_7) = 4$, $e(v_8) = 5$, $e(v_9) = 6$

$e(v_{10}) = 6$, $e(v_{11}) = 5$, $e(v_{12}) = 6$, $e(v_{13}) = 6$

Now vertices with minimum eccentricity.

V_5 only, which is called as center of T, the minimum eccentricity is called as radius and maximum eccentricity is diameter.

Example 4.15 : *Find center of above tree without finding eccentricity for a vertex.*

Solution : We know T and T – {v/v is leaf in T} has same center.

Now we find center by deleting leaves step by step.

Iteration 1 : Deleting leaves in T, we get T_1 as

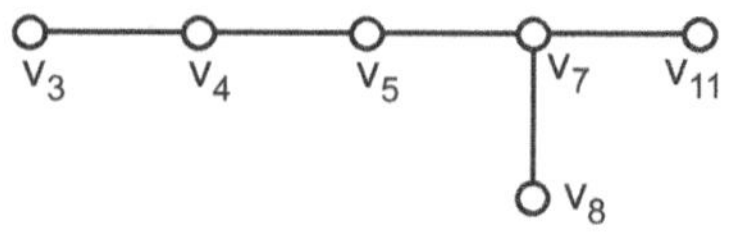

Fig. 4.48

Iteration 2 : Deleting leaves in T_1, we get T_2

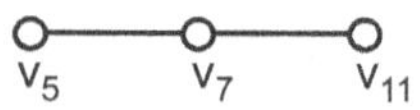

Fig. 4.49

Iteration 3 : Deleting leaves in T_2, we get v_5.

∴ v_5 is center of T_2 and hence of T_1 and hence of T.

Example 4.16 : *Find spanning tree of the following graph.*

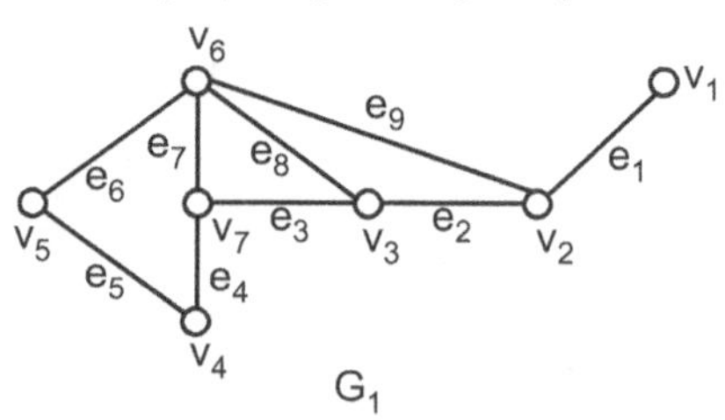

Fig. 4.50

Solution : Here number of vertices of G are 7.

∴ Any spanning tree of G has six edges contain no cycle and connected.

Now, we list all spanning tree of G as below.

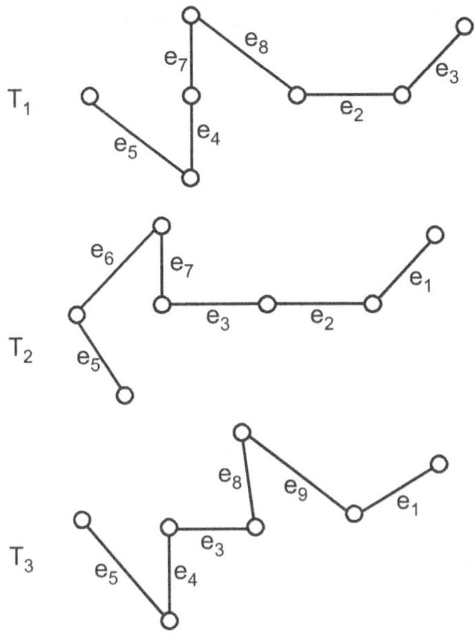

Fig. 4.51

Example 4.17 : *Consider the connected graph G and its spanning tree T. Find all the fundamental cycles and all fundamental cutsets of G with respect to T.*

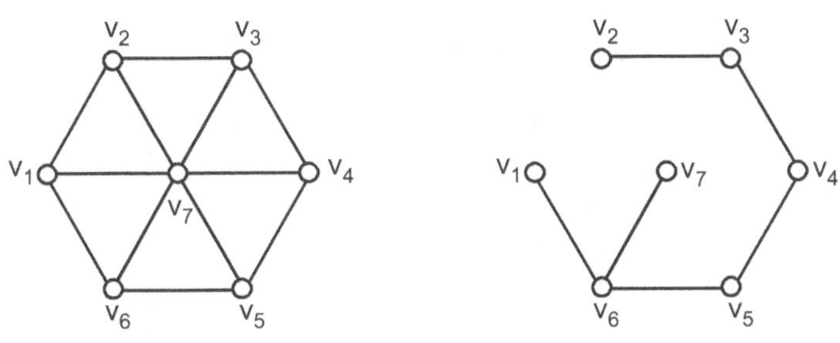

Fig. 4.52

Solution : The chords of G with respect to T are

$$\{(v_1, v_2), (v_2, v_7), (v_3, v_7), (v_4, v_7), (v_5, v_7), (v_1, v_7)\}$$

The branches of G with respect to T are

$$\{(v_1, v_6), (v_6, v_7), (v_5, v_6), (v_4, v_5), (v_3, v_4)\}$$

Now fundamental cycle corresponding to each chords is as shown below.

There are 12 – (7 – 1) = 6 chords and hence 6 fundamental cycles.

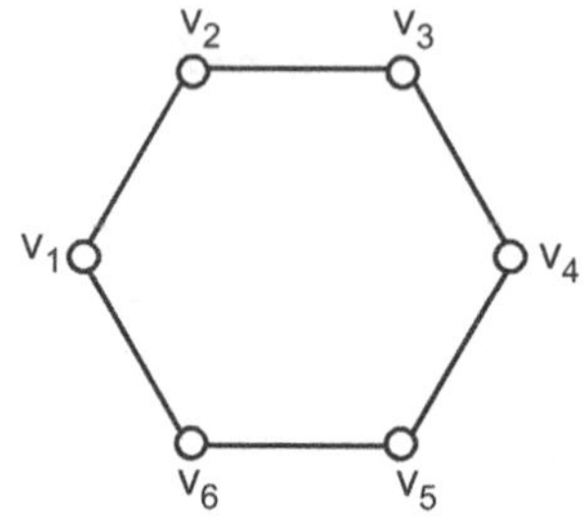

ie. T + (v_1, v_2)

(a)

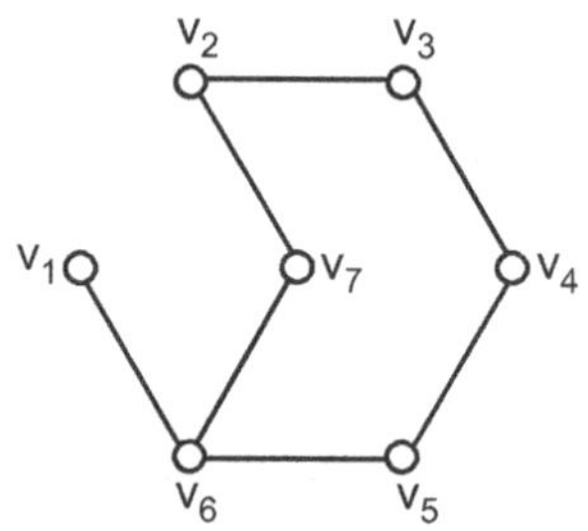

ie. T + (v_7, v_2)

(b)

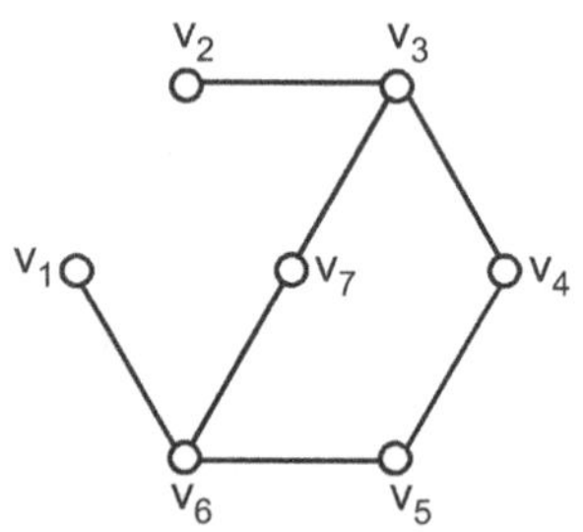

ie. T + (v_7, v_3)

(c)

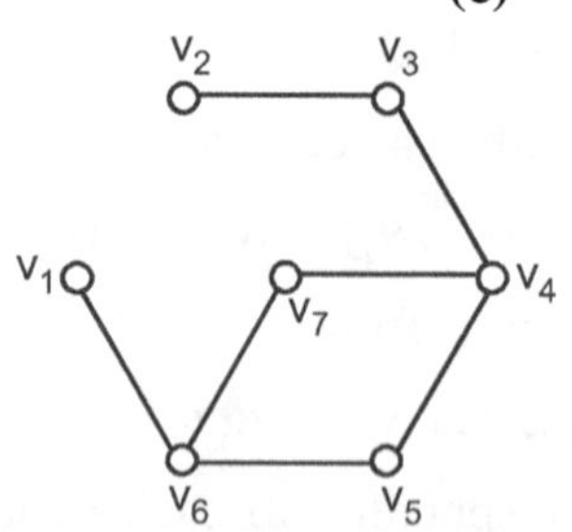

ie. T + (v_4, v_7)

(d)

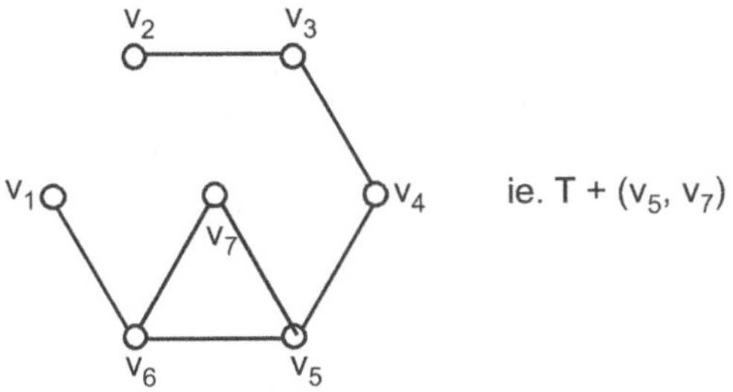

(e)

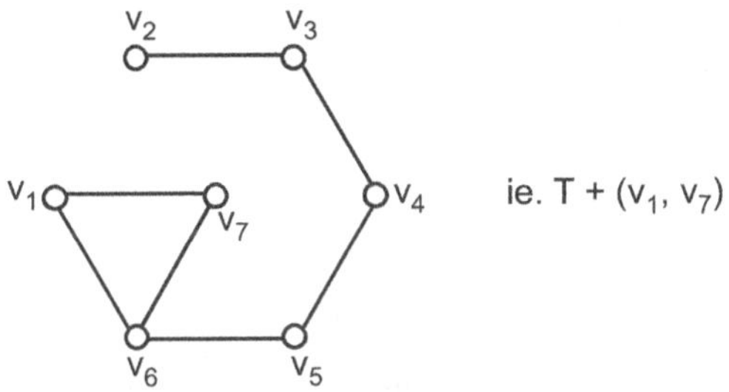

(f)

Fig. 4.53

Example 4.18 : *Can you draw a binary tree on 7 vertices and height 2 ? Justify.*

Solution : Yes.

Since a binary tree with height 2 contains atmost $2^0 + 2^1 + 2^2 = 7$ vertices.

This shown as below.

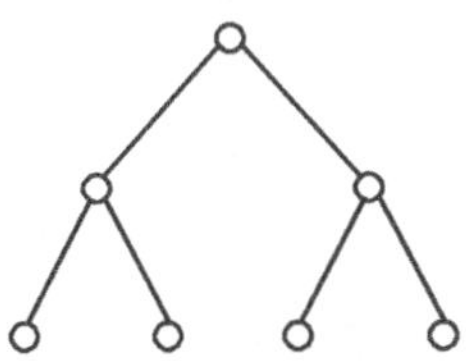

Fig. 4.54

Example 4.19 : *Can you draw a binary tree with 17 vertices of height 3 ? Justify.*

Solution : No.

Since a binary tree with height 3 contains at most $2^0 + 2^1 + 2^2 + 2^3 =$ 15 vertices

This shown as below.

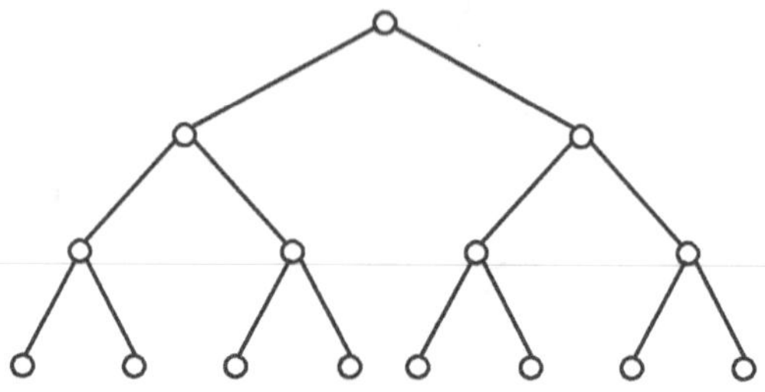

Fig. 4.55

Example 4.20 : *How many leaves does a complete binary tree on 100 vertices have ?*

Solution : In a binary rooted tree, there is only one vertex of degree even, particularly of degree 2, other vertices of degree 3 and 1. By handshaking lemma, sum of degrees must be even.

$\therefore$ Total number of vertices in binary tree are odd always.

$\therefore$ There does not exist a binary tree on 100 vertices.

Example 4.21 : *A chain letter starts when a person sends a letter to five others. Each person who receives the letter either it to 5 others or to none. Suppose 1000 people send out the letters before the chain ends on no are receives more than one letter. How many people receive the letter, but do not send out ?*

Solution : We have tree with each middle vertex (person) and root has five childrens to whom he sends letter. If this tree has height 5 then

$$5^0 + 5^1 + 5^2 + 5^3 + 5^4 < 1000 \text{ and } 5^0 + 5^1 + 5^2 + 5^3 + 5^4 + 5^5 > 1000$$

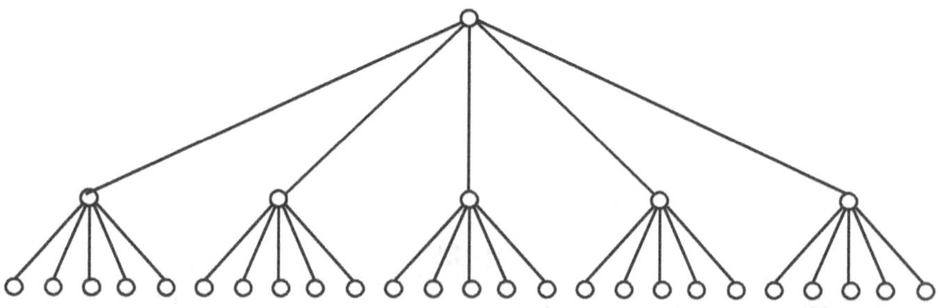

Fig. 5.56

Now upto level 4 there are $(5^4 + 5^3 + 5^2 + 5 + 1) = 781$ people.

Now at level five, we have persons receives letter but do not send iff. They are

$$1000 - 781 = 219 \text{ in number}$$

Think Over It

A tree with n vertices is called **graceful** if its vertices can be labeled with the integers 1, 2, …, n such that the absolute values of the difference of the labels of adjacent vertices are all different.

1. Show that the following trees are graceful.

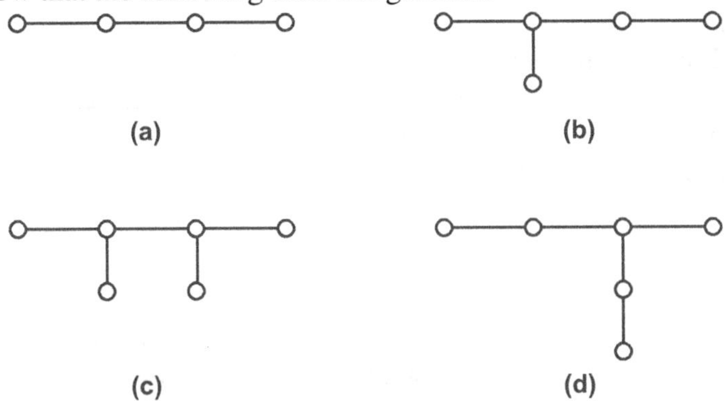

Fig. 4.57

A **caterpillar** is a tree that contains a simple path such that every vertex not contained in this path is adjacent to a vertex in the path.

2. Which graphs from (a), (b), (c), (d) are caterpillars ?
3. How many non-isomorphic caterpillars are there with six vertices ?

Summary

1. A **tree** is a connected undirected graph with no simple circuits.
2. An undirected graph is a tree if and only if there is a unique simple path between any two of its vertices.
3. A **rooted tree** is a tree in which one vertex has been designated as the root and every edge is directed away from the root.
4. A tree with n vertices has n – 1 edges.
5. A full m-ary tree with i internal vertices contains n = mi + 1 vertices.
6. There are at most m^h leaves in an m-ary tree of height h.
7. A sorting algorithm based an binary comparisons requires at least [log n!] comparisons.

8. Procedures for systematically visiting every vertex of an ordered rooted tree and called **traversal algorithms.**
9. In a rooted tree with root r, the **preorder traversal** begins by visiting r. It continues by traversing subtrees T_1, T_2, …, T_n in preorder from left to right.
10. In a rooted tree with root r, the **inorder traversal** begins by traversing subtree T_1 in order, then visiting r, traversing T_2 in inorder, …, finally T_n in inorder (T_1, T_2, …, T_n are subtrees from left to right).
11. Let T be an ordered rooted tree with root r and T_1, T_2, …, T_n are subtrees at r from left to right. The **postorder traversal** begins by traversing T_1 in postorder, then T_2 in postorder, …, then T_n in postorder, and ends by visiting r.
12. Let G be a simple graph. A **spanning tree** of G is a subgraph of G that is a tree containing every vertex of G.
13. A simple graph is connected if and only if it has a spanning tree.
14. A minimum spanning tree in a connected weighted graph is a spanning tree that has the smallest possible sum of weights of its edges.

Exercise

[A] Say True or False : Justify !

1. Every graph has atleast one spanning tree.
2. Any graph G(V, E) has atmost ${}^{|E|}C_{|V|-1}$ number of spanning tree.
3. There is binary rooted tree on 10 vertices.
4. Maximum height of a binary tree with 25 vertices is 12.
5. Minimally connected subgraph of a connected graph is tree.
6. For any connected graph, rank + nullity = total number of edges.
7. The rank of a connected graph is independent of spanning trees of graph.
8. Kruskal's algorithm is a greedy algorithm.
9. Every tree is bipartite graph.
10. Complete bipartite graphs which are trees are only $k_{1,\,n}$ for any $n \in \mathbb{N}$.
11. A graph with n vertices and e edges; $e = n - 1$; need not be a tree.

[B] Multiple Choice Questions : Choose the Correct Alternative

1. Which of the following choices is not a spanning tree of a graph ?

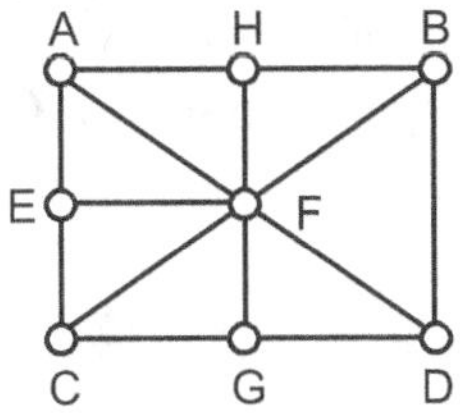

(a) 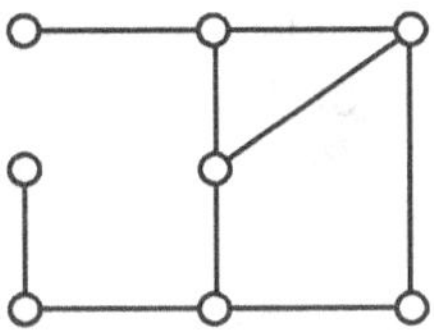

(b) 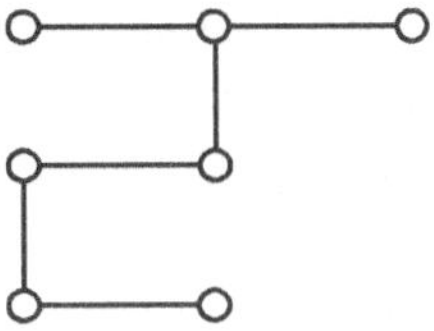

(c) 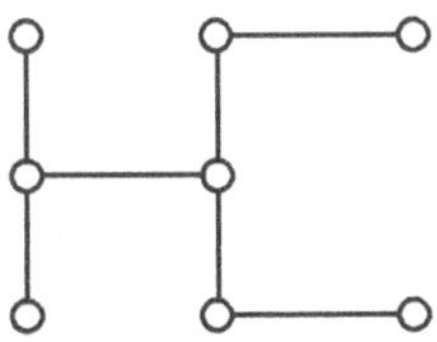

(d) 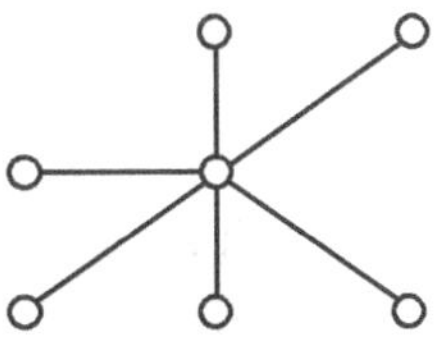

2. Examine the weighted graph. If the graph shows cost in rupees associated with each edge, what is the minimum cost spanning tree for the graph ?

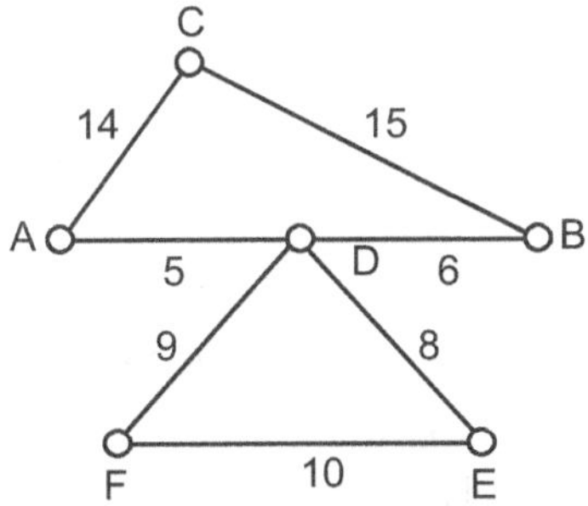

(a) 43 (b) 42
(c) 38 (d) 20

3. The idea of Kruskal's algorithm is to always pick the smallest edge but avoid creating any cycle. The statement is
(a) True (b) False
(c) Sometimes true (d) None of these

4. In a tree every edge is
(a) bridge (b) a part of cycle
(c) not a bridge (d) none of these

5. A connected subgraph H of G that consists all vertices of G, but not any cycle then
   (a) H is a spanning tree of G
   (b) H is tree but not a spanning tree of G
   (c) H is not a tree itself
   (d) None of these
6. Let H is subgraph of tree T, which forms center of T, then
   (a) H consist single vertex
   (b) H contains only one edge
   (c) Both (a) and (b) are true
   (d) None of these
7. In which case the graph G(V, E) is a tree
   (a) $|V| = |E|$
   (b) $|V| > |E|$
   (c) $|V| = |E| - 1$
   (d) $|E| = |V| - 1$
8. Let v is vertex of tree T. It is cut vertex iff
   (a) $d(v) \geq 2$
   (b) $d(v) \geq 3$
   (c) $d(v) = 1$
   (d) $d(v) = 0$
9. Complete graph k_n has a_n number of spanning trees then a_n satisfies
   (a) $a_n = a_{n-1} + n$
   (b) $a_n = a_{n-1} + a_{n-2}$
   (c) $a_n = a_n^2$
   (d) None of these
10. Number of spanning tree of graph 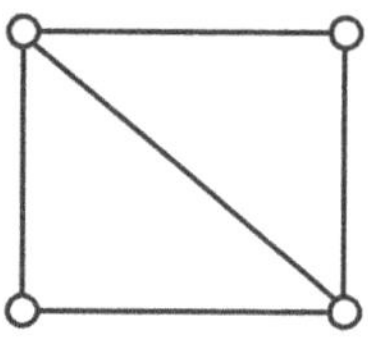 upto isomorphism are
   (a) 2
   (b) 3
   (c) 4
   (d) 5
11. A tree having 35 vertices has
   25 vertices of degree 1,
   2 vertices of degree 2,
   3 vertices of degree 4,
   1 vertex of degree 5,
   2 vertices of degree 6,
   2 vertices of degree x.
   Then the value of x is
   (a) 4
   (b) 5
   (c) 6
   (d) 8

[C] Theory Questions :

1. Show that a connected graph with n vertices and n – 1 edges is cycle free.
2. Show that, if G is a tree then it is minimally connected.
3. Show that center of any tree consists of atmost two vertices.
4. Show that every connected graph has a spanning tree.
5. State and prove rank-nullity theorem for a connected graph.
6. Prove that every circuit in a connected graph G has even number of edges in common with every cut set of G.
7. Prove that a binary rooted tree has odd number of vertices.
8. Let T be a binary tree with n vertices then show that height of T always greater than or equal to $\log_2 (n + 1) - 1$.
9. Prove that the spanning tree given by Kruskal's algorithm has the minimum of weights of all spanning tree in a weighted connected graph.
10. Determine the order in which a preorder traversal visits the vertices of the given ordered rooted tree.

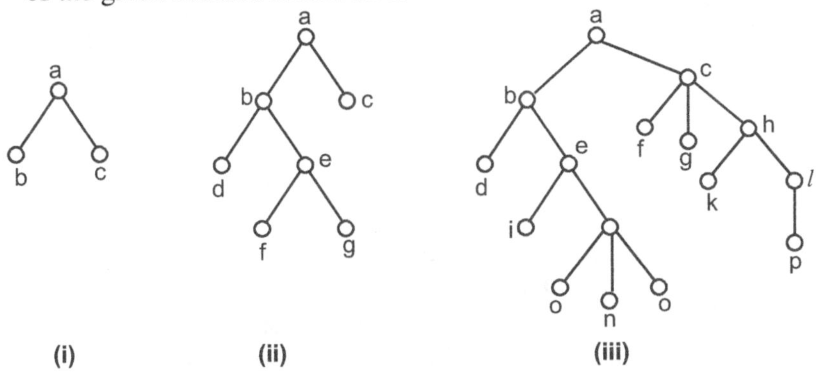

Fig. 4.58

11. In which order are the vertices of the ordered rooted tree in above example visited using an inorder traversal ?
12. In which order are the vertices of the ordered rooted tree in Ex. 1 Visited using a postorder traversal ?
13. (a) Represent the expression
    $((x + 2) \uparrow 3) \times (4 - (3 + x)) - 5$ using a binary tree, write this expression in
    (b) prefix notation
    (c) postfix notation
    (d) infix notation

14. Above example replace expression (x + xy) + (x/y).
15. Draw the ordered rooted tree corresponding to each of these arithmetic expressions written in prefix notation. Then write each expression using infix notation.
    (a) + * + – 5 3 2 1 4 (b) ↑ + 2 3 – 5 1
    (c) * 1 9 3 + * 2 4 – 7 6
16. What is the value of each of these postfix expressions ?
    (a) 5 2 1 – – 3 1 4 + + *
    (b) 9 3 / 5 + 7 2 – *
    (c) 3 2 * 2 ↑ 5 3 – 8 4 / * –
17. Use Prim's algorithm to find a minimum spanning tree for the given weighted graph.

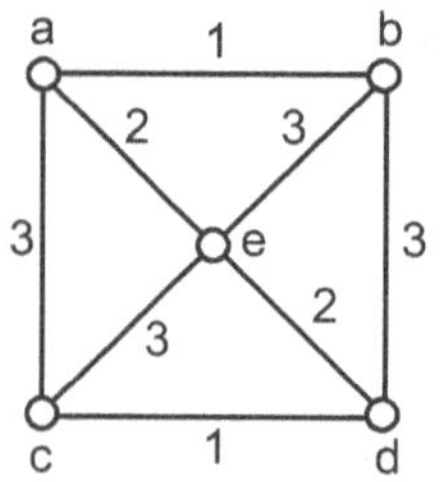

(a)

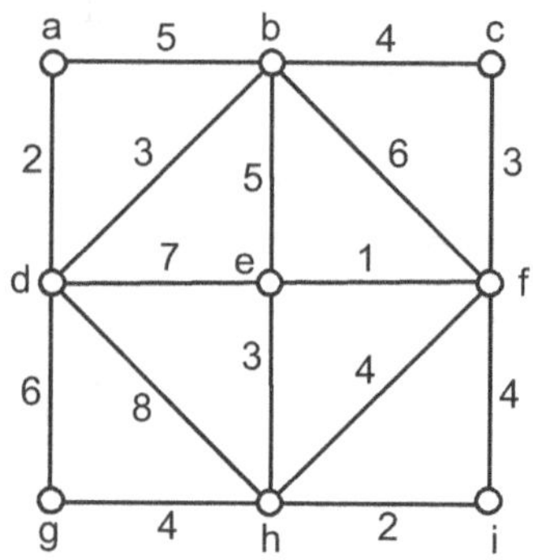

(b)

Fig. 4.59

[D] Numerical Problems :

1. A tree has 2 vertices of degree 2, 1 vertex of degree 3 and 3 vertices of degree 4. Find the number of vertices of degree 1.
2. A tree has n_2 vertices of degree 2, n_3 vertices of degree 3, … and n_k vertices of degree k.
   Find the number of vertices of degree 1.
3. How many possible trees are there with 6 vertices; out of which 3 are pendant vertices ? Draw them.
4. Draw all possible non-isomorphic trees on :
   (a) 4 vertices (b) 5 vertices (c) 6 vertices
5. Prove that the maximum number of pendant vertices in an n-vertex tree is n – 1.
6. G is a connected graph such that d (v) ≥ 2 for every vertex v in G. Prove that G contains a circuit.

7. Prove that every tree is a bipartite graph. State which trees are complete bipartite graphs.
8. Prove that a vertex v of a tree is a cut vertex iff d(v) > 1.
9. Find the eccentricity of each vertex of the tree given below. Hence, find its centre.

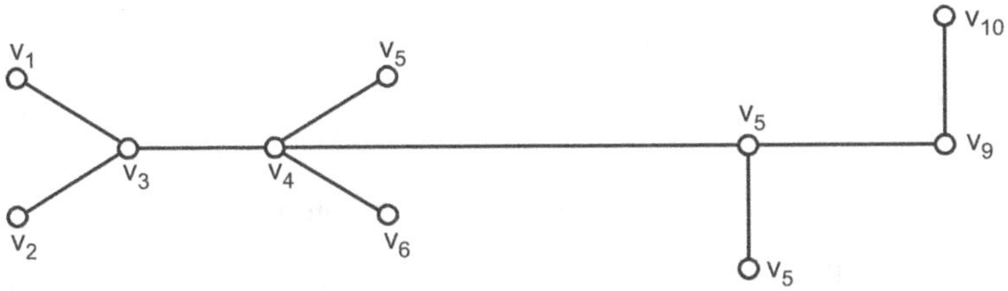

Fig. 4.60

10. Find the degree and eccentricity of each vertex of the tree given below. Find its centre by two methods.

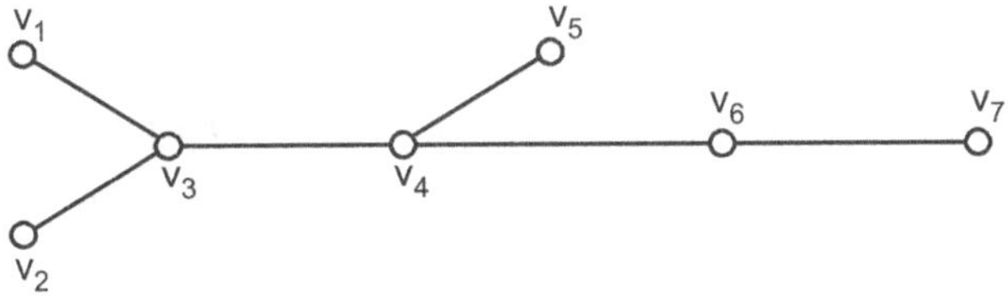

Fig. 4.61

11. Find all spanning trees of the graph given below.

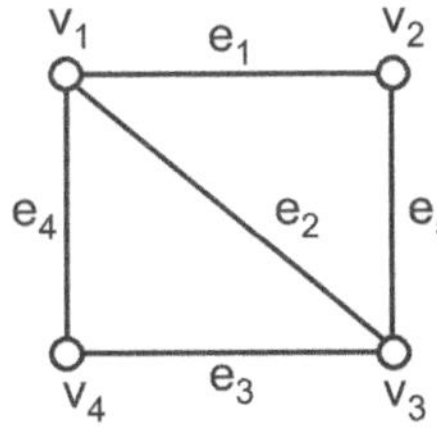

Fig. 4.62

12. Draw all possible spanning trees of the following graph.

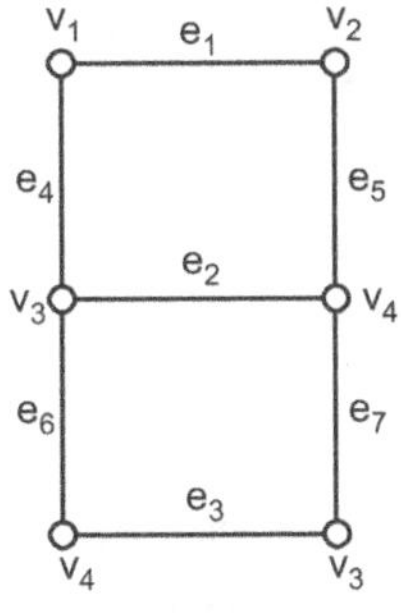

Fig. 4.63

13. Draw two spanning trees of Peterson's graph.
14. Prove that every connected graph has at least one spanning tree.
15. In a connected graph G, prove
    (a) e is a bridge ⇔ e is in every spanning tree of G
    (b) e is a loop ⇔ e is not in any spanning tree of G.
16. Prove that a connected graph having exactly one spanning tree is a tree.
17. What is the nullity of a complete graph k_n on n vertices ?
18. Let T and T' be two spanning trees of a connected graph G. Suppose that an edge x is in T but not in T'. Show that there is an edge y in T' but not in T such that $(T - x) \cup y$ and $(T' - y) \cup x$ are both spanning trees of G.
19. Find all fundamental circuits and fundamental cutsets of connected graph G w.r.t. the given spanning tree T given below :

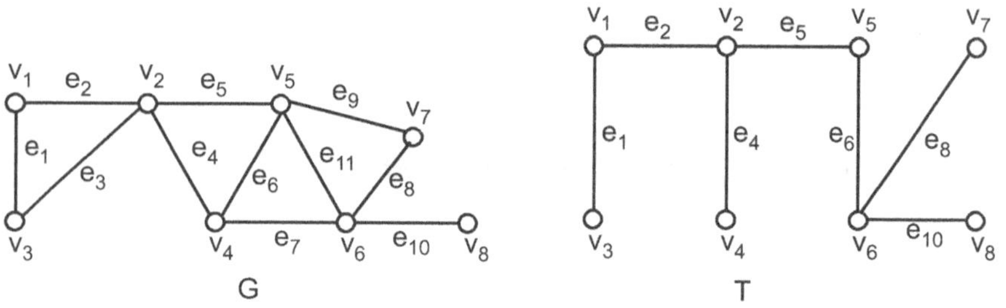

(a)

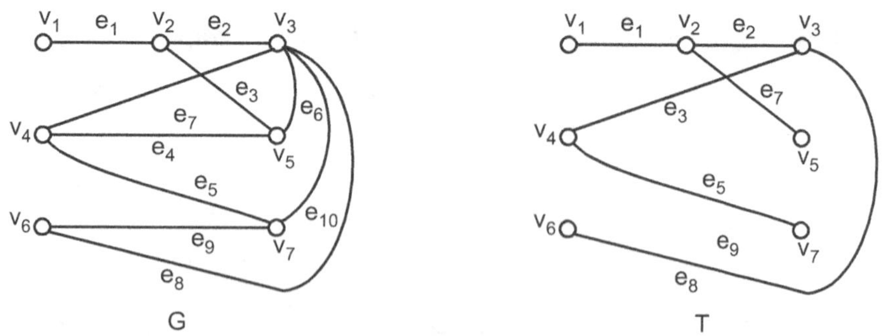

(b)

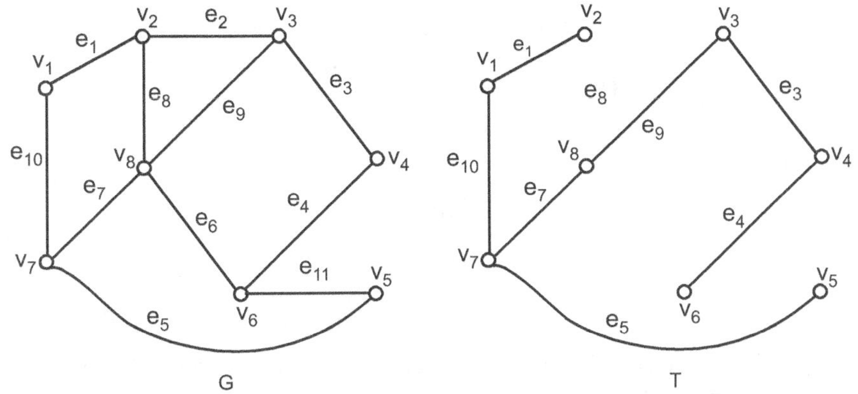

(c)

Fig. 4.64

20. Draw binary trees of 21 vertices with maximum height and minimum height.
21. What is the height of a balanced binary tree with 51 vertices ?
22. Show that the sum of the level numbers of all l leaves in a binary tree is at least $l \log_2 l$ and hence the average leaf level is at least $\log_2 l$.
23. By using Kruskal's algorithm, find a shortest spanning tree of the given graph. State the weight of the shortest spanning tree.

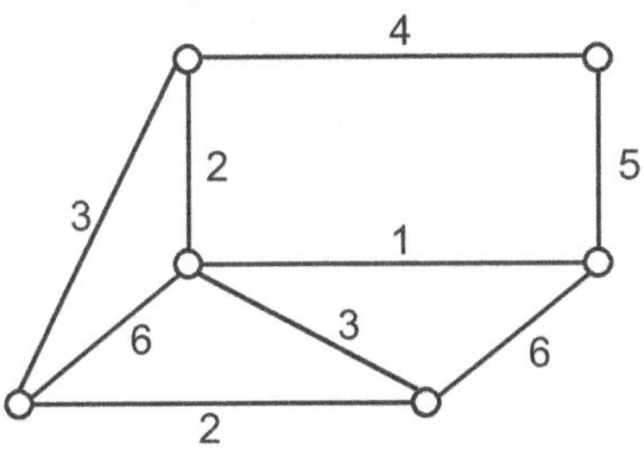

(a)

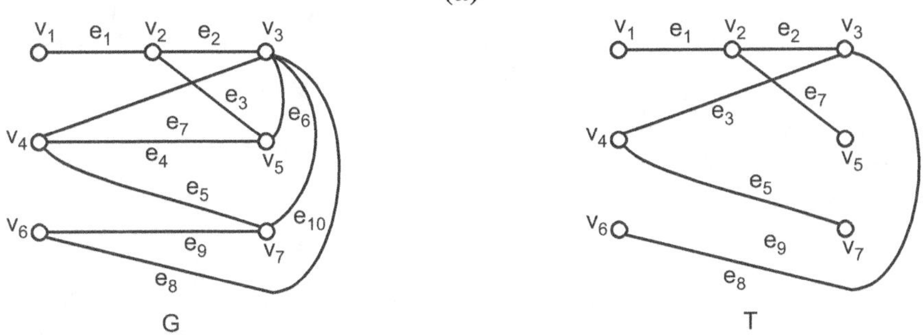

(b)

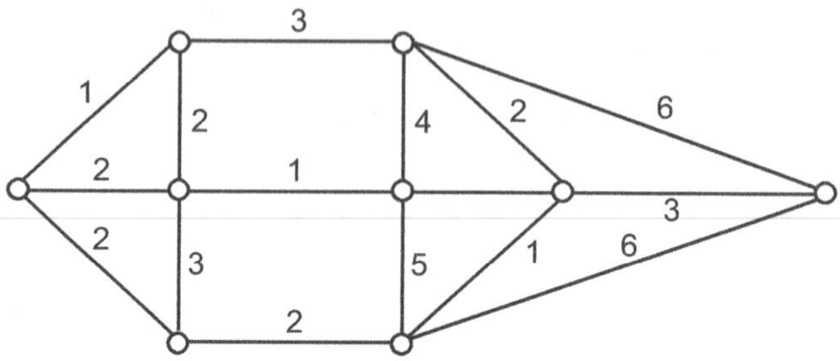

(c)

Fig. 4.65

24. Let T be a tree with $n \geq 4$ vertices and v be a vertex of maximum degree in T. Show that T is a path if and only if $d(v) = 2$.
25. A tree T with 50 end vertices has equal number of vertices of degree 2, 3, 4, 5 and there are no vertices of degree more than 5. Find the number of vertices of T.

Answers

[A] (1) False (2) True (3) False (4) True (5) True (6) True (7) True (8) True (9) True (10) True (11) True

[B] (1) - (a) (2) - (b) (3) - (a) (4) - (a) (5) - (a) (6) - (c) (7) - (c) (8) - (a) (9) - (a) (10) - (a) (11) - (b)

[C] 1. 9

2. $n_3 + 2n_4 + \ldots + (k - 2)\, n_k + 2$.

3.

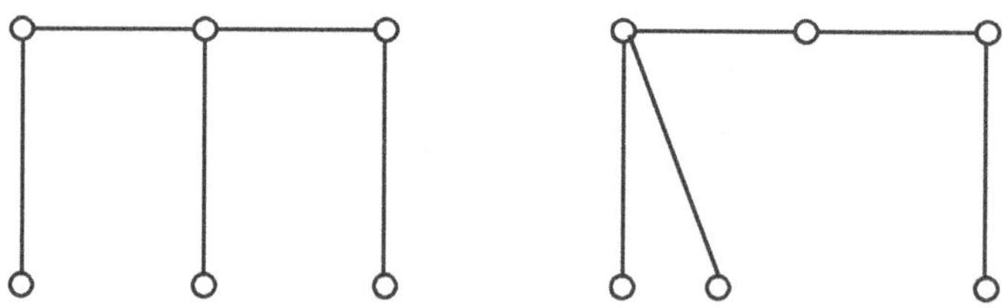

Fig. 4.66

4. (a)

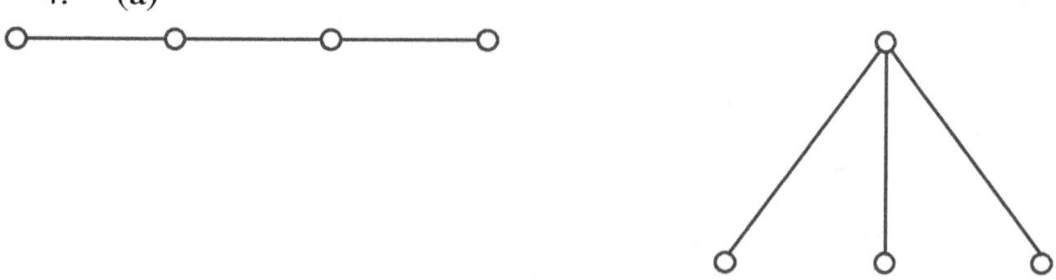

Fig. 4.67 (a)

(b)

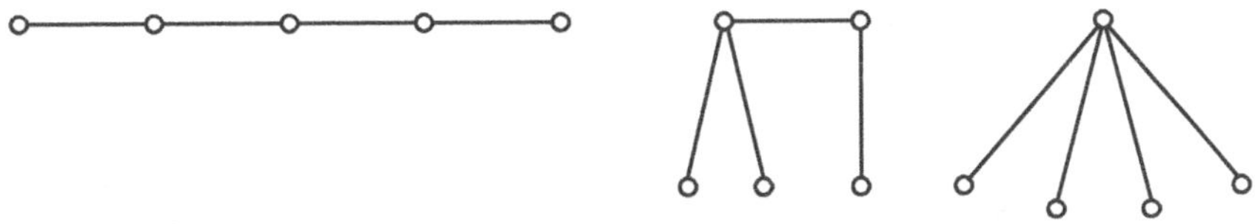

Fig. 4.67 (b)

(c)

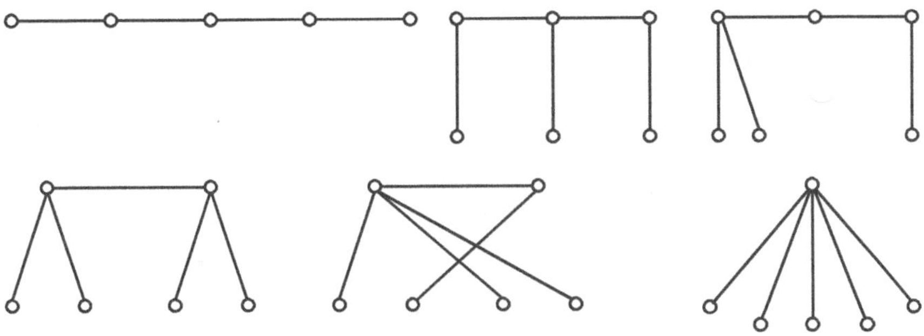

Fig. 4.67 (c)

7. The star graph $k_{1,\,n}$ is a complete bipartite graph.

9. $E(v_1) = 5$, $E(v_2) = 5$, $E(v_3) = 4$, $E(v_4) = 3$, $E(v_5) = 4$, $E(v_6) = 4$, $E(v_7) = 3$, $E(v_8) = 4$, $E(v_9) = 5$, $E(v_{10}) = 5$.

   Centre is

Fig. 4.68

10. $d(v_1) = 1$, $d(v_2) = 1$, $d(v_3) = 3$, $d(v_4) = 3$, $d(v_5) = 1$, $d(v_6) = 2$,

    $d(v_7) = 1$

    $E(v_1) = 4$, $E(v_2) = 4$, $E(v_3) = 3$, $E(v_4) = 2$, $E(v_5) = 3$, $E(v_6) = 3$,

    $E(v_7) = 4$.

    Centre is $^{o}v_4$.

11.

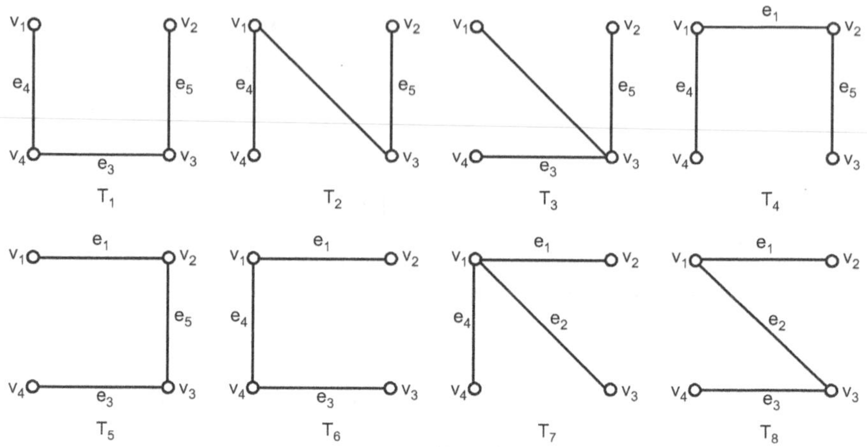

Fig. 4.69

12.

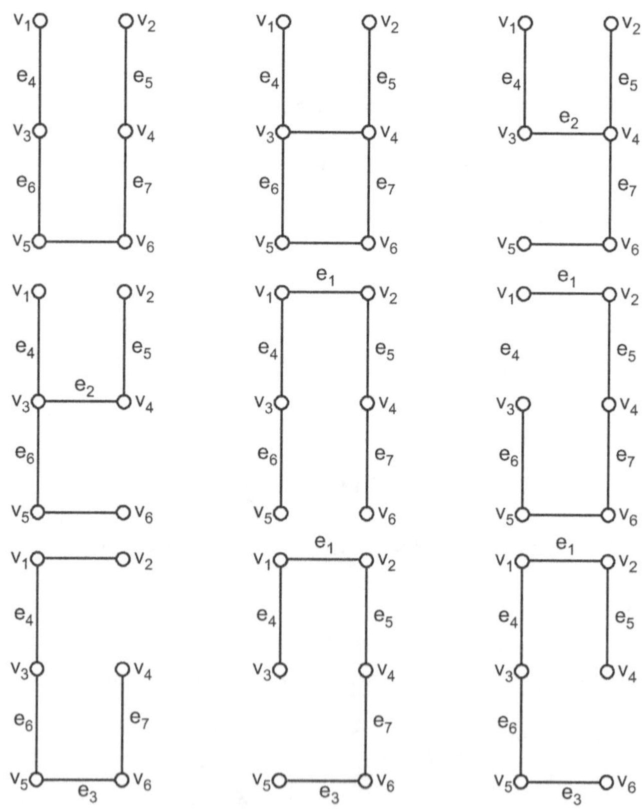

Fig. 4.70 (a)

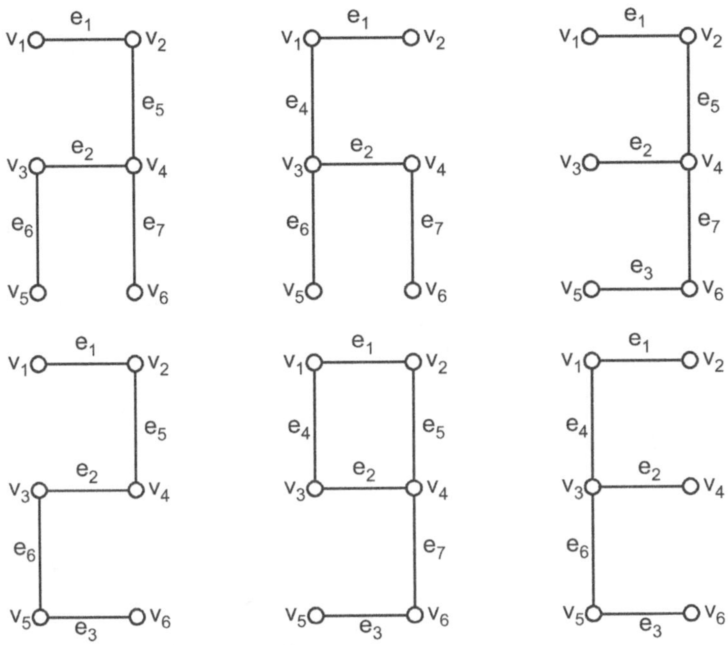

Fig. 4.70 (b)

17. $\frac{(n-1)\ (n-2)}{2}$.

20.

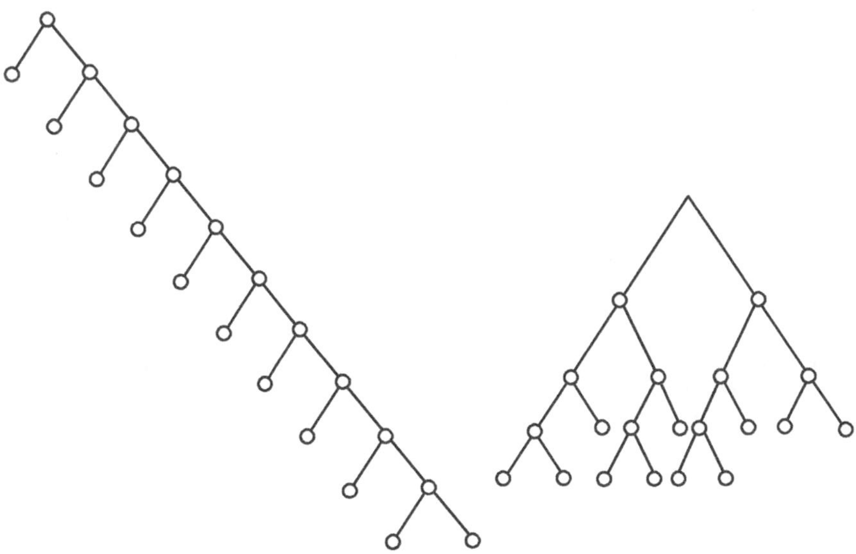

Fig. 4.71

21. 5

23. (a)

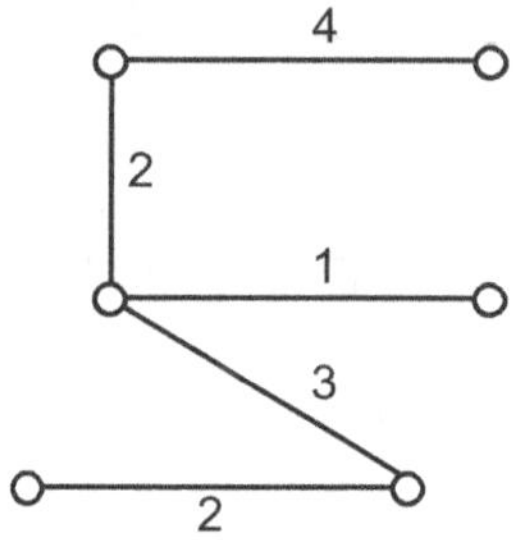

Fig. 4.72 (a) : W = 12

(b)

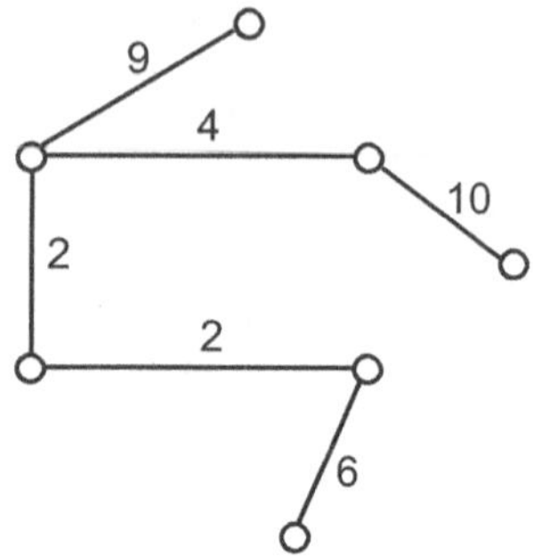

Fig. 4.72 (b) : W = 33

(c)

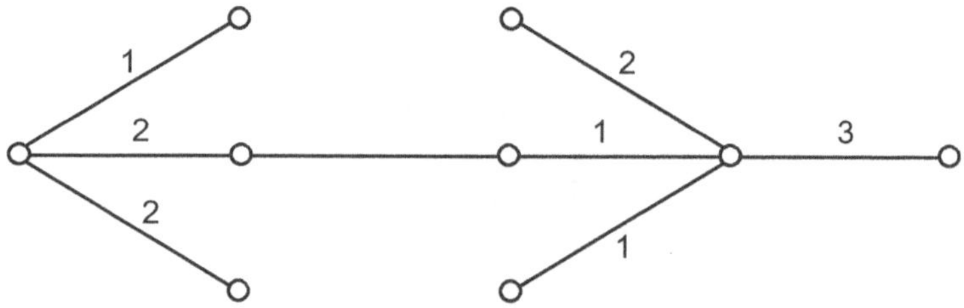

Fig. 4.72 (c) : W = 13

25. 82

✍✍✍

Appendix

Practical Problems

(A) Graphs - I

Q.1. (a) Draw the graph whose incidence matrix is given below :

$$I(G) = \begin{pmatrix} 1 & 0 & 1 & 0 & 0 & 0 \\ 1 & 1 & 0 & 1 & 0 & 0 \\ 0 & 1 & 1 & 1 & 1 & 1 \\ 0 & 0 & 0 & 0 & 1 & 1 \end{pmatrix}$$

(b) Draw the graph represented by the adjacency matrix :

$$A(G) = \begin{pmatrix} 0 & 1 & 2 & 2 & 0 \\ 1 & 0 & 1 & 0 & 0 \\ 2 & 1 & 0 & 1 & 1 \\ 2 & 0 & 1 & 0 & 1 \\ 0 & 0 & 1 & 1 & 2 \end{pmatrix}$$

Q.2. Which is the smallest integer n such that the complete graph K_n has at least 55 edges ?

Q.3. Draw the following types of graphs :

(a) 4 - Regular graph (Two examples).

(b) Complete graph K_6 and K_5.

Q.4. Does there exist a simple graph on five vertices with the following sequence of degrees of the vertices? If so, give an example of such a graph.

(a) 1, 1, 1, 2, 3 (b) 1, 2, 2, 4, 5 (c) 1, 2, 2, 2, 4

Q.5. Draw the graphs :

(a) K_7 (b) W_7 (c) Q_4

Q.6. Determine whether or not the following graphs are bipartite.

(a)

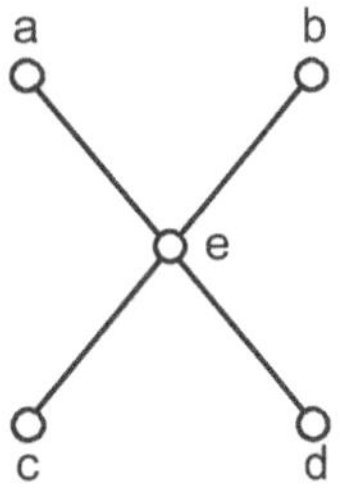

Fig. 1

(b)

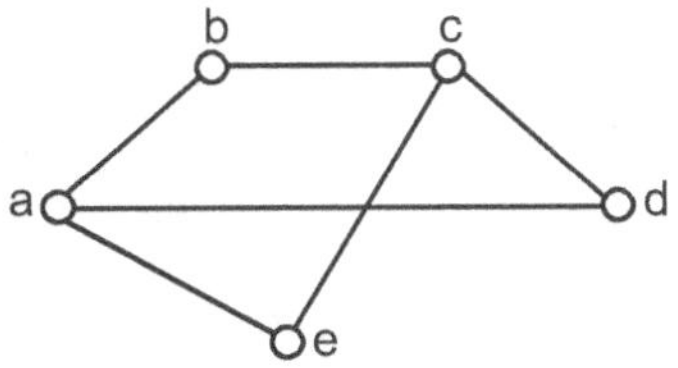

Fig. 2

(B) Graphs - II

Q.1. Draw a graph with the following adjacency matrix :

(a) $\begin{bmatrix} 0 & 0 & 1 & 1 \\ 0 & 0 & 1 & 0 \\ 1 & 1 & 0 & 1 \\ 1 & 1 & 1 & 0 \end{bmatrix}$ (b) $\begin{bmatrix} 1 & 1 & 1 & 0 \\ 0 & 0 & 1 & 0 \\ 1 & 0 & 1 & 0 \\ 1 & 1 & 1 & 0 \end{bmatrix}$

Q.2. Represent the given graph using an adjacency matrix.

(a)

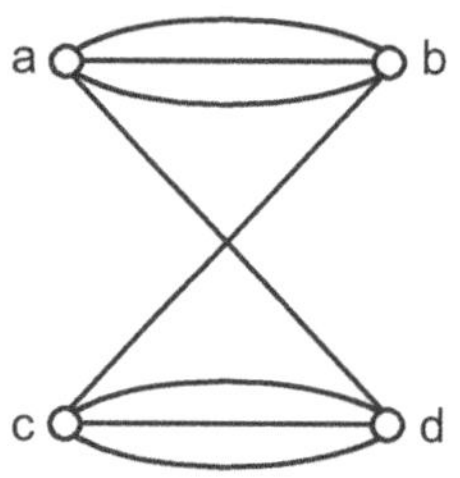

Fig. 1

(b)

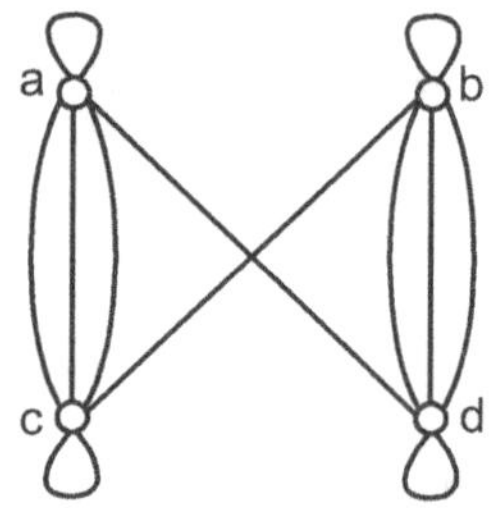

Fig. 2

Q.3. Draw an undirected graph represented by the given adjacency matrix.

(a) $\begin{bmatrix} 1 & 2 & 0 & 1 \\ 2 & 0 & 3 & 0 \\ 0 & 3 & 1 & 1 \\ 1 & 0 & 1 & 0 \end{bmatrix}$ (b) $\begin{bmatrix} 0 & 1 & 3 & 0 & 4 \\ 1 & 2 & 1 & 3 & 0 \\ 3 & 1 & 1 & 0 & 1 \\ 0 & 3 & 0 & 0 & 2 \\ 4 & 0 & 1 & 2 & 3 \end{bmatrix}$

Q.4. Determine whether the given pair of graphs is isomorphic. Exhibit an isomorphism or provide a rigorous argument that none exists.

(a)

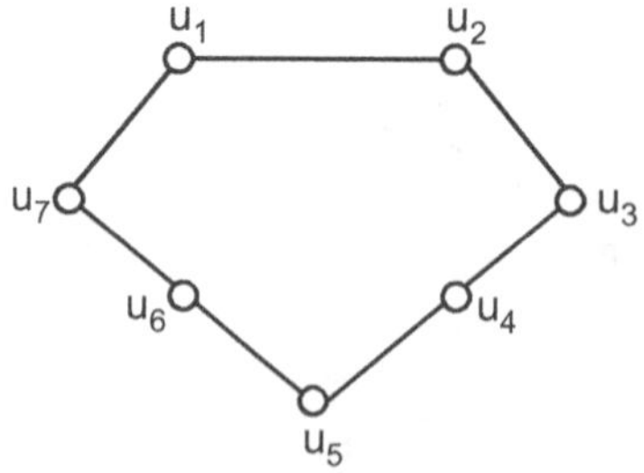

Fig. 3

(b)

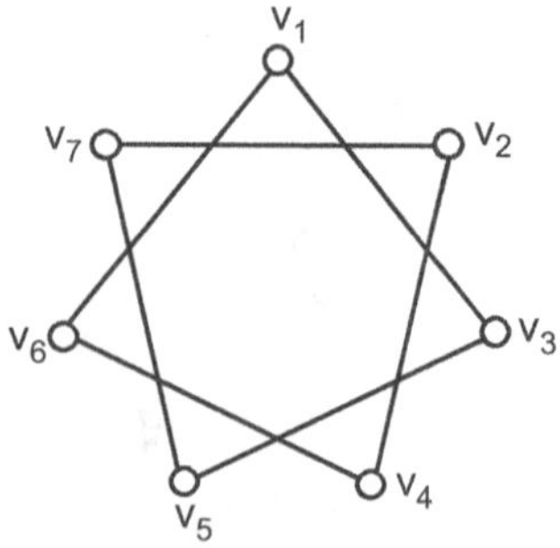

Fig. 4

Q.5. How many non-isomorphic simple graphs are there with n vertices, when n is

(a) 2 ? (b) 3 ? (c) 4 ?

Q.6. Are the simple graphs with the following adjacency matrices isomorphic ?

(a) $\begin{bmatrix} 0 & 0 & 1 \\ 0 & 0 & 1 \\ 1 & 1 & 0 \end{bmatrix}, \begin{bmatrix} 0 & 1 & 1 \\ 1 & 0 & 0 \\ 1 & 0 & 0 \end{bmatrix}$

(b) $\begin{bmatrix} 0 & 1 & 0 & 1 \\ 1 & 0 & 0 & 1 \\ 0 & 0 & 0 & 1 \\ 1 & 1 & 1 & 0 \end{bmatrix}, \begin{bmatrix} 0 & 1 & 1 & 1 \\ 1 & 0 & 0 & 1 \\ 1 & 0 & 0 & 1 \\ 1 & 1 & 1 & 0 \end{bmatrix}$

(C) Connected Graphs

Q.1. Find the maximum edge connectivity and the maximum vertex connectivity that can be achieved in graphs with :

(a) 5 vertices and 3 edges

(b) 8 vertices and 16 edges

Q.2. Consider the graph G given below.

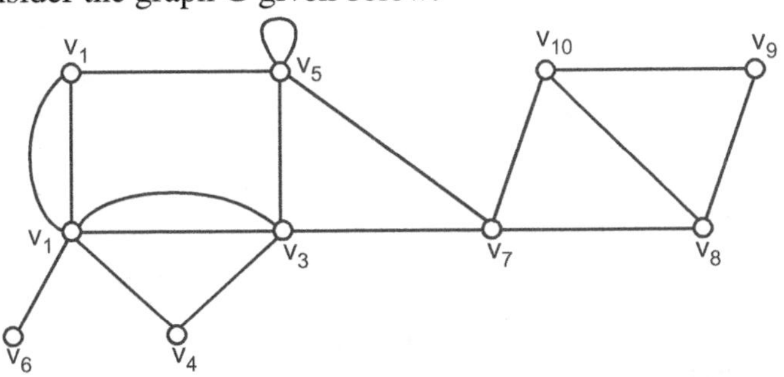

Fig. 1

(a) Find a walk of length 5.

(b) A path of length 9.

(c) Circuits of lengths 5, 6 and 8.

Q.3. Let V = {0, 1, 2, …, 20} be the vertex set of a graph G. An edge between x and y exists when x – y is divisible by 5. Draw the graph G. Explain why G is not connected. What do the components of G represent ?

Q.4. Using Dijkstra's algorithm, find the shortest path from 'a' to each of the remaining vertices in the weighted connected graphs given below.

(a)

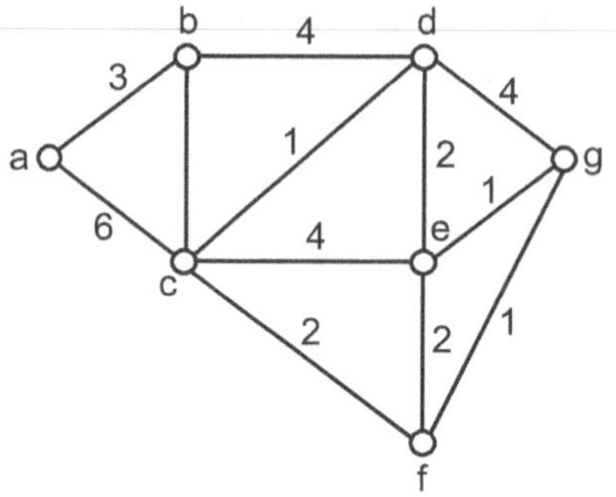

Fig. 2

(b)

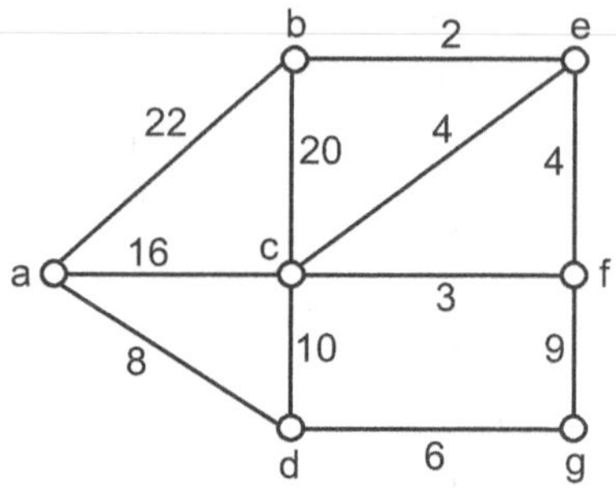

Fig. 3

(D) Euler and Hamilton Path

Q.1. Determine whether the directed graph shown below has an Euler circuit. Construct an Euler circuit if one exists.

(a)

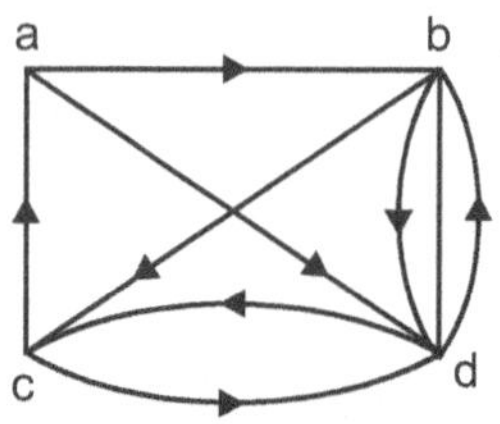

Fig. 1

(b)

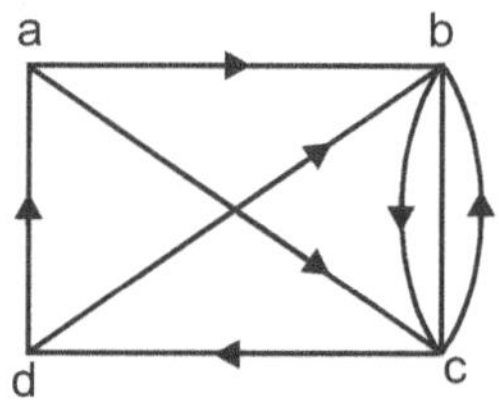

Fig. 2

Q.2. Determine whether the given graph has a Hamilton circuit. If it exists find such a circuit.

(a)

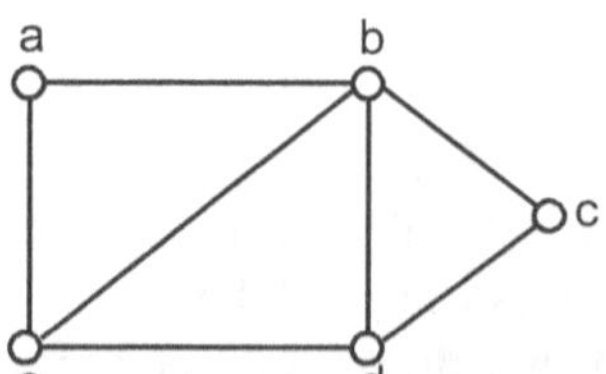

Fig. 3

(b)

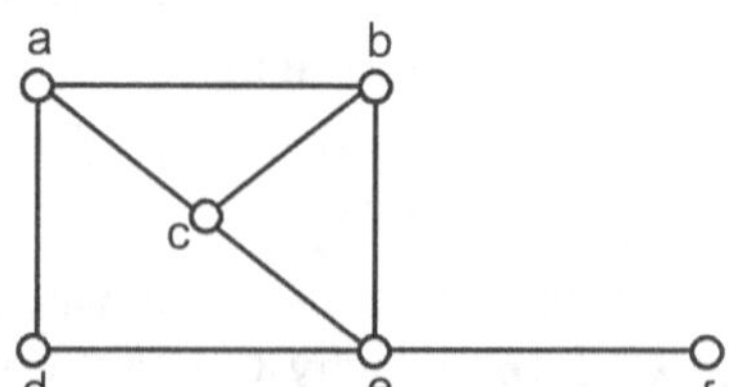

Fig. 4

Q.3. For which values of n do the following graphs have an Euler circuits?

(a) K_n (b) C_n

(c) W_n (d) Q_n

Q.4. Solve the travelling salesman problem for the following graph by finding the total weight of all Hamilton circuits and determining a circuit with minimum total weight.

(a)

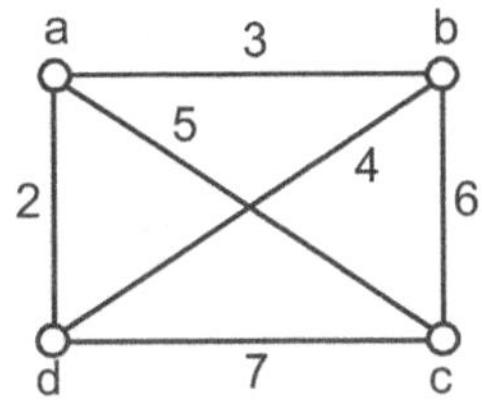

Fig. 5

(b)

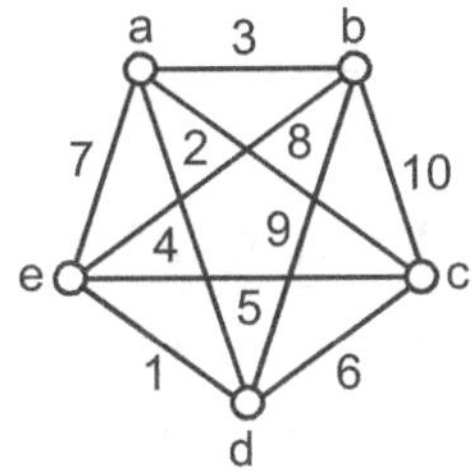

Fig. 6

Q.5. Apply Fleury's algorithm to find Eulerian tour in the graph.

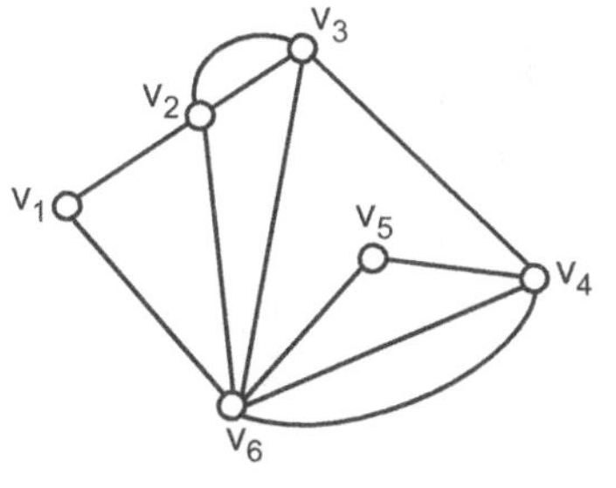

Fig. 7

(E) Trees

Q.1. Find the maximum and minimum height of a binary tree on 23 vertices and illustrate with examples.

Q.2. Draw all possible non-isomorphic trees on 7 vertices.

Q.3. Find all spanning trees of the graph given below.

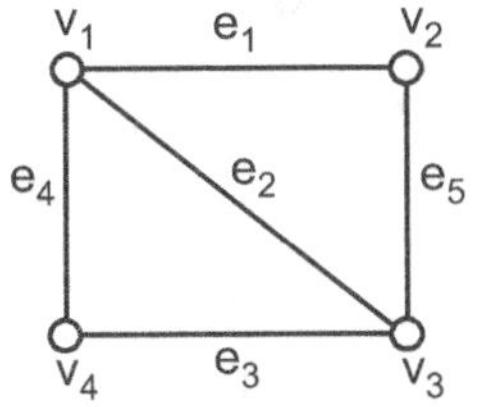

Fig. 1

Q.4. Find the eccentricity of each vertex of the tree given below. Hence, find its centre.

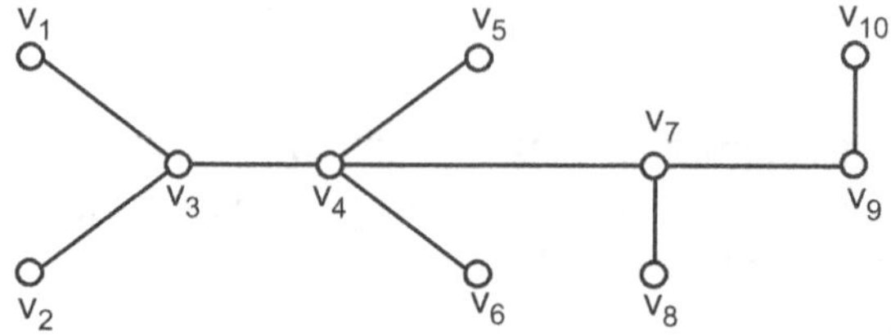

Fig. 2

(F) Kruskal's Algorithm and Binary Trees

Q.1. Determine the order in which a preorder traversal visits the vertices of the given ordered rooted tree.

(a)

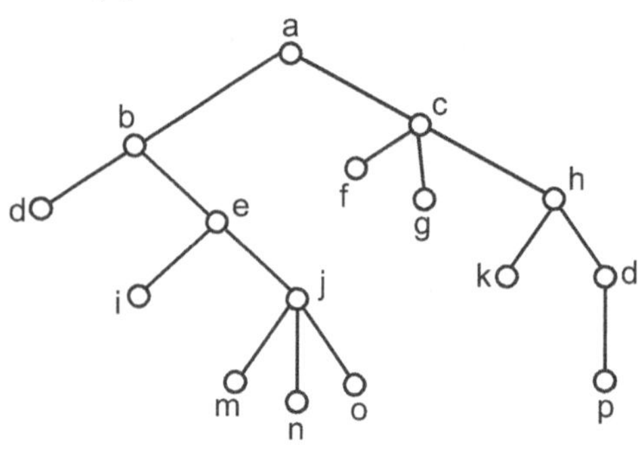

Fig. 1

(b)

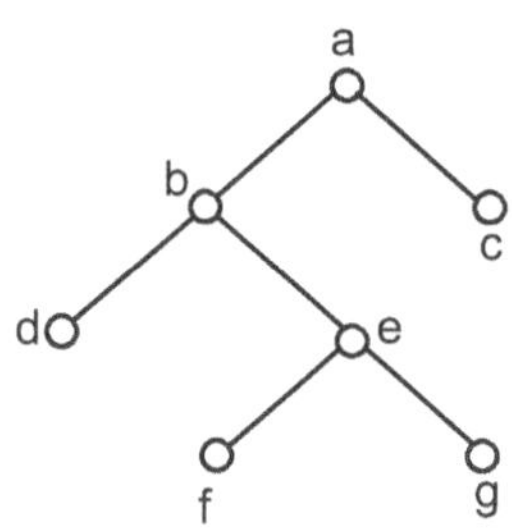

Fig. 2

Q.2. In which order are the vertices of the ordered rooted tree visited using an inorder traversal.

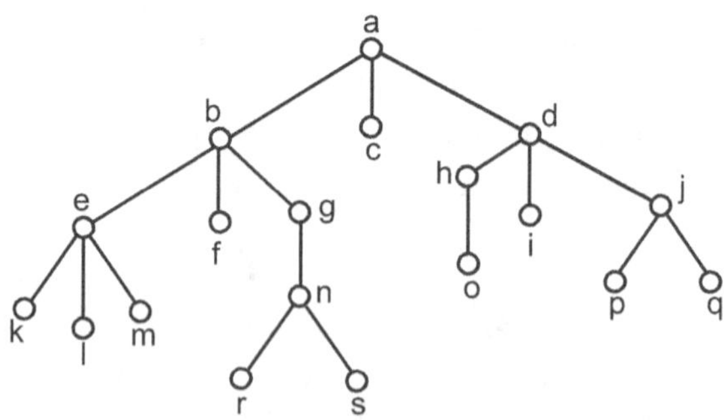

Fig. 3

Q.3. Represent the expression $((x + 2) \uparrow 3) * (y - (3 + x)) - 5$ using a binary tree.

Write this expression in :

(a) Prefix notation (b) Postfix notation

(c) Infix notation

Q.4. Draw the ordered rooted tree corresponding the following arithmetic expression written in prefix notation. Then write each expression using infix notation

(a) $+ * + - 53214$ (b) $\uparrow + 23 - 51$

Q.5. What is the value of the following postfix expressions ?

(a) $521 - - 314 + + *$ (b) $93/5 + 72 - *$

Q.6. Use prim's algorithm to find a minimum spanning tree for the following weighted graph.

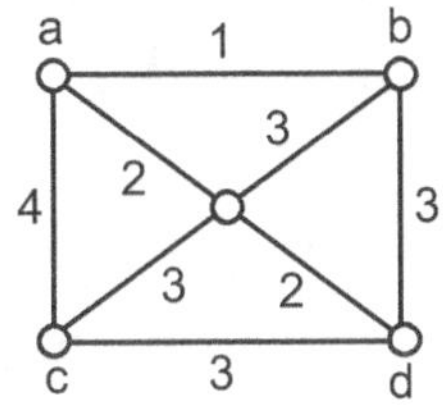

Fig. 4

Q.7. Use Kruskal's algorithm to find a minimum spanning tree for the following weighted graph.

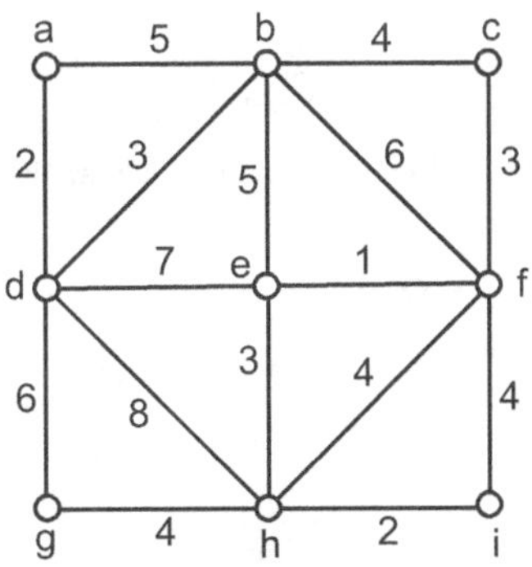

Fig. 5

✍ ✍ ✍

MODEL QUESTION PAPER - I

F.Y.B.Sc. Computer Science

MTC - 122 : Graph Theory

Time : 2 Hours **Total Marks : 35**

Note : 1. All questions are compulsory.
2. Figures to the right indicate full marks.

Q.1. Attempt any five of the following : **[5]**

(a) How many edges are there in a graph with 10 vertices each of degree 6 ?

(b) Draw a regular graph which is not complete.

(c) Find the vertex connectivity of the following graph.

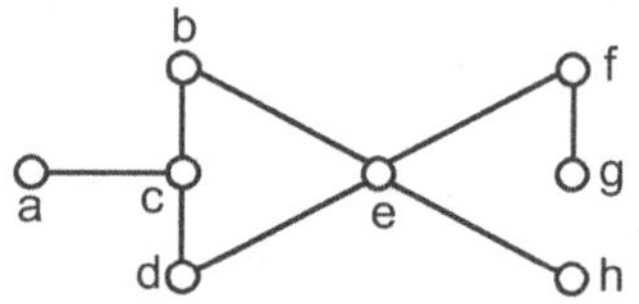

Fig. 1

(d) Find a spanning tree of the following graph.

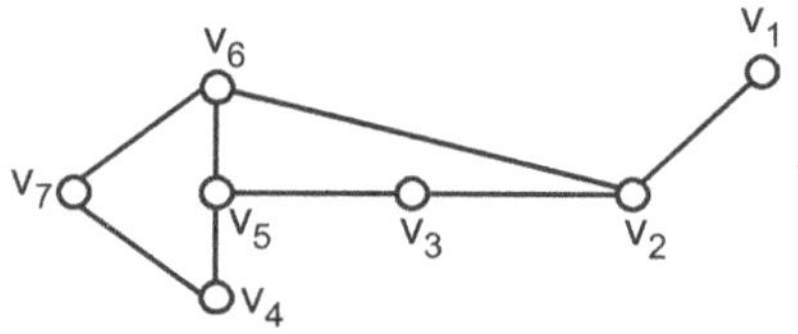

Fig. 2

(e) Find the degree and eccentricity of the vertex u_3 of the following graph.

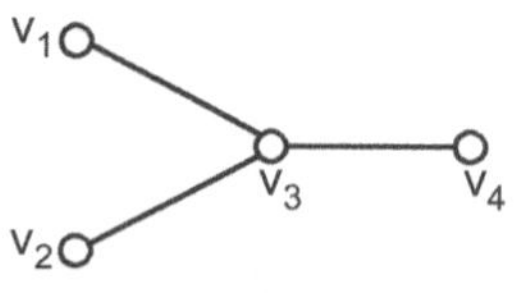

Fig. 3

(f) What is the ordered rooted tree that represents the expression $(x + y) \uparrow 2$?

(g) What is the value of the post fix expression 7 2 3 $*$ – ?

Q.2. Attempt any two of the following : [10]

(a) Find the adjacency matrix and incidence matrix of the graph.

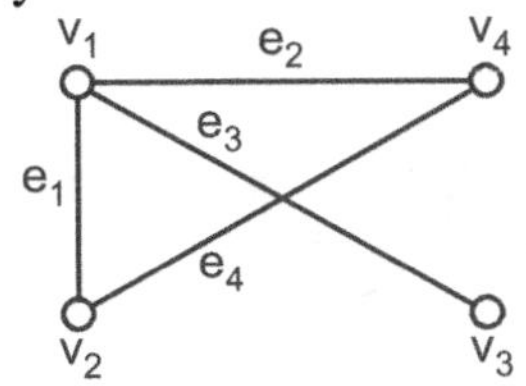

Fig. 4

(b) Let G be a connected graph with at least three vertices. Prove that, if G has a bridge then G has a cut vertex.

(c) Determine whether the following graphs are isomorphic.

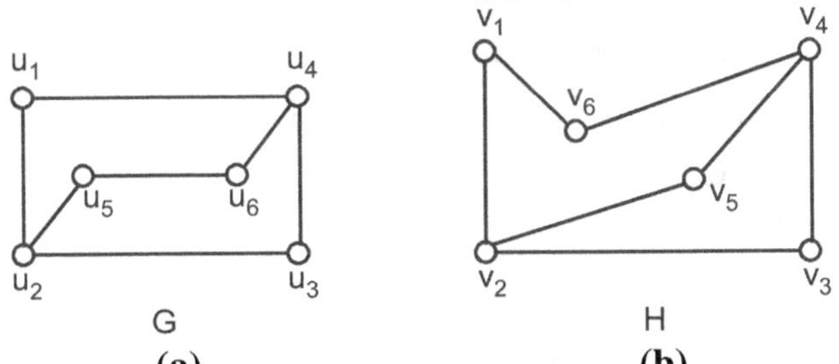

Fig. 5

Q.3. Attempt any two of the following : [10]

(a) Determine whether the directed graph shown below has an Euler circuit. Construct an Euler circuit if one exists.

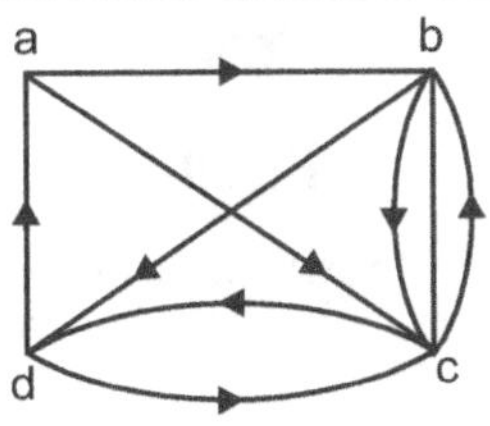

Fig. 6

(b) Determine whether the given graph has a Hamilton circuit. If it does, find such a circuit.

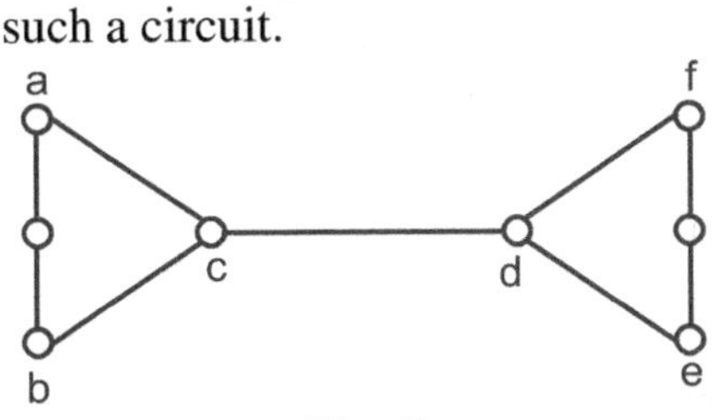

Fig. 7

(c) In which order does a preorder traversal visit the vertices in the ordered rooted tree T shown below.

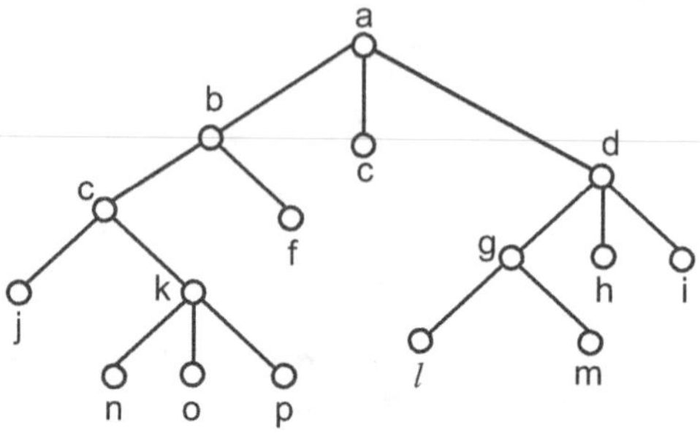

Fig. 8

Q.4. Attempt any one of the following : [10]

(a) By using Dijkstra's algorithm, find the shortest path from the vertex a to e.

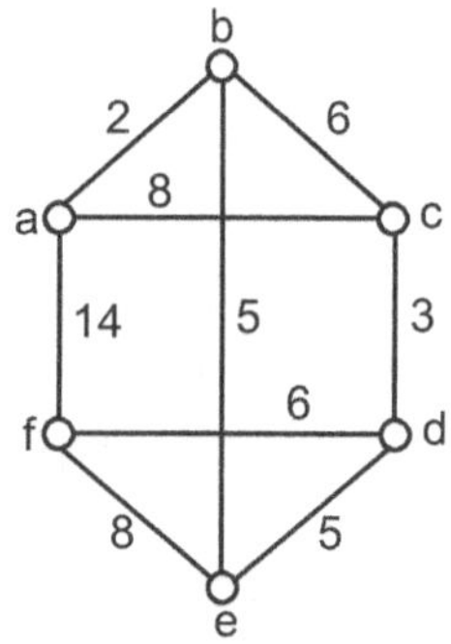

Fig. 9

(b) By using Kruskal's algorithm find the shortest spanning tree of the following graph.

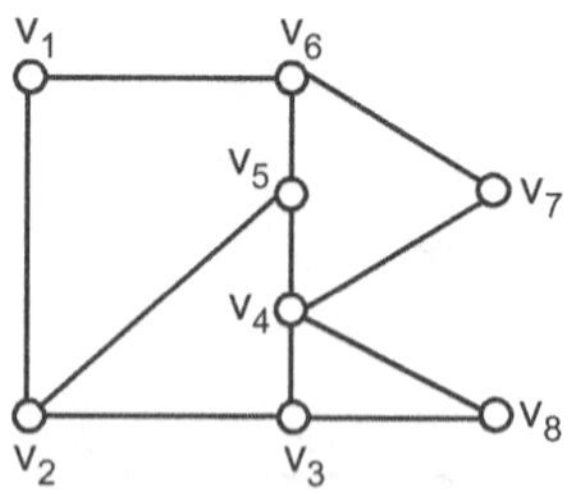

Fig. 10

✍ ✍ ✍

MODEL QUESTION PAPER - II

F.Y.B.Sc. Computer Science

MTC - 122 : Graph Theory

Time : 2 Hours **Total Marks : 35**

Note : 1. All questions are compulsory.
2. Figures to the right indicate full marks.

Q.1. Attempt any five of the following : **[5]**

(a) Can a simple graph exists with 15 vertices each of degree five ? Justify.

(b) Draw the following graphs.

(i) K_7 (ii) $K_{4,4}$

(c) How many connected components does the following graph have ?

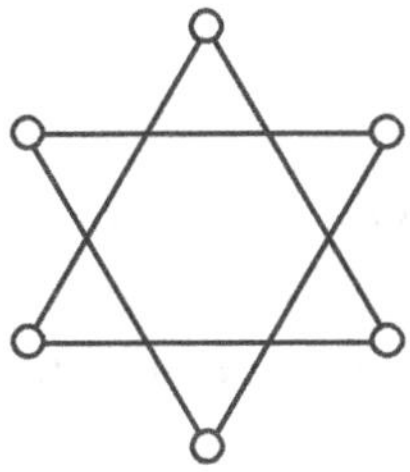

Fig. 1

(d) For which values of n do the graph K_n have an Euler circuit ?

(e) Which of the graphs are trees ?

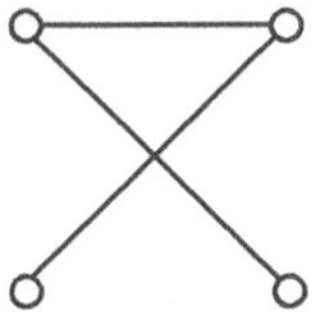

Fig. 2

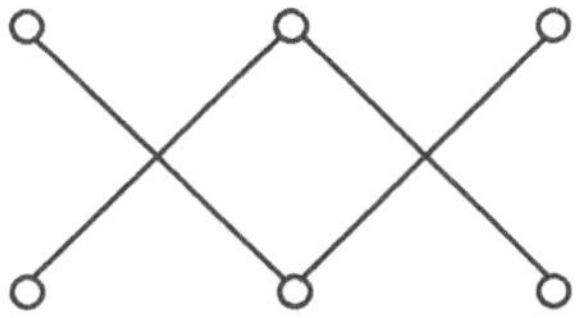

Fig. 3

(f) What is the ordered rooted tree that represents the expression $\frac{(x-4)}{3}$?

(g) Draw all spanning trees of the following graph.

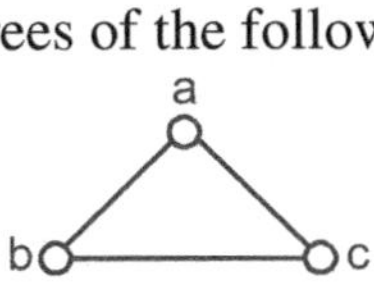

Fig. 4

Q.2. Attempt any two of the following : [10]

(a) Draw a graph with the following adjacency matrix.

$$\begin{bmatrix} 0 & 0 & 1 & 1 \\ 0 & 0 & 1 & 0 \\ 1 & 1 & 0 & 1 \\ 1 & 1 & 1 & 0 \end{bmatrix}$$

(b) Determine whether the given pair of graphs is isomorphic.

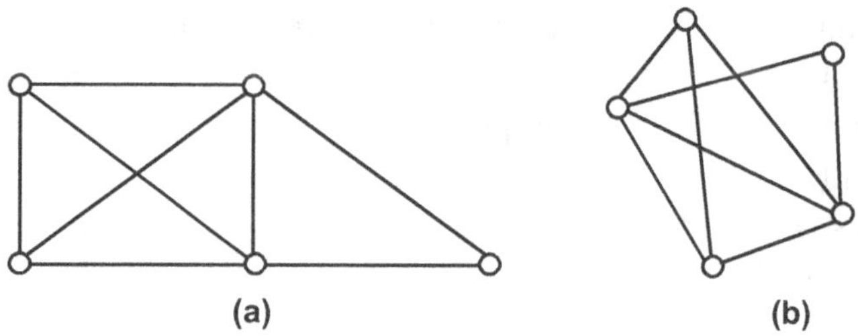

Fig. 5

(c) Let G be a graph with adjacency matrix A with respect to the ordering 1, 2, …, n. Show that (an integer) the number of different paths of length r from i to j, equals the $(i, j)^{th}$ entry of A^r.

Q.3. Attempt any two of the following : [10]

(a) Prove that in a cubic graph, vertex connectivity equals the edge connectivity.

(b) Apply Fluery's algorithm to find Eulerian tour in the graph.

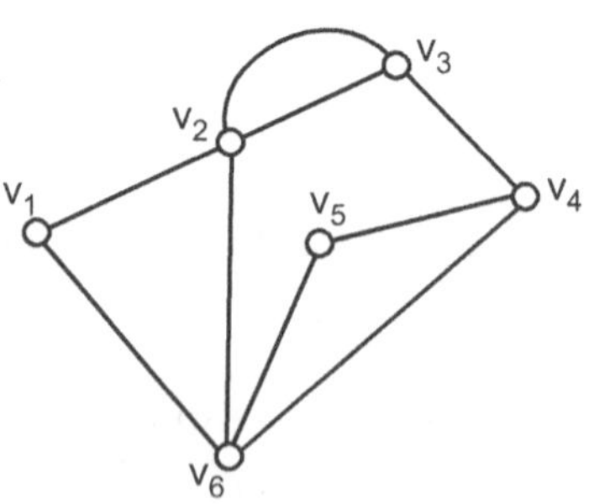

Fig. 6

(c) In which order are the vertices of the ordered rooted tree given below visited using an inorder traversal ?

Q.4. Attempt any one of the following : [10]

(a) Use Prim's algorithm to find a minimum spanning tree in the graph shown below.

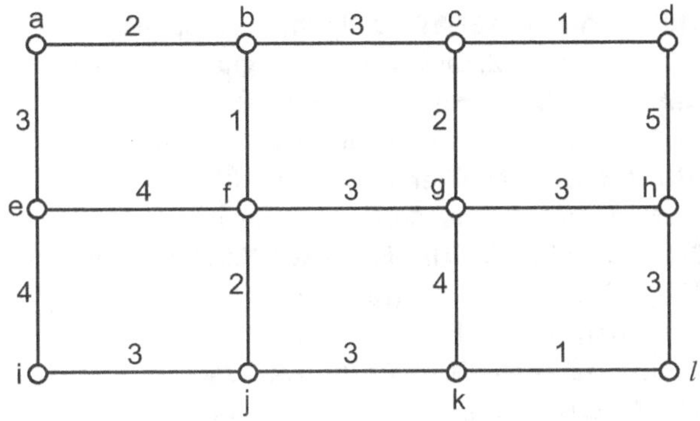

Fig. 7

(b) Use Kruskal's algorithm to find a minimum spanning tree for the following weighted graph.

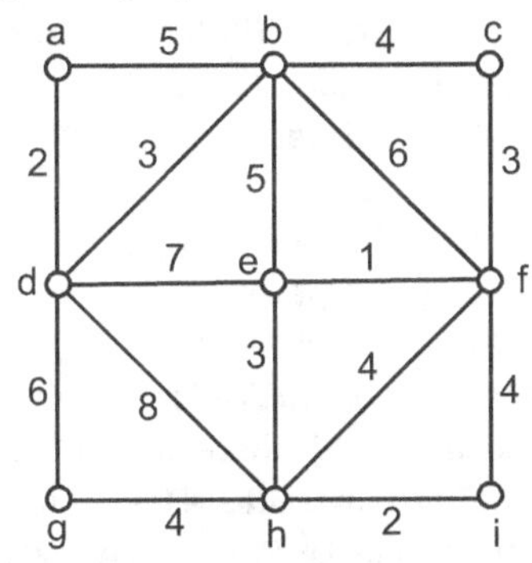

Fig. 8

✍ ✍ ✍

www.ingramcontent.com/pod-product-compliance
Lightning Source LLC
LaVergne TN
LVHW082343171026
850499LV00040B/1311
* 9 7 8 9 3 8 9 5 3 3 6 8 2 *